A MAP HISTORY OF THE
BRITISH PEOPLE
SINCE 1700

A MAP HISTORY
OF THE BRITISH PEOPLE
SINCE 1700

Brian Catchpole

Second Edition

Maps and diagrams by
Regmarad

HEINEMANN EDUCATIONAL BOOKS
LONDON

Other books by the same author

A Map History of the Modern World
A Map History of the United States
A Map History of Russia
A Map History of China
The Clash of Cultures

Heinemann Educational Books Ltd
22 Bedford Square London WC1B 3HH

LONDON EDINBURGH MELBOURNE AUCKLAND
HONG KONG SINGAPORE KUALA LUMPUR NEW DELHI
IBADAN NAIROBI JOHANNESBURG
EXETER (NH) KINGSTON PORT OF SPAIN

ISBN 0 435 31160 3
© Brian Catchpole 1971, 1975
First published 1971
Second edition 1975
Reprinted 1977
Reprinted with additions, 1980, 1983

Printed in Great Britain by
Fletcher & Son Ltd, Norwich

Contents

Preface

Because they created the world's first industrial nation, the British people have had a particularly interesting history. They were the first to experience the effect a prolonged war could have upon young, developing industries; the first to suffer the degradation of massive industrial unemployment and the misery of unexpected price fluctuations. The British had their share of riot, protest and conspiracy; but they never had the revolution predicted by Karl Marx. They evolved a pattern of education and a Welfare State still envied by many countries. They were the only people to fight throughout and win the two World Wars which have scarred the twentieth century. Their vast colonial possessions in Africa and Asia have been transformed into an independent Commonwealth of Nations.

The aim of this history is to tell these and other stories by means of maps and diagrams directly related to the text. Each self-contained page of narrative faces illustrations and source material designed to contribute to the understanding and amplification of a specific topic. Many of the themes have a special relevance to British and world affairs today. For example, the problem of law and order in our society may be traced from London's eighteenth century mob to the tragedy of Ulster in the 1970s. Themes such as The Clamour for Improvement or The Lost Peace offer opportunities for centre of interest studies; while the use of several related topics (such as Nos. 8, 27, 37, 50, 63, 67 and 77 on Empire and Commonwealth) provides rapid guidance for the development of project work.

Acknowledgements

The author and publishers are grateful for permission from the following to reproduce the photographs used in this book:
Associated Press Ltd, p. 171
Mr Leslie Baily, p. 89
BBC Hulton Picture Library, pp. 54, 73, 79, 131
Imperial War Museum, p. 101
London Express News and Features Service, p. 157
The Sunday Times, p. 165
The Times, p. 169

Abbreviations

ASRS	Amalgamated Society of Railway Servants
BEA	British European Airways
BEF	British Expeditionary Force
BOAC	British Overseas Airways Corporation
CND	Campaign for Nuclear Disarmament
DD	Duplex Drive (see P. 129)
DORA	Defence of the Realm Acts
EEC	European Economic Community
EFTA	European Free Trade Association
ELDO	European Launcher Development Organization
HMSO	His/Her Majesty's Stationery Office
IRC	Industrial Reorganization Corporation
ITMA	'It's that Man again' – Wartime Radio Show
LCC	London County Council
LEA	Local Education Authority
NATO	North Atlantic Treaty Organization
NEDC	'Neddy' – National Economic Development Council
OEEC	Organization for European Economic Co-operation
PLUTO	Pipe Line Under the Ocean
RAF	Royal Air Force
SAS	Special Air Service (their motto is 'Who dares wins')
SDF	Social Democratic Federation
TUC	Trades Union Congress
UDI	Unilateral Declaration of Independence (Rhodesia 1965)
UNO	United Nations Organization
USAF	United States Air Force
USSR	Union of Soviet Socialist Republics
VE-Day	Victory in Europe 1945
VJ-Day	Victory over Japan 1945
V-1	Pilotless bomb (German 1944–5)
V-2	Supersonic rocket missile (German 1944–5)
WAACS, WRAFS, WRNS	Womens Services (World War 1 – Army, Air Force, Navy)

PART 1

The British people on the eve of industrial change

During the eighteenth century the British people experienced the beginnings of an 'industrial revolution'. They were increasing in numbers and becoming far more mobile. They were better fed and on the whole healthier than people had been in previous centuries. Talented individuals were expanding existing industries such as *mining* and *textiles* and this expansion involved the use of new forms of transport, new kinds of power and new methods of production. By about 1780 the British people were about to 'take-off', as one economist has put it, into a period of sustained economic growth.

Such industrial expansion had never happened to any other country before; the British were the first people to experience rapid industrial change. It was their bad luck that this change happened to coincide with a long period of international warfare.

Why were the British the first to industrialize? Historians are not too sure about the answer to this question. They cannot, for example, explain why the population of England and Wales zoomed from below 6 million in 1700 to over 9 million in 1801. They cannot agree whether the industrial revolution did more harm than good. Socialist historians argue that wealthy capitalists, who paid meagre wages and provided appalling working conditions, deliberately exploited millions of workers and caused untold misery. Other historians argue, perhaps less forcibly but no less convincingly, that this is an exaggerated view. They point out that the human suffering of the early industrial age was not simply the result of deliberate capitalist exploitation, but of the interplay of many important historical events such as an unprecedented population explosion, a series of poor harvests and a long period of warfare in Europe. Surely these matters, they say, were beyond the control of factory owners and the landed gentry.

It is very important for you to realize that the history of the British people has been written from several points of view; and that it is very difficult to generalize about people who lived two hundred years ago. Not many records have survived and it is always difficult to talk meaningfully about 'the worker', 'the middle class' and 'the industrialists'. These groups were made up of all kinds of people just as 'students', 'immigrants' and 'old age pensioners' are today.

1: The population, 1700–1750

Increasing numbers

In 1700 England was still a rural community. Most people worked on the land or in the prosperous sea-ports and trading centres. The manufacturing industries were largely concerned with the production of 'primary products'—of relatively simple goods made from wood, textiles, leather, pewter and iron. About 5.75 million people lived in England and Wales in 1700; over the next fifty years they increased to about 6.75 million.

This increase was due partly to immigration from Ireland and Scotland and partly to *improving infant mortality rates*. Very young children seemed less prone to fevers and disease; they survived and grew up into healthy young adults. They spurned long apprentice-ships, married early and produced more children. Older people did not seem to fare so well. A harsh winter or a brief spell of famine would wipe out those with a low resistance to disease; and until the government clamped down with some strict *Licensing Laws* in 1751 thousands of gin-drinkers drank themselves to death. Generally speaking, when there were 'hard times' in the land deaths increased and births decreased; in 'good times' deaths decreased and births increased. The overall effect was a marked increase in the number of people living in England.

Increasing mobility

In 1700 most people lived on or close to the good farm-lands of the South or crowded into the main commercial centres such as London, Bristol, Exeter and Norwich. The North could boast only two densely populated areas: Lancashire and the West Riding of Yorkshire. It needed more labour, not just from Scotland and Ireland, but from the main reservoir of labour in the South. In 1700, however, families needed a compelling reason to migrate North. Poor roads, the menace of highwaymen and the sheer cost of removals deterred most families. Another reason kept most families at home: the regulations of the Elizabethan Poor Law Act (1601). This had placed the responsibility of helping the sick and unemployed paupers squarely on the shoulders of Justices of the Peace and parish officials. They levied a tax called the Poor Rate on parish residents and used the money to help the needy. By the 1662 Act of Settlement, paupers could expect help in the form of money 'relief' or work-house accommodation—but *only* in their own parish. No other parish would help them. This explains why rate-payers were anxious to keep poor people out; lots of paupers wandering around looking for jobs would drain parish funds and put the poor rate up. Clearly, these laws helped to make the population immobile.

Then in 1697 an Act of Parliament allowed parish officials to issue a certificate to any family wishing to move. The certificate confirmed that the family was legally settled in the 'home' parish and would not be a financial burden on the new parish. The certificate opposite was carried by a George Evinns when he, his wife, and two children moved from Derbyshire into York. It was one of the first to be issued.

Gradually families began to move just as the Evinns had done. Usually they did not move far—just a few miles and a few parishes away. But they left gaps which others filled and in this way the *expanding* population rippled across the countryside into the northern areas where developing industry was creating a demand for labour.

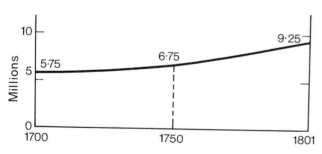

POPULATION INCREASE — England and Wales 1700–1801

GAIN IN POPULATION
1. Immigrants
2. Increased birth rate
3. Less infant mortality

LOSS OF POPULATION
1. Emigrants to the Colonies
2. Emigrants to Europe

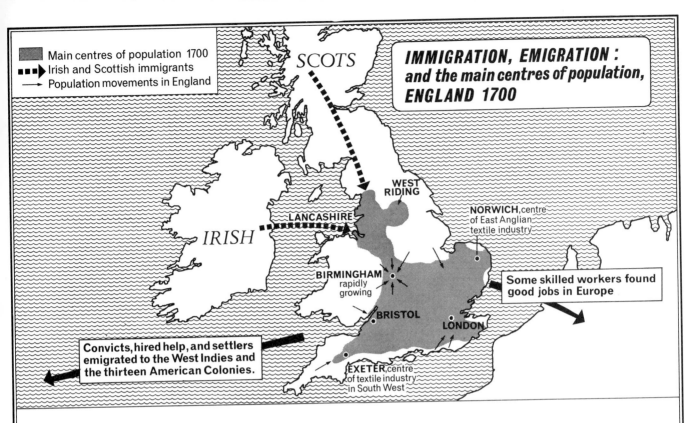

Main centres of population 1700
Irish and Scottish immigrants
Population movements in England

SCOTS

IRISH

LANCASHIRE

WEST RIDING

NORWICH, centre of East Anglian textile industry

BIRMINGHAM rapidly growing

BRISTOL

LONDON

EXETER, centre of textile industry in South West

IMMIGRATION, EMIGRATION : and the main centres of population, ENGLAND 1700

Some skilled workers found good jobs in Europe

Convicts, hired help, and settlers emigrated to the West Indies and the thirteen American Colonies.

A RESETTLEMENT CERTIFICATE ISSUED TO THE EVINNS FAMILY IN 1699

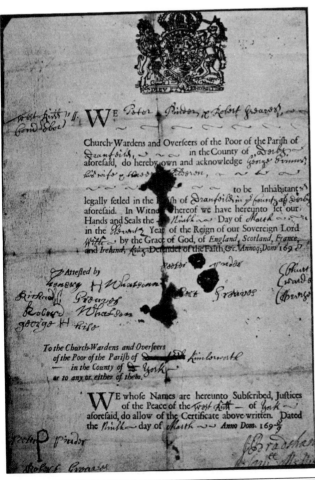

— The Churchwardens and Overseers of the poor

— George Evinns, his wife and two children

— Signatures of Churchwardens and overseers of the poor

— DATE

— Signatures of Justices of the Peace

3

2: The farmers, 1700–1780

Social Classes

British farmers came from every social class. Most were freeholders who owned the land they farmed. Many were tenant farmers who leased their land from the gentry—the squires and the country parsons. Prosperous tenants might farm hundreds of acres and employ a dozen or more farmservants. At the other end of the scale were those with five or six acres, feeding their own families and selling milk, eggs and perhaps a pig or two at the local market. Farmservants were tending to leave the big farmhouses and move into rented cottages. Some would have a few rods of land to cultivate, or the right of pasturing animals on common and waste land. But more and more were becoming labourers for hire, dependent upon wages which often fell below the level enjoyed by town workers.

Seventeenth century improvements

By 1750, despite the fact that a great deal of farming was carried out under the 'open-field' system, British farmers were among the most successful in the world. They were growing enough food to support the slowly increasing population; they had a surplus for export to Europe. Their success had its roots in the previous century when many farmers adopted Dutch agricultural methods and improved their grasslands and fodder crops. By 1650 it was customary, for example, to sow clover seed with the barley: once the crop was harvested, they turned cattle out to graze on the clover. The clover renewed the nitrogen in the soil, the cattle fattened on the clover, and the animal manure increased the fertility of the fields. Of course, the farmers did not describe the process in these words—they simply knew that the system worked. In the 1660s, they began to grow turnips. Turnips needed constant weeding and the hand-hoeing created a good tilth. The turnips provided a sound winter fodder for animals. Norfolk and Suffolk became famous for their 'crop-rotations'—wheat, barley, turnips, clover, ryegrass, was a typical rotation—and the farmers produced consistently good crops and reared fatter livestock without having to leave fields fallow for long periods.

Eighteenth century improvements

Other ideas developed in the eighteenth century. Lord 'Turnip' Townshend (1674–1738) won his nickname by growing turnips on his Norfolk estates. He was equally well-known for his use of 'marl' which he spread on fields to increase their fertility. Around 1750 several farmers began selective stock-breeding in Leicestershire. Best known were Joseph Allom and Robert Bakewell; the latter's farm at Dishley became famous for New Leicester sheep and sturdy breeds of Shire horses. Near Darlington, Charles Colling developed his shorthorn breed of cattle. Gradually, both the quality and the quantity of grain and stock improved. This was supplemented by thousands of cattle driven in from Wales and Scotland for the annual fattening on rich English grasslands. It all added up to profit and a general improvement in the national diet. Famine, though not completely absent (1709–10 and 1740–1 were especially bad times), was rare during the first half of the eighteenth century. Contemporary writers such as Arthur Young publicised the new methods. Young travelled the countryside and wrote at great length on farming matters; his enthusiasm and personality aroused tremendous interest wherever he went—far more so than did his voluminous reports which the government's Board of Agriculture sponsored after 1793.

Enclosure

Farming is profitable when it is efficient. The old open-field system with its scattered strips and dividing baulks was basically inefficient. Yet in 1700 half of England's arable land was still under open-fields. The answer was to enclose small, scattered holdings into larger farming units. There was nothing new in the idea; enclosures had been going on for five hundred years. But in the 1700s, the process accelerated. Between 1750 and 1780, for instance, more than 1,200 Acts of Parliament (Enclosure Acts) enclosed more than three million acres of strips, waste and common land. It was costly because enclosure involved careful surveys, fencing and hedging operations. Many small farmers sold out to make a quick profit or because they could not afford the costs of enclosure and a lot of these joined the ranks of landless labourers. Enclosure happened to coincide with a rapid increase in population after 1780 and thus it contributed to, even if it did not cause, the growth of poverty in the countryside.

The absence of farm machinery

Very few of the changes in this agricultural revolution depended on the use of new farm machinery. Jethro Tull (1664–1741) had invented a seed-drill and a horse-drawn hoe. In 1733 he published *Horse-hoeing Husbandry* to advertise his ideas. At the same time a number of new plough designs came on the market. But before 1780 very few farmers used any such machinery. The success of British farmers in the eighteenth century was almost entirely rooted in the field improvements and not in the use of new farm machinery.

A SAMPLE ENCLOSURE AWARD

"ETTON... in the East Riding of the County of York, divided in the year One Thousand Eight Hundred and Nineteen."

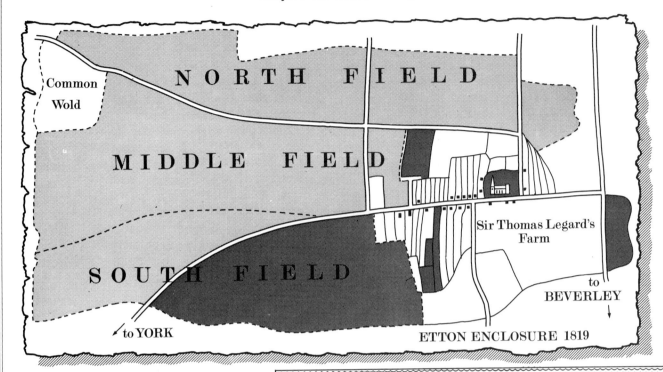

Common Wold

N O R T H   F I E L D

M I D D L E   F I E L D

S O U T H   F I E L D

Sir Thomas Legard's Farm

to YORK

to BEVERLEY

ETTON ENCLOSURE 1819

ENCLOSURE AWARDS

1. Many villages, such as Etton, were enclosed gradually. Villagers referred to "old" and "new" enclosures.

2. The wealthiest landowners paid for the cost of enclosure. They rented their newly acquired farms to tenant farmers who, in turn, hired landless farm labourers.

3. In Etton, the three fields were divided as follows:

NORTH FIELD

a   Lord Hotham
b   William Schoolcroft
c   Robert Belt (took Common Wold also)
d   Henry Grimston

MIDDLE FIELD

a   Lord Hotham
b   Sir Thomas Legard
c   Robert Belt
d   The Vicar

SOUTH FIELD

a   Lord Hotham
b   Sir Thomas Legard
c   Robert Belt
d   The Vicar

The Vicar was the Rev. Gilby —his lands are shaded ■ on the top map

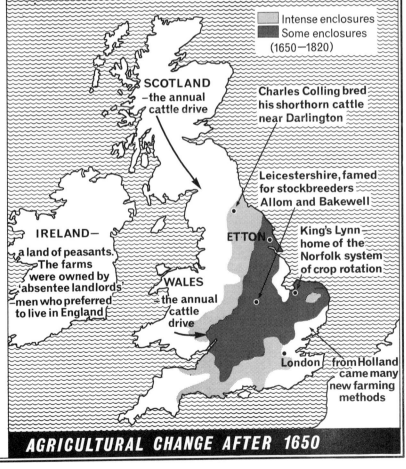

Intense enclosures
Some enclosures
(1650—1820)

SCOTLAND
–the annual cattle drive

Charles Colling bred his shorthorn cattle near Darlington

Leicestershire, famed for stockbreeders Allom and Bakewell

IRELAND—
a land of peasants. The farms were owned by 'absentee landlords' —men who preferred to live in England

ETTON

King's Lynn home of the Norfolk system of crop rotation

WALES
–the annual cattle drive

London   from Holland came many new farming methods

AGRICULTURAL CHANGE AFTER 1650

3: The commercial revolution

Overseas trade

In 1700 England and Holland were the two most progressive trading nations in Europe. After three wars against the Dutch in the seventeenth century, the English copied many of their rival's commercial ideas. Moreover, by imposing the Navigation Acts (1651, 1660, 1663) they robbed the Dutch of much of the world's 'carrying trade'; all cargoes entering England or her colonies now had to be carried in English ships or in ships of the country in which the cargoes originated. This helped England not only to expand overseas trade with the colonies but also to embark on the re-export trade with Europe.

The expanding ports

London was the country's biggest port, but by 1700 it was becoming overcrowded as the East Indiamen, colliers, lighters and barges jostled for a berth. On the west coast other ports began to rival the capital. From Bristol and Liverpool the slavers set out in search of human cargoes on the first leg of the 'Triangular Trade'. Whitehaven was handling 100,000 tons of shipping annually by 1750. Newcastle, Hull, King's Lynn, Yarmouth and Ipswich shared the same prosperity on the east coast. And as the ports expanded so they needed more docks and warehouses. All of these activities brought increased wealth to the port areas in general and to the merchant class in particular.

The merchants

Defoe once described the merchant as 'the most intelligent man in the world and consequently the most capable, when urged by necessity, to contrive new ways to live'. The eighteenth century merchant certainly found new ways of making profits. Some, such as Walter Litwidge of Whitehaven, had obscure origins. Around 1705 he was a wine-dealer; after 1710 he specialized in Virginian tobacco imports. By 1740 he owned a small fleet of ships and boasted that he traded with all parts of the world. When he retired from commerce in 1746 he said he had made £30,000 and was 'a man of opulency'. He became the Sheriff of Cumberland in 1747—a typical eighteenth-century self-made man. A different kind of man was Edward Colston of Bristol. He made a fortune from the West Indian trade and then gave thousands away every year to charities; and when he died in 1721 he still left a vast fortune.

Small groups of wealthy merchants came to dominate the port areas. In Hull, the Maister and Crowle families ran the Baltic trade. In Newcastle, the Ridley and Liddell families controlled coal exports. These were the men who could afford to build the fine Georgian mansions, who landscaped the gardens on their new country estates. They were the new landed gentry who had the surplus capital to invest in transport and industrial schemes. In this way, the profits from trade acted as a spur to England's manufacturing industries.

Money matters

Most merchants found money matters difficult to handle. Problems of buying and selling goods at home and abroad, finding shipping space, arranging insurance were beyond the powers of one man. So they turned to specialists—shipping merchants who chartered the ships, brokers who handled specialized cargoes, agents who would insure them against damage and loss. These experts could be found in the ports, for example, in Liverpool at the Cotton Exchange and in London at Edward Lloyd's Coffee Shop.

But the most important specialist was the banker. The Bank of England dated from 1694 and during the eighteenth century other banks opened in the provinces. Their main function was to discount bills of exchange. A merchant often found it inconvenient to pay cash for a transaction; instead he issued a bill of exchange which promised to pay the creditor the sum due in three month's time. But the creditor might need the cash at once. This was where the banker played his part. If the merchant were 'credit-worthy' the bank would discount—or cash—the bill. So bills of exchange acted as a sort of currency; merchants were less dependent on supplies of gold and silver coin; and it all helped to lay the foundations of business credit as we know it today.

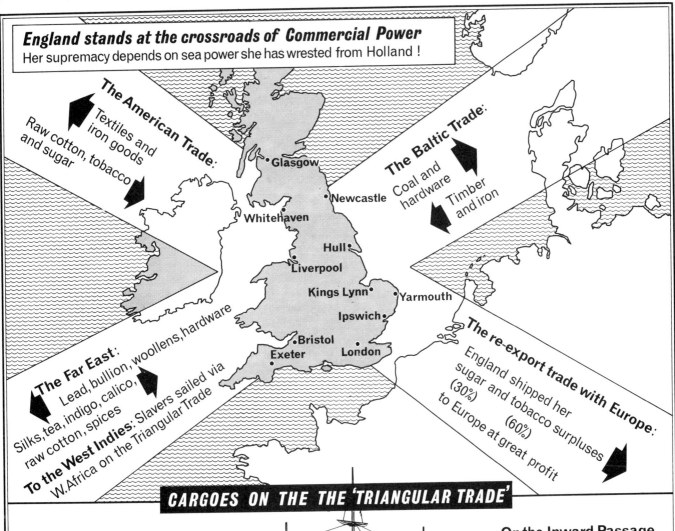

England stands at the crossroads of Commercial Power
Her supremacy depends on sea power she has wrested from Holland!

The American Trade:
Textiles and iron goods
Raw cotton, tobacco and sugar

The Baltic Trade:
Coal and hardware
Timber and iron

The Far East:
Lead, bullion, woollens, hardware
Silks, tea, indigo, calico, raw cotton, spices

To the West Indies: Slavers sailed via W. Africa on the Triangular Trade

The re-export trade with Europe:
England shipped her sugar and tobacco surpluses (30%) (60%) to Europe at great profit

Glasgow · Newcastle · Whitehaven · Hull · Liverpool · Kings Lynn · Yarmouth · Ipswich · Bristol · Exeter · London

CARGOES ON THE THE 'TRIANGULAR TRADE'

A SLAVER c.1780

On the Outward Passage to West Africa:—

Brandy
Rolls of Cloth
Muskets
Gunpowder
Bar-iron

— for the African kings in exchange for Slaves

Handcuffs, Leg-irons
—to shackle the slaves

Beans—food for the slaves on the Middle Passage

On the Inward Passage to Liverpool:—

"Load up with One Hundred Cask good Muscovado Sugars for the ground tier, the remainder with first and second White Sugars and betwixt Decks with good Cotton and Coffee."
—and in Jamaica— "as much Broad sound mahogany as will serve for dunnage."

(Orders to a Liverpool slaver captain, 1762)

On the Middle Passage to the West Indies:—
The main deck M held about 100 slaves. The ship's carpenter specially built a 'shelf' S to hold another 100 negroes," .... like books in a row", was how John Newton, a slaver captain, described the unhappy negroes.

7

4: The rise of the cotton industry

The established woollen industry

Since the middle ages the most widespread industry in the land had been the spinning and weaving of wool. For centuries the quality of British fleeces and the skill of the woollen workers had been renowned in Europe. Yet almost every part of the manufacturing process was carried out by ordinary people in their own homes. They bought or hired their spinning wheels, stocking frames and handlooms. They either purchased outright the raw wool and yarn or contracted with merchant suppliers to produce finished cloth at an agreed price. This is the classic example of the 'domestic system' of textile manufacture before the age of industrial expansion. Of course, specially built mills and workshops carried out many of the fulling and dyeing processes. Nevertheless, it is fair to say that in 1700 Britain's most valuable export commodity was made by hand in the cottages of the countryside.

The challenge from cotton

Around 1680 substantial imports of cotton fabrics arrived from the Far East. They were lightweight, easily washed and attractive when compared with their linen and woollen counterparts. But they were also expensive—and this encouraged Lancashire spinners to experiment with raw cotton imported via Liverpool. They soon discovered how difficult it was to spin cotton thread in quantities big enough to keep the handloom weavers supplied. Their problem was a technical one; how could the simple spinning wheel be modified to make cotton production a profitable investment? There was no immediate answer. In fact the first major textile inventions benefited weaving rather than spinning and so made the problem worse.

The textile inventors

In 1733 John Kay improved production at his father's woollen mill in Colchester by inventing a *flying shuttle*. This speeded up the weaving process and enabled the weaver to work singlehanded at his loom. Though the flying shuttle was adopted gradually, by 1760 there was an urgent need for faster spinning equipment. James Hargreaves, a Blackburn weaver, patented his *spinning jenny* in 1767. Still operated by hand, it could spin eight spindles of cotton thread at once. However, the spun thread was too weak to form a vertical warp on a handloom. Richard Arkwright, a Preston barber, solved this problem in 1769. He built a *water-frame* which spun and twisted cotton threads into a strong warp. But the water-frame was big and complex; it had to be sited next to a source of water power. Clearly, water-frame spinning was beyond the scope of the 'domestic system'. Then in 1779 Samuel Crompton, a Bolton weaver, 'crossed' Hargreaves' jenny with Arkwright's water-frame and produced a *spinning mule* which could produce large quantities of cotton thread as good as any Oriental imports. Eight years later, the Rev. Edmund Cartwright devised a *power-operated loom* for the weavers. Now the technical innovations existed for the expansion of the cotton industry.

The textile factories

If he had plenty of capital and faith in the new technical inventions, the ambitious cotton manufacturer could find inspiration from the silk-mills at Derby. John Lombe, who had stolen the designs of silk-throwing machines while working in Italy, joined forces with his half-brother, Thomas, to build the mills during 1717–19. They were still the wonder of the age in 1771:

> In these Mills are 26,586 wheels and 97,746 movements, continually working except on Sundays. This grand Machine is disposed in four stories of large rooms above one another; and the whole is actuated by one great Waterwheel which goes round three times in one minute. In each time of its going round 73,728 yards of Silk are twisted.... Wond'rous Machine! (James Ferguson, 1771)

That very year, Arkwright built the first water-powered cotton-mill at Cromford. Five years later he built another—then a third at Belper. They prospered; he won a knighthood and became Sheriff of Derbyshire. Sir Richard Arkwright was one of the first of the new style businessmen—the cotton industrialist.

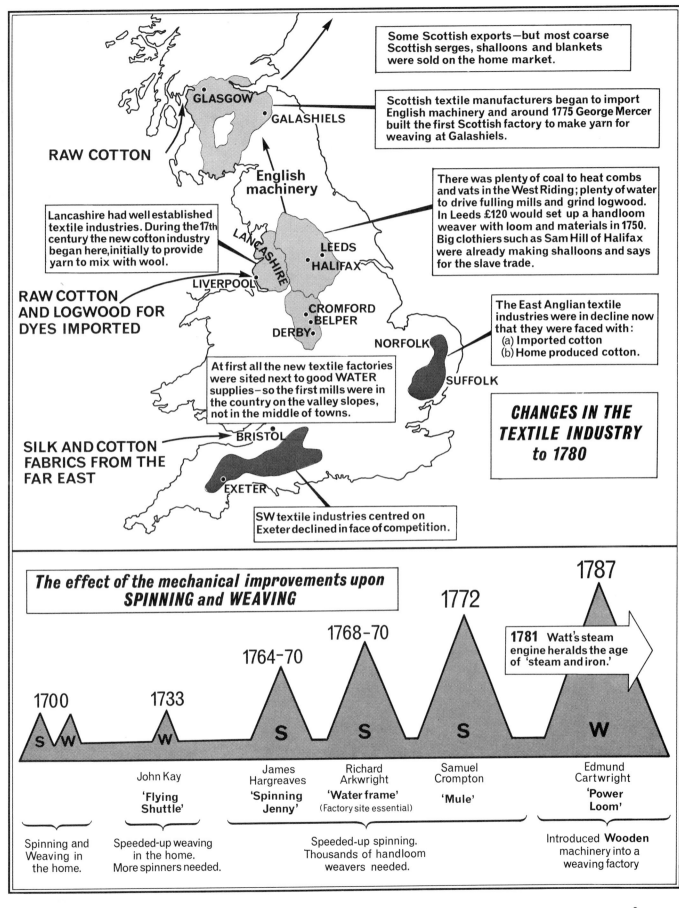

Some Scottish exports—but most coarse Scottish serges, shalloons and blankets were sold on the home market.

Scottish textile manufacturers began to import English machinery and around 1775 George Mercer built the first Scottish factory to make yarn for weaving at Galashiels.

GLASGOW
GALASHIELS

RAW COTTON

English machinery

There was plenty of coal to heat combs and vats in the West Riding; plenty of water to drive fulling mills and grind logwood. In Leeds £120 would set up a handloom weaver with loom and materials in 1750. Big clothiers such as Sam Hill of Halifax were already making shalloons and says for the slave trade.

Lancashire had well established textile industries. During the 17th century the new cotton industry began here, initially to provide yarn to mix with wool.

LANCASHIRE
LEEDS
HALIFAX
LIVERPOOL

RAW COTTON AND LOGWOOD FOR DYES IMPORTED

CROMFORD
BELPER
DERBY

The East Anglian textile industries were in decline now that they were faced with:
(a) Imported cotton
(b) Home produced cotton.

NORFOLK
SUFFOLK

At first all the new textile factories were sited next to good WATER supplies—so the first mills were in the country on the valley slopes, not in the middle of towns.

CHANGES IN THE TEXTILE INDUSTRY to 1780

SILK AND COTTON FABRICS FROM THE FAR EAST

BRISTOL
EXETER

SW textile industries centred on Exeter declined in face of competition.

The effect of the mechanical improvements upon SPINNING and WEAVING

1787

1772

1768–70

1764–70

1781 Watt's steam engine heralds the age of 'steam and iron.'

1700

1733

S W

W

S

S

S

W

	John Kay **'Flying Shuttle'**	James Hargreaves **'Spinning Jenny'**	Richard Arkwright **'Water frame'** (Factory site essential)	Samuel Crompton **'Mule'**	Edmund Cartwright **'Power Loom'**

Spinning and Weaving in the home.

Speeded-up weaving in the home. More spinners needed.

Speeded-up spinning. Thousands of handloom weavers needed.

Introduced **Wooden** machinery into a weaving factory

5: The coal industry

'The soul of English manufactures'

From 1300 onwards coalmining was well established in many parts of the country. Coal was in constant demand and by 1750 the annual production was about 5 million tons. At the time, coal was called 'the soul of English manufactures': soap-boilers, sugar-refiners, brick-makers, glass-blowers and, above all, iron and copper workers depended on it. Just as important was the domestic demand. Householders, especially in London, wanted coal to burn on their traditional open fireplaces—a wasteful habit that persisted well into the mid-twentieth century. Long before 1750, the miner had exhausted most of the shallow seams and opencast mines. Land-owners in the coal-bearing regions were forced to sink shafts and the deep mines brought with them the hazards of flooding, chokedamp (lack of oxygen) and firedamp (explosive gas). Moreover, as both population and industry increased so the demand for coal soared. In turn, the problem of distributing bulky coal deliveries to the consumer market seemed insoluble.

Working the coal

The most productive mines were in the North-East where access to the sailing colliers made the transport of coal easier. Here the pitmen hewed coal by the 'board and pillar' method. The *board* was the section in which the miner worked; the *pillar* was the unworked coal left in position to support the roof. According to an early report (1747) on the Gateshead Fell pits 'Ye Boards are from 4 to 5 yards broad, headways some $2\frac{1}{2}$ yards and some 3 yards wide; the Pillar's length from 20 to 30 yards and some $4\frac{1}{2}$ yards in thickness'. Sometimes the miners were able to hew out the pillars to avoid waste. In contrast, the miners of Shropshire were able to use wooden pit props to support the roof because the coal seams were very thin, while in the Black Country, where the South Staffordshire seams rose ten yards high, miners had to leave huge pillars of coal to keep the roof up.

Mining hazards

The deeper men went, the greater the dangers they faced. Sometimes crude ventilation systems cured the choke-damp, but firedamp remained a menace. As Professor Ashton has said: 'It was sometimes dealt with by a fire-man who, clad in leather or wet rags, carried a long pole with a lighted candle at the end, with which, at some personal risk, he exploded the gas'. Miners' wives and children shared the hardships at the coal face and on the surface. They pushed the heavy corves and tubs or carried baskets of coal on their backs. Accidents due to cave-ins, shaft falls and explosions were common and the parish registers of the mining communities bear witness to the tragedies that so often struck families whose livelihood depended on the pit.

Steam power in the mines

Flooded workings hampered the miners more than any-thing else. Existing pumps, either water or horse powered, could not lift from depths of 300 feet or more. Then, just at the right moment, a steam driven pump met the miners' demands. In 1705 Thomas Newcomen, a Devonshire blacksmith, devised a steam engine for pumping water. He adapted a design by Thomas Savery who in 1698 had invented a steam driven piston for pumping out flooded tin mines in Cornwall. Newcomen's version was an atmospheric steam engine—that is, he brought atmospheric pressure to bear on the piston to create a working stroke. A rocking beam connected the piston to the pump. Newcomen's engine was a techno-logical breakthrough. Of course, it had its limitations. The engine components were crudely made; they cost a lot—about £1000; the engine burnt vast quantities of coal. Nevertheless, the mine-owners bought it when pro-duction got into swing after 1715. They found that it pumped water from great depths and that it was easy to maintain and operate. By the time Newcomen died in 1729 he was meeting export orders. By 1780 about 140 Newcomen engines were pumping in the North-East coalfields alone, whilst another 220 had been installed in Yorkshire, the Black Country and South Wales.

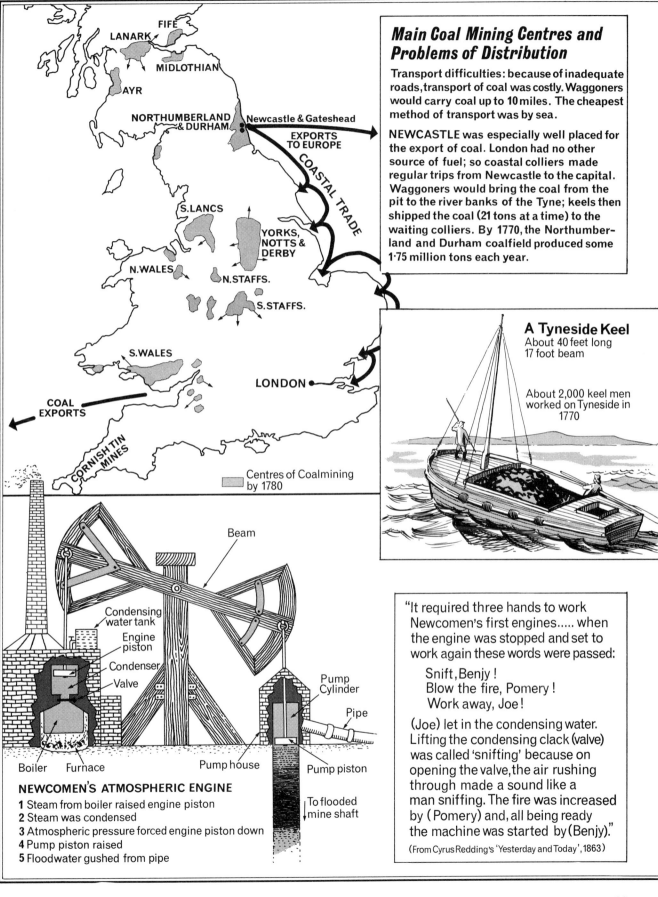

Main Coal Mining Centres and Problems of Distribution

Transport difficulties: because of inadequate roads, transport of coal was costly. Waggoners would carry coal up to 10 miles. The cheapest method of transport was by sea.

NEWCASTLE was especially well placed for the export of coal. London had no other source of fuel; so coastal colliers made regular trips from Newcastle to the capital. Waggoners would bring the coal from the pit to the river banks of the Tyne; keels then shipped the coal (21 tons at a time) to the waiting colliers. By 1770, the Northumberland and Durham coalfield produced some 1·75 million tons each year.

FIFE
LANARK
MIDLOTHIAN
AYR
NORTHUMBERLAND & DURHAM — Newcastle & Gateshead
EXPORTS TO EUROPE
COASTAL TRADE
S.LANCS
YORKS, NOTTS & DERBY
N.WALES
N.STAFFS.
S.STAFFS.
S.WALES
LONDON
COAL EXPORTS
CORNISH TIN MINES

Centres of Coalmining by 1780

A Tyneside Keel
About 40 feet long
17 foot beam

About 2,000 keel men worked on Tyneside in 1770

Beam
Condensing water tank
Engine piston
Condenser
Valve
Pump Cylinder
Pipe
Pump house
Pump piston
Boiler   Furnace
To flooded mine shaft

NEWCOMEN'S ATMOSPHERIC ENGINE
1 Steam from boiler raised engine piston
2 Steam was condensed
3 Atmospheric pressure forced engine piston down
4 Pump piston raised
5 Floodwater gushed from pipe

"It required three hands to work Newcomen's first engines..... when the engine was stopped and set to work again these words were passed:

Snift, Benjy !
Blow the fire, Pomery !
Work away, Joe !

(Joe) let in the condensing water. Lifting the condensing clack (valve) was called 'snifting' because on opening the valve, the air rushing through made a sound like a man sniffing. The fire was increased by (Pomery) and, all being ready the machine was started by (Benjy)."

(From Cyrus Redding's 'Yesterday and Today', 1863)

6: The iron industry

The decline of Wealden iron

In 1700 blacksmiths and other craftsmen in the iron industry were widely scattered throughout the land. They supplied the farmers with their ploughshares and wheelrims. They made the cutlery, pots and pans for the housewife. They cast the cannon, forged the swords and handguns for the services. In the Midlands nailers specialized in heavy duty nails for export to the American colonies. The best English iron had once come from the Weald, where the charcoal-fired furnaces were just ending their long history. The main reason for this was the steep rise in charcoal prices; as farmers cleared the young woodlands and other industries clamoured for timber fuel, the ironworkers' costs soared until, by 1746, charcoal accounted for 80% of their overheads! Another totally unexpected factor which hastened their decline was the run of hot summers between 1737 and 1750 which dried up many Wealden streams and brought the waterwheels to a standstill.

Expansion in the Midlands

However, in the Midlands iron production increased. Quality bar-iron came in from Sweden—costs actually fell after the improved Hull-Bawtry river route was completed in the seventeenth century. There was plenty of water power and the small blast furnaces poured forth a steady stream of pig iron which, after forging and slitting, became the raw material for thousands of nailers. But the major expansion in the Midlands—and later on in the North and South Wales also—awaited the developments which would enable the iron industry to use not only local ore but *local coal* as well.

The ironmasters

In 1709 Abraham Darby, founder of a line of famous ironmasters, discovered how to smelt iron by using coke as his fuel. This freed him from dependence on charcoal supplies, but Darby, a Quaker, kept this revolutionary discovery a secret. After he died in 1717, his son expanded the family works at Coalbrookdale and specialized in building Newcomen engines. Then the demands of the Seven Years War with France (1756–63) spurred other ironmasters to increase production. The Wilkinson brothers built coke-fired blast furnaces at Bersham, Broseley and Bradley. In 1760 John Roebuck opened his iron works at Carron. Visiting the works in 1765 a French metallurgist, Gabriel Jars, admired Roebuck's choice of site:

> Everything tends to the advantage of this establishment. The owners themselves exploit a large coal mine near the furnace. They have a very fine stream of water; in addition the foundry is very near a sea-port.

Roebuck won several military contracts and in 1769 the Royal Navy adopted his cannons (the famous carronades) as standard equipment.

The turning point

Until 1776 the iron industry had used all its steam engines for pumping water. Nobody had been skilful enough to apply the cumbersome Newcomen engine for use in hammering and rolling pig iron, for example. Then, that year, John Wilkinson installed a new kind of steam engine to drive the bellows of his blast furnace at Broseley. This new engine was the brainchild of a brilliant Scottish instrument maker, James Watt. He had made several important modifications to the Newcomen engine so that it could run on comparatively small supplies of water and coal and, above all, be installed anywhere. It took Watt four years of experiment (1765–9) to perfect the separate steam condenser, the essential feature of his new design. But it was not until 1775, when he went into partnership with Matthew Boulton, the Birmingham manufacturer, that he made contact with the knowledgeable ironmasters who helped him produce his prototype engine. Boulton and Watt steam engines were destined to transform the whole of British industry—especially after 1781 when Watt added rotary motion to his engine. But it was the iron industry that made the immediate gains: the big hammers, rollers and bellows were easy to adapt to the new engine. And when during 1783–4 an ironmaster called Henry Cort devised his method of 'puddling' or purifying molten iron and then rolling it into the required shape, the age of Steam and Iron had truly begun.

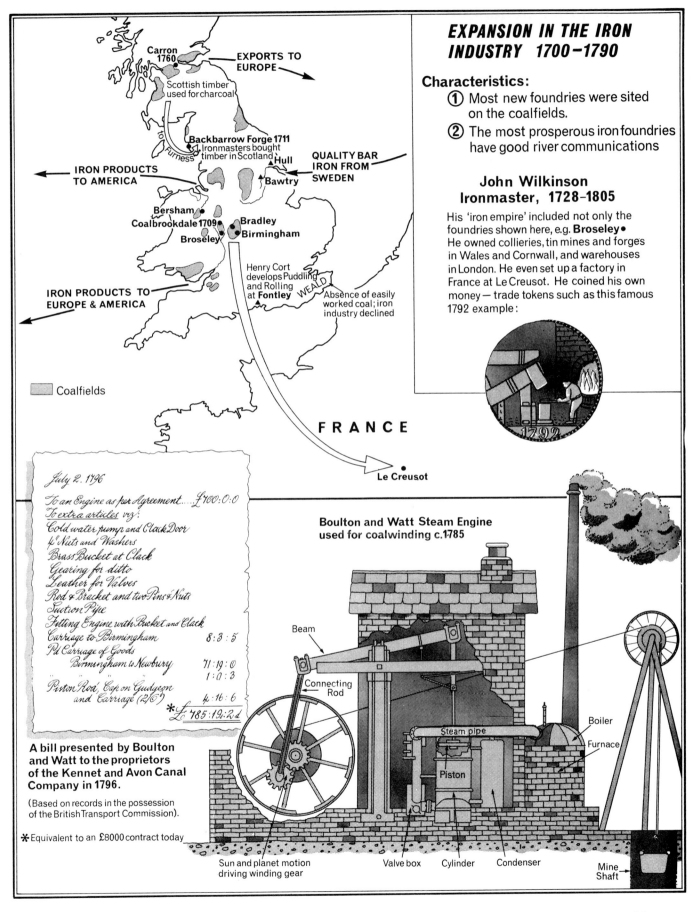

EXPANSION IN THE IRON INDUSTRY 1700–1790

Carron 1760

EXPORTS TO EUROPE

Scottish timber used for charcoal

Backbarrow Forge 1711
Ironmasters bought timber in Scotland

to Furness

▲ Hull

IRON PRODUCTS TO AMERICA

QUALITY BAR IRON FROM SWEDEN

Bawtry

Bersham
Coalbrookdale 1709

Bradley
Birmingham

Broseley

IRON PRODUCTS TO EUROPE & AMERICA

Henry Cort develops Puddling and Rolling at **Fontley**

WEALD

Absence of easily worked coal; iron industry declined

Coalfields

F R A N C E

Le Creusot

Characteristics:
① Most new foundries were sited on the coalfields.
② The most prosperous iron foundries have good river communications

John Wilkinson Ironmaster, 1728–1805

His 'iron empire' included not only the foundries shown here, e.g. **Broseley** ●
He owned collieries, tin mines and forges in Wales and Cornwall, and warehouses in London. He even set up a factory in France at Le Creusot. He coined his own money — trade tokens such as this famous 1792 example:

1792

July 2. 1796

To an Engine as per Agreement.....£700:0:0
To extra articles viz:
Cold water pump and Clack Door
4" Nuts and Washers
Brass Bucket at Clack
Gearing for ditto
Leather for Valves
Rod & Bracket and two Pins & Nuts
Suction Pipe
Fitting Engine with Bucket and Clack
Carriage to Birmingham   8:3:5
Pd Carriage of Goods
    Birmingham to Newbury   71:19:0
                                       1:0:3
"Piston Rod, Cap on Gudgeon
    and Carriage (2/6")   4:16:6
                           *£ 785:19:2d

A bill presented by Boulton and Watt to the proprietors of the Kennet and Avon Canal Company in 1796.

(Based on records in the possession of the British Transport Commission).

✱ Equivalent to an £8000 contract today

Boulton and Watt Steam Engine used for coalwinding c.1785

Beam

Connecting Rod

Steam pipe

Boiler

Furnace

Piston

Sun and planet motion driving winding gear

Valve box

Cylinder

Condenser

Mine Shaft

13

7: Improvements in transport, 1700–1790: canals and roads

The need for canals

The expense involved in moving raw materials and industrial products was a permanent trial to mine-owners and manufacturers at the beginning of the eighteenth century. Traditionally, they used river transport as the easiest and cheapest method available and they had always been willing to invest money in schemes to improve river navigation. But now many mines and textile mills were sited in districts ill-served by existing river systems. Direct access to seaports, better ways of carrying increasing quantities of coal, bricks, iron ore and food supplies were vital for industrial progress. Many industrialists were aware of successful canal-building schemes on the Continent—especially in France—and soon groups began to sponsor 'cuts' as the first canals were called. The first English canal, the tiny Exeter cut, had a history going back to 1564. In Ireland, the Lough Neagh canal opened in 1742. Between 1757 and 1761 Liverpool merchants financed the Sankey Brook Cut. But the best known of these early ventures was Brindley's Worsley Canal, constructed between 1759 and 1761.

James Brindley 1716–72

At Worsley, the Duke of Bridgewater owned rich deposits of coal. At Manchester, a rapidly increasing population demanded regular quantities of cheap coal. The Duke's problem was simply one of transporting coal to Manchester at an economical price. He was convinced that a private canal was the answer—and hired Brindley to build it in 1759. Brindley was by trade a millwright but he had a genius for unusual, large-scale construction work. He was a born organizer and knew how to handle men; and though he had little formal education, he ranks as one of Britain's first civil engineers. His canal covered seven miles of difficult terrain and was, said the *Annual Register*, 'the most extraordinary thing in the kingdom'.

As soon as the Worsley canal barges arrived in Manchester, the price of coal dropped dramatically. Other manufacturers, spurred on by the prospect of a 50% reduction in fuel costs, clamoured for Brindley's expertise. He undertook the Bridgewater Cut to Runcorn in 1762. He dreamed of a system of internal waterways linking all the major rivers and in 1766 he began the Great Trunk. By 1772 he had worked himself to death, but over the next sixteen years others completed his plans.

The condition of the roads

By 1700 most British roads were in a terrible condition. As early as 1555 the 'Statute for Mending the Highways' had ordered each parish to keep its own roads in good condition. Most found the task beyond their resources and although Justices of the Peace levied regular fines on offending villages very little was done to improve the roads. But with the expansion of trade and the growth of towns in the eighteenth century, more and more pack-horses, wagon-teams, stage-coaches and herds of animals used the roads and caused conditions to become chaotic. Yet the 1753 regulation which ruled that all wagons must be fitted with wheelrims of at least nine inches in width was simply attempting to preserve conditions rather than improve them. Moreover, when a parish tried to repair its roads by filling in the ruts or laying a few paving stones, it was not unknown for the road-materials to disappear in the middle of the night. One Nottinghamshire labourer, arrested for digging pits across a road, explained that he was only searching for coal!

The turnpike builders

That some roads did improve was due to the work of the turnpike trusts—groups of wealthy individuals who, after 1706, received Parliamentary permission to build or repair stretches of highway along which they would be allowed to charge tolls. Gates and turnstiles—sometimes topped by ferocious pikes or spikes—barred each end of the turnpike where a tollkeeper would collect fees from the road users. Parliament authorized nearly 2000 turnpikes between 1706 and 1790. But in no sense was there any national planning involved and no national system of roads resulted. In fact many turnpikes were quite short and sometimes badly built. Two of the more distinguished turnpike engineers were John Metcalfe (1717–1810) and Thomas Telford (1757–1834). Metcalfe, who lost his sight as a child after an attack of small-pox, was better known as 'Blind Jack of Knaresborough'. He built nearly 200 miles of turnpikes in Yorkshire, Lancashire and Derbyshire. Telford worked mainly in Shropshire before 1790. His great engineering works did not materialize until the early nineteenth century.

The benefits

The contribution of canals to industrial expansion was spectacular. That of the roads was very necessary. Road-building did not attract so much investment as did the canals, mainly because the advantages of bulk carriage and quick profits were absent. However, the roads enabled Mat Pickford to move freight from Manchester to London in 'flying wagons' in a record-breaking $4\frac{1}{2}$ days. In 1706 a coach journey from York to London took four days; in 1790 the 'Highflyer' coach was clocking 31 hours. By 1790 mail coaches connected most of the major towns and their combined *daily* mileage was just under 7000 miles.

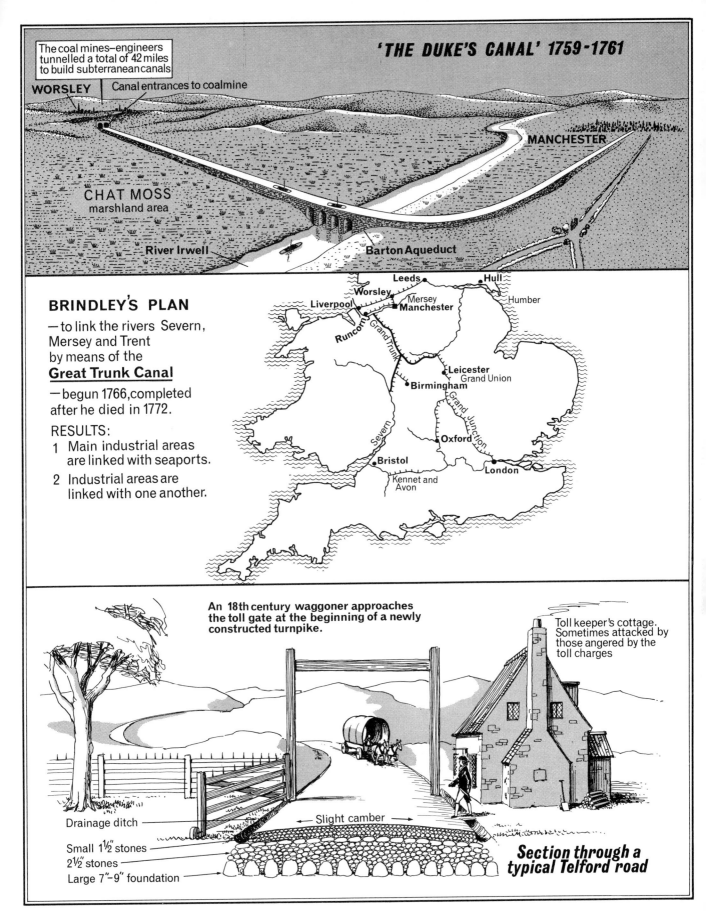

'THE DUKE'S CANAL' 1759-1761

The coal mines—engineers tunnelled a total of 42 miles to build subterranean canals

WORSLEY Canal entrances to coalmine

MANCHESTER

CHAT MOSS marshland area

River Irwell **Barton Aqueduct**

BRINDLEY'S PLAN

—to link the rivers Severn, Mersey and Trent by means of the

Great Trunk Canal

—begun 1766, completed after he died in 1772.

RESULTS:

1 Main industrial areas are linked with seaports.

2 Industrial areas are linked with one another.

Leeds Hull
Worsley Mersey Humber
Liverpool Manchester
Runcorn Grand Trunk
Leicester
Grand Union
Birmingham
Grand Junction
Severn
Oxford
Bristol London
Kennet and Avon

An 18th century waggoner approaches the toll gate at the beginning of a newly constructed turnpike.

Toll keeper's cottage. Sometimes attacked by those angered by the toll charges

Drainage ditch

Small 1½" stones

2½" stones

Large 7"–9" foundation

Slight camber

Section through a typical Telford road

8: The American War of Independence, 1775–1783

The colonial problem

Whilst the British engaged in industrial expansion, their trading empire received a shattering blow. Thirteen American colonies declared their independence, won a revolutionary struggle and emerged as the United States of America. About 2½ million settlers lived in these thirteen colonies and, in accordance with the Navigation Acts, imported most of their manufactured goods from Britain. Birmingham gunmakers, Dudley nailers and Staffordshire potters had substantial export markets in America. For them, colonies meant profit. For the government, colonies could mean financial loss. Fighting the French in Canada during the Seven Years' War (1756–63) had been a costly business; and there was still the threat of Redskin troubles. It was vital to retain an army in the colonies—but it would cost £350,000 a year. This was too much for British taxpayers (mainly the landed gentry) to bear alone; the colonists would have to pay something towards their own defence costs.

No taxation without representation

After 1763 the British tried to raise the necessary revenue inside the colonies. In 1764 Parliament approved a Revenue Act which, by raising sugar duties, would bring in £45,000 a year. In 1765 Parliament passed the Stamp Act which would yield £60,000 from stamp duties on newspapers, advertisements and legal contracts. This seemed a reasonable tax to the British—they had suffered it since 1694. In 1765 Parliament authorized the Mutiny Act which required settlers to contribute to the day-to-day needs of troops stationed in America. These measures caused an uproar in the colonies. The settlers insisted that a Parliament located in Westminster had no right to levy taxes on free British subjects, unless those free British subjects gave their consent. Consent was unobtainable as the colonists neither had nor wanted representatives in Westminster. They boycotted British goods and forced the British to repeal the Stamp Act in 1766. But next year saw the Chancellor of the Exchequer, Lord Townshend, attempting to raise £40,000 by extra duties on American imports. Again the colonists protested and in 1770 the Townshend duties were repealed. Nothing had been achieved apart from the alienation of the colonists and, in Britain, the build-up of anti-colonist prejudice.

Revolution

Several incidents escalated the ill-will into revolt. In 1770 a Boston mob provoked a British patrol; it opened fire, causing twelve casualties in this 'Boston Massacre'. In 1772 a British revenue schooner called the *Gaspée* ran aground off Providence; the Americans rowed out and burnt it. And when the British allowed the East India Company to sell tea in America at a cut-price rate *below* the price of smuggled tea, irate American merchants organized a protest. On 16 December 1773 150 men disguised in Redskin warpaint boarded three tea-ships berthed in Boston harbour. They tipped £18,000 worth of tea overboard. It took more than six weeks for news of the 'Boston Tea Party' to reach Westminster; when it did the government reacted firmly. It closed down the harbour (Boston Port Act 1774) and placed the government of Massachusetts colony in the hands of General Gage of the British army. Gage was unable to cope with the unruly population around Boston and when he sent a detachment to destroy an illegal gunpowder store at Concord in April 1775 the moment of truth arrived. On the way in there was a firefight at Lexington; on the way out the British lost 244 dead and wounded to sustained sniper fire. The revolution had begun.

The war 1775–83

It was an unwinnable war for the British. The Americans fought for a cause, for their homes and families, for civil rights and, after the Declaration of Independence in 1776, for their own country. After they formed their Continental Congress in 1775, they had an executive body capable of waging war. They found inspiration in their army commander, George Washington. Their British opponents had no such advantages: they faced huge natural obstacles, for the terrain was difficult and poorly mapped. All supplies had to be ferried across the Atlantic. Even with Hessian mercenaries, Indian scouts and Canadian volunteers, the army was too small. Then Britain's commercial rivals joined the Americans: France (1778), Spain (1779), Holland (1780). French warships controlled the eastern American seaboard; French soldiers aided Washington. Spaniards attacked Florida; French ships rampaged through the West Indies. Gradually, British resistance declined on the mainland and in 1781 most of the army surrendered to a superior Franco-American force at Yorktown. After this disaster, the British sought to regain control of the sea and to salvage their West Indian possessions. In 1782 Admiral Rodney defeated the French at the Battle of the Saints; he had saved Jamaica and given Britain an advantage at the peace talks which led to the 1783 Treaty of Versailles and the recognition of American independence.

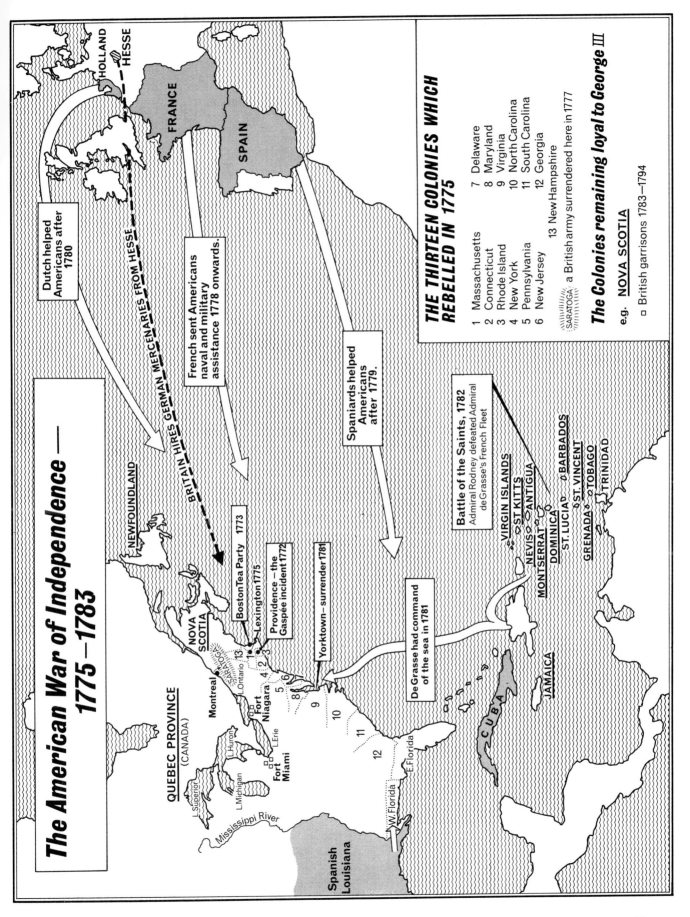

The American War of Independence — 1775–1783

HOLLAND

HESSE

FRANCE

SPAIN

Dutch helped Americans after 1780

BRITAIN HIRES GERMAN MERCENARIES FROM HESSE

French sent Americans naval and military assistance 1778 onwards.

Spaniards helped Americans after 1779.

Battle of the Saints, 1782
Admiral Rodney defeated Admiral deGrasse's French Fleet

VIRGIN ISLANDS
ST KITTS
NEVIS — ANTIGUA
MONTSERRAT — DOMINICA
ST. LUCIA — BARBADOS
ST. VINCENT
GRENADA — TOBAGO
TRINIDAD

DeGrasse had command of the sea in 1781

JAMAICA

CUBA

NEWFOUNDLAND

NOVA SCOTIA

Boston Tea Party 1773

Lexington 1775

Providence — the Gaspée incident 1772

Yorktown – surrender 1781

QUEBEC PROVINCE
(CANADA)

Montreal

SARATOGA

L.Ontario

Fort Niagara

L.Huron

L.Erie

Fort Miami

L.Superior

L.Michigan

Mississippi River

E.Florida

W. Florida

Spanish Louisiana

THE THIRTEEN COLONIES WHICH REBELLED IN 1775

1 Massachusetts
2 Connecticut
3 Rhode Island
4 New York
5 Pennsylvania
6 New Jersey
7 Delaware
8 Maryland
9 Virginia
10 North Carolina
11 South Carolina
12 Georgia
13 New Hampshire

SARATOGA – a British army surrendered here in 1777

The Colonies remaining loyal to George III

e.g. NOVA SCOTIA

☐ British garrisons 1783–1794

9: War and the British economy, 1775–1793

Conditions in Britain during the war

The American war saw the usual waste of human life and equipment. Grievous though such losses were, they were less important than the effect the war had on the economy. Britain had already begun her industrial expansion. The war interrupted this process. Fighting on land and sea meant a reduction in imports and exports just when Britain's expanding population was growing more dependent upon imported food. So the war caused food shortages; and the shortages caused price increases. Moreover, military contracts attracted money away from peaceful investments, with the result that canal and turnpike construction diminished. Economists call this sort of industrial decline a recession—and the British suffered their worst recession since 1700 during the American war.

Of course, a lot of people did well out of the war. Silk weavers who had always been troubled by French competitors found that this competition disappeared after 1778. The Carron works profited from the demand for guns. Ship's carpenters commanded good wages as the Royal Navy's losses mounted—at the Yorktown surrender in 1781 the Americans claimed to capture 'a 40 gun ship, a frigate, an arm'd sloop and a hundred transports'. Sailors' wages doubled between 1775 and 1780, while leather and textile workers were kept busy making boots and uniforms. But for lots of people, times were hard. When tobacco stopped coming in from Virginia and when the sugar imports from the West Indies dwindled, Bristol and Glasgow suffered hardship whilst Whitehaven was almost ruined. One section of the community, the Midland nailers, depended on the American trade. There were thousands of nailers; Arthur Young, travelling between Birmingham and West Bromwich in 1776, noted that there was 'for five or six miles . . . one continued village of nailers'. They averaged a subsistence wage of about 6/- a week (about 7,000 nailers were women and children) for a tiring 14-hour day at the nail forges. The trade was easy to pick up and wages were always depressed because penniless Irish immigrants were always eager to take a nailer's job. Yet during the war, these meagre wages went even lower. This was how the war disturbed the pattern of industrial growth and brought suffering to large sectors of the population.

*In 1797 the government commissioned him to issue a copper coinage for Britain and between 1797 and 1806 he made 4,200 tons of copper coins. He then built the Royal Mint near Tower Hill in London.

Gradual recovery

The immediate post-war years were understandably gloomy for defeated Britain. But once it was clear that overseas buyers still wanted British goods—between 1787 and 1790 the Americans bought nearly 90% of their manufactured goods from Britain—the merchants and industrialists grew more optimistic. The earlier advances in coal and iron production, the low transport costs were now paying off—British manufactures were cheap to make and easy to sell. Now canal-building resumed, so intensively that in the boom years (1790–3) it was called 'canal mania'. The big manufacturers were responsible: Abraham Darby III backed the Shropshire Canal in 1788; Sir Richard Arkwright proposed the new Crompton cut in 1789. By 1790 it was easy to persuade investors to part with their money when a canal could pay, as the Birmingham Canal did in 1789, dividends of 23%!

One interesting feature of this period was the serious shortage of copper coin with which to pay the industrial workers. Lots of firms resorted to the issue of copper 'tokens' which men used as currency. In 1792 Matthew Boulton* installed eight steam presses at his Birmingham Soho works expressly for their manufacture. His machines needed 1,200 tons of copper a year and the metal's value rose to £6 a ton. The local button manufacturers said this put up their costs; and their reaction was to *lower* their workers' wages, explaining that the wage cut was something 'for which they must thank Mr. Boulton'. The button makers took to the streets and rioted. Boulton was terrified, recruited a private bodyguard and bitterly complained that he was neither competing with the button makers nor was he to blame for their hardships. But this cut no ice with the rioters who, as products of the new industrial age, had no organized means of bargaining for better wages and working conditions. The riot, the street commotion, was their only weapon; it was, in fact, a normal feature of life in this country at the time.

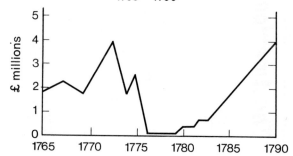

VALUE OF BRITISH EXPORTS TO AMERICA
1765–1790

£ millions

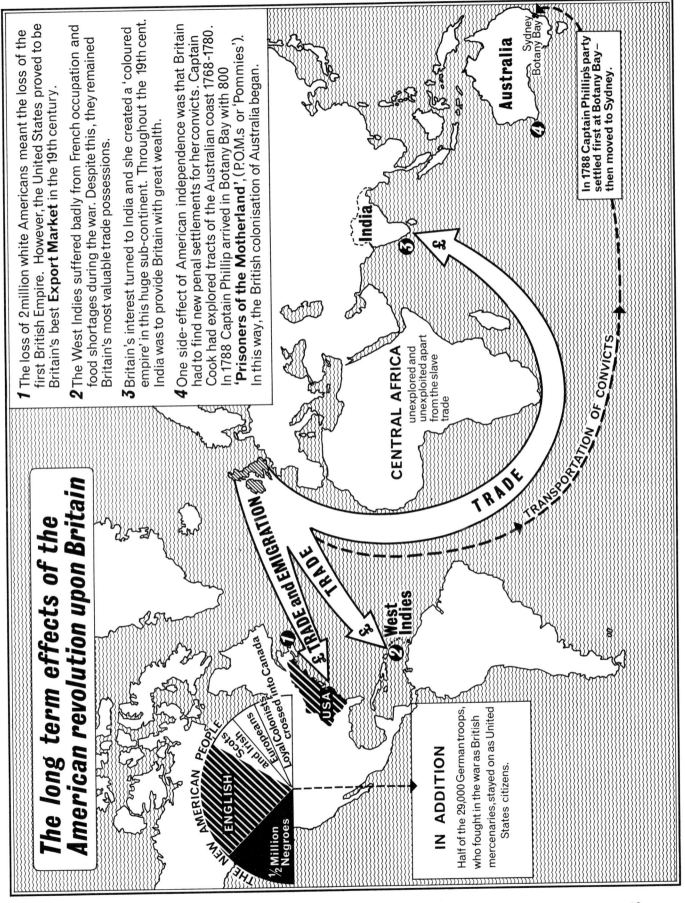

The long term effects of the American revolution upon Britain

1 The loss of 2 million white Americans meant the loss of the first British Empire. However, the United States proved to be Britain's best **Export Market** in the 19th century.

2 The West Indies suffered badly from French occupation and food shortages during the war. Despite this, they remained Britain's most valuable trade possessions.

3 Britain's interest turned to India and she created a 'coloured empire' in this huge sub-continent. Throughout the 19th cent. India was to provide Britain with great wealth.

4 One side-effect of American independence was that Britain had to find new penal settlements for her convicts. Captain Cook had explored tracts of the Australian coast 1768-1780. In 1788 Captain Phillip arrived in Botany Bay with 800 **'Prisoners of the Motherland'**, (P.O.M.s or 'Pommies'). In this way, the British colonisation of Australia began.

THE NEW AMERICAN PEOPLE
ENGLISH
Scots and Irish
Europeans
Loyal Colonists crossed into Canada
½ Million Negroes

£ TRADE and EMIGRATION

£ TRADE

① USA

③ West Indies

② West Indies

IN ADDITION

Half of the 29,000 German troops, who fought in the war as British mercenaries, stayed on as United States citizens.

CENTRAL AFRICA
unexplored and unexploited apart from the slave trade

TRADE

TRANSPORTATION OF CONVICTS

£ ⑤

India

Australia

Sydney
Botany Bay ④

In 1788 Captain Phillip's party settled first at Botany Bay— then moved to Sydney.

10: Law and order

London

England in the eighteenth century was notorious for her unruly mobs. With no organized police forces, the magistrates and country squires responsible for law and order had to call on troops to handle mob violence. Justice was rough and ready: the bayonet or musket ball on the spot; and for those arrested and found guilty a fine, transportation, or death. A few jails, such as London's Newgate, Clerkenwell and Fleet (for debtors) existed; but as death was the penalty for scores of crimes, the prison population remained small. London was 'peculiarly turbulent'. It was one of the most difficult cities in Europe to keep under control. Londoners had all sorts of grievances and prejudices. They distrusted Methodists and Catholics, resented the Irish and, understandably, hated the press gang. Anything which put up the price of food or housing infuriated them. And as well as violence in the streets, there was plenty of criminal violence. Highwaymen were still operating *inside* the City of London. Punishments were barbaric: whipping and branding were quite common. An aimless crowd, bored with prizefighting and bearbaiting, might wander down Charing Cross to pelt some helpless villain in the stocks, or go along to 'Tyburn Fair' to see the hangings. But the dangerous time was usually the summer; and during the hot June days of 1780 the worst outburst of violence took place.

The Gordon Riots, June 1780

Lord George Gordon, Member of Parliament, mistakenly believed that some of his fellow M.P.s were secretly pro-Catholic and, moreover, that there was a plan afoot to massacre London's Protestants. His extraordinary views aroused plenty of support among the Londoners and on Friday, 2 June 1780 Gordon led a crowd to Westminster where he presented a petition deploring 'the Catholic threat'. Parliament threw it out. That evening some rioters, most of whom had nothing to do with the petition, burnt some Catholic chapels used by foreign embassy staffs. On Sunday, gangs moved into East London and set fire to several Irish areas. By Monday several parts of the city were ablaze and on Tuesday the mob released the prisoners from Newgate Jail. They then moved on to Clerkenwell and Fleet so that, by Wednesday, all semblance of law and order had vanished. So had all the magistrates who could have done something

about it. It was generally, but wrongly, assumed that before soldiers could be used against a mob a magistrate must first read the 1715 Riot Act. Alderman Kennet, the Lord Mayor, openly admitted why he hadn't done this: 'I must be cautious what I do lest I bring the mob to my house'. In desperation the government called out the troops by Royal Proclamation—but they could not stop Fleet Prison from going up in flames. However, after John Wilkes* successfully defended the Bank of England against the rioters, the soldiers began to restore law and order. They arrested 160 people; 25 were hanged. In 1781 the judges cleared Gordon of complicity in the riots; but six years later he was back in jail for libelling Marie Antoinette, the Queen of France. He adopted the Jewish faith while languishing in Newgate and in 1793 died there after an outbreak of typhus—a strange fate for the Protestant fanatic who saw Catholic plotters everywhere.

The French Revolution

Most eighteenth-century commotions, such as Nottingham's famous 'Great Cheese Riot' of 1764, were essentially food riots. A few were genuinely concerned with religious and political grievances—though many a rioter got away with murder by screaming 'For Church and King!' and 'No Popery!' None made the impact as did the revolutionary crowd in Paris. When it stormed the Bastille on 14 July 1789 it sparked off a revolution that led to the creation of the First French Republic in 1792. No comparable movement existed in Britain where the first effect of the French Revolution was to arouse some 'intellectual discontent'. Many people admired the French bid for liberty, fraternity and equality. They read Tom Paine's *Rights of Man* (published 1791–2) and wondered about *their* lack of political rights. A few formed 'Corresponding Societies' in Sheffield, Derby, Manchester and London during 1792 and exchanged political ideas. Thomas Hardy, a shoemaker and founder of the London Corresponding Society, had enrolled 2000 people by the end of the year. That ordinary people should identify with revolutionaries abroad alarmed the government and, after France declared war on Britain in 1793, it quickly clamped down on these societies.

*Wilkes had himself been a very effective agitator in the 'sixties and 'seventies and a constant thorn in the government's side.

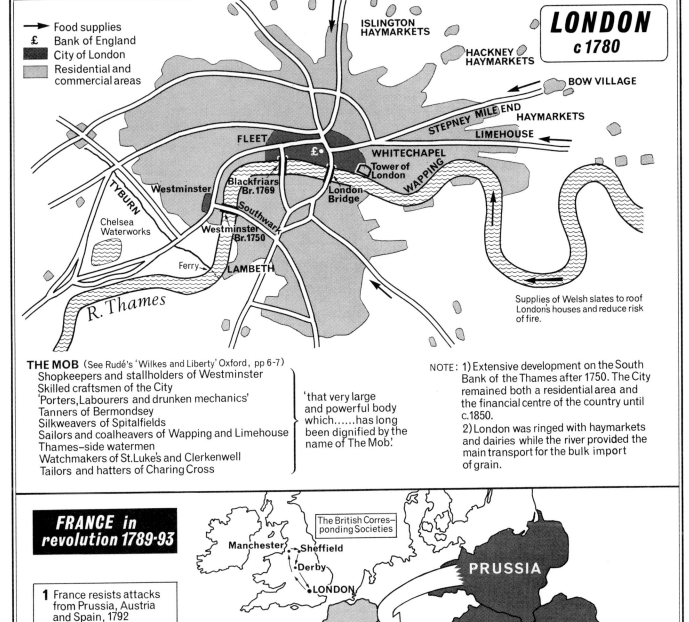

LONDON c 1780

- → Food supplies
- £ Bank of England
- City of London
- Residential and commercial areas

ISLINGTON HAYMARKETS

HACKNEY HAYMARKETS

BOW VILLAGE

STEPNEY MILE END HAYMARKETS

LIMEHOUSE

FLEET

£

WHITECHAPEL

Tower of London

WAPPING

TYBURN

Westminster

Blackfriars Br. 1769

London Bridge

Chelsea Waterworks

Southwark

Westminster Br. 1750

Ferry

LAMBETH

R. Thames

Supplies of Welsh slates to roof London's houses and reduce risk of fire.

THE MOB (See Rudé's 'Wilkes and Liberty' Oxford, pp 6-7)
Shopkeepers and stallholders of Westminster
Skilled craftsmen of the City
'Porters, Labourers and drunken mechanics'
Tanners of Bermondsey
Silkweavers of Spitalfields
Sailors and coalheavers of Wapping and Limehouse
Thames–side watermen
Watchmakers of St. Luke's and Clerkenwell
Tailors and hatters of Charing Cross

'that very large and powerful body which......has long been dignified by the name of The Mob.'

NOTE: 1) Extensive development on the South Bank of the Thames after 1750. The City remained both a residential area and the financial centre of the country until c.1850.
2) London was ringed with haymarkets and dairies while the river provided the main transport for the bulk import of grain.

FRANCE in revolution 1789-93

The British Corresponding Societies

Manchester · Sheffield
· Derby
· LONDON

1 France resists attacks from Prussia, Austria and Spain, 1792
2 Guillotined her king, Louis XVI, in 1793
3 Declared war on Britain, 1793

PARIS

FRANCE in revolution

PRUSSIA

AUSTRIA

SPAIN

Part 1 – The British people on the eve of industrial change

Spread

1. *The Industrial Revolution***   T. S. Ashton   HUL
2. *The Agrarian Revolution*   J. Addy   Longmans
   The Agricultural Revolution 1750–1880   Chambers & Mingay   Batsford
3. *Commercial Revolution*   Historical Association Pamphlet

   *The Slave Trade***   Jackdaw Publication
   *English People***   Dorothy Marshall   Longmans
4. *The First Industrial Revolution*   P. Deane   CUP
   *A Textile Community in the Industrial Revolution***   E. Power   Longmans
5. *The Industrial Revolution***   T. S. Ashton   HUL
6. *Iron and Steel***   W. Gale   Longmans
7. *British Canals***   R. Hadfield   Phoenix
8. *The American War of Independence***   P. Wells   ULP
9. *The First Industrial Revolution*   P. Deane   CUP
10. *Wilkes and Liberty*   George Rudé   Oxford

**Especially useful for project and topic work

PART 2

The Impact of War
1793–1822

Between 1793 and 1815, with one brief respite, the British people fought the French in the Revolutionary and Napoleonic Wars. This continual warfare hindered *trade* and *industry* and coincided with the *population explosion* and a *prolonged food shortage*. These were therefore crisis years in which the government ruled according to the well-established principles of the 'mercantile system'; that is, it regulated trade and controlled food prices so that the financial and military well-being of the State, rather than that of individuals, was preserved. The system had so many weaknesses that it was constantly under attack by contemporary economists.

As early as 1776 Adam Smith (1723–90) had published his famous *Wealth of Nations* in which he urged the government to free trade and industry from regulations and taxes. He argued that '*consumption* is the sole end of all production' and deplored the fact that the interest of the consumer 'is almost constantly sacrificed to that of the producer'. Another writer, Thomas Malthus (1766–1834), was more interested in the dangers from the population explosion. In his *First Essay on Population* (1798) he tried to demonstrate that the government's policy of poor relief actually *caused* distress when it was supposed to relieve it! He argued that the more you help poor families to survive by doling out money and food, the more you encourage poor people to marry and have more children. The government was following a policy of creating more mouths to feed when it should be encouraging *small* families. Reduce poor relief; war, disease and poverty will do the rest. A third writer, David Ricardo (1772–1823), thought that 'laws of nature', not man-made laws, should control production, prices and wages. The government shouldn't try to interfere in such matters; leave them alone, he said, and they will look after themselves. In their different ways, these writers were saying the same thing; the government should play a smaller part in the economics of the nation. It should take as its motto the phrase 'laissez-faire'—'leave things alone to take their own course'.

However, the government was not then disposed to adopt any of these suggestions. It felt a duty to support the producers—especially the arable farmers who had a very powerful influence in government circles. But it did not feel any duty to improve the condition of the *consumers* apart from providing poor relief.

This is why discontent and violence on the part of the consumers—the ordinary people—dominate this period. The British people could neither join trade unions nor send their own M.P.s to Parliament. They had no way of making their voices heard. So they protested, demonstrated, went on strike or joined the Luddites. The government, totally inexperienced in these matters and ill-equipped to handle the *human* problems of an industrialized society, had no answer other than repression.

11: The revolutionary and Napoleonic Wars, 1793–1815, (a) To the death of Pitt (1806)

Pitt's victory plan

Pitt the Younger, Prime Minister of Britain since 1783, had no wish to fight France. Yet once hostilities began he followed the usual pattern for fighting a continental war. He offered gold subsidies to European allies, who would bear the brunt of the land fighting. He attacked France's colonies, raided her trade routes and blockaded her ports. He was convinced that these tactics would soon bring about the collapse of Revolutionary France.

The ascendancy of France

Pitt was over-optimistic. The fighting men of France were imbued with the spirit of a successful revolution; they believed passionately in their new Republic and were ready to die for her. Pitt soon realized that he was fighting men of a different calibre from those who had served in the armies of the Bourbon kings. The French were not dismayed by the size of Pitt's First Coalition (1793: Britain, Holland, Prussia, Spain, Austria). They managed to break the Royal Navy's blockade when their grainships eluded the British frigates during the Battle of the Glorious First of June (1794). They overran Holland, deterred the Prussians and Spaniards from making war in 1795 and forced the Austrians to make peace in 1797. As for the main British effort out in the West Indies, they simply ignored it. Between 1794 and 1798, thousands of British servicemen died from dysentery and yellow fever on the French island of San Domingue. Toussaint L'Ouverture, former slave and negro nationalist, contemptuously expelled the remnants of the British force.

The survival of Britain

The threat of revolution existed at home as well as abroad. Two mutinies occurred in the Royal Navy during 1797. The April mutiny among the ships of the Channel Fleet at Spithead was a protest against the press-gang, arrears of pay and abominable conditions below deck. But the May mutiny at the Nore was a direct challenge to naval authority. Its ringleader, Richard Parker, was a professed revolutionary, and for a few days his 'floating republic' blockaded London. He and 28 accomplices were hanged. Then Ireland flared into revolt. One of the leaders, Wolfe Tone, considered 'the connexion between Ireland and Great Britain as the curse of the Irish nation'. Thousands of depressed peasants rallied to the cause of a free Ireland and stormed the British garrison at Wexford in 1798. Fortunately for Pitt, the local Yeomanry crushed the rebels in a savage civil war; the small French army which landed arrived too late to sway the issue. Wolfe Tone achieved martyrdom by committing suicide. So Pitt managed to ride the dangers at home and abroad and Britain survived in a sufficiently strong position to form the Second Coalition against France (1798: Britain, Russia, Austria, Turkey).

The threat from Napoleon 1798–1805

From 1798 onwards Napoleon's military ambitions were a menace to British security. The French Directors (leaders of the French Republic) authorized an attack upon Egypt. Napoleon landed at Alexandria and posed a threat to the whole Middle East—a threat which Nelson removed by his victory over the French fleet at the Battle of the Nile (1 August 1798). Napoleon returned to France in 1799, overthrew the Directors and set himself up as First Consul. He wrote a most beguiling letter to George III:

> Why should the two most enlightened countries . . . go on sacrificing their trade, their prosperity and their domestic happiness to false ideas of greatness?

But it was three years before they made peace at Amiens (27 March 1802). Pitt was no longer Prime Minister, but Napoleon remained the prime source of danger. Relishing his 'Grand Design'—the invasion of England, he declared war on Britain in May 1803. Pitt, now a sick man, returned as Prime Minister in 1804 and set to work to build the Third Coalition against France (1805: Britain, Austria, Russia). But he knew that this would be no protection against a French invasion. Again Nelson settled the issue. On 21 October 1805 he destroyed the Franco-Spanish fleets at the Battle of Trafalgar and thus robbed Napoleon of any chance of ever dominating the English Channel.

The death of Pitt, 23 January 1806

Shortly after Trafalgar, the Lord Mayor of London toasted Pitt as the saviour of Europe. Pitt replied with one of the shortest and most famous speeches in British history:

> I return you many thanks for the honour you have done me; but Europe is not to be saved by any single man. England has saved herself by her exertions and will, I trust, save Europe by her example.

He was dead within two months. Napoleon, victorious over the Austrian and Russian armies at the Battles of Ulm and Austerlitz, was now supreme in Europe.

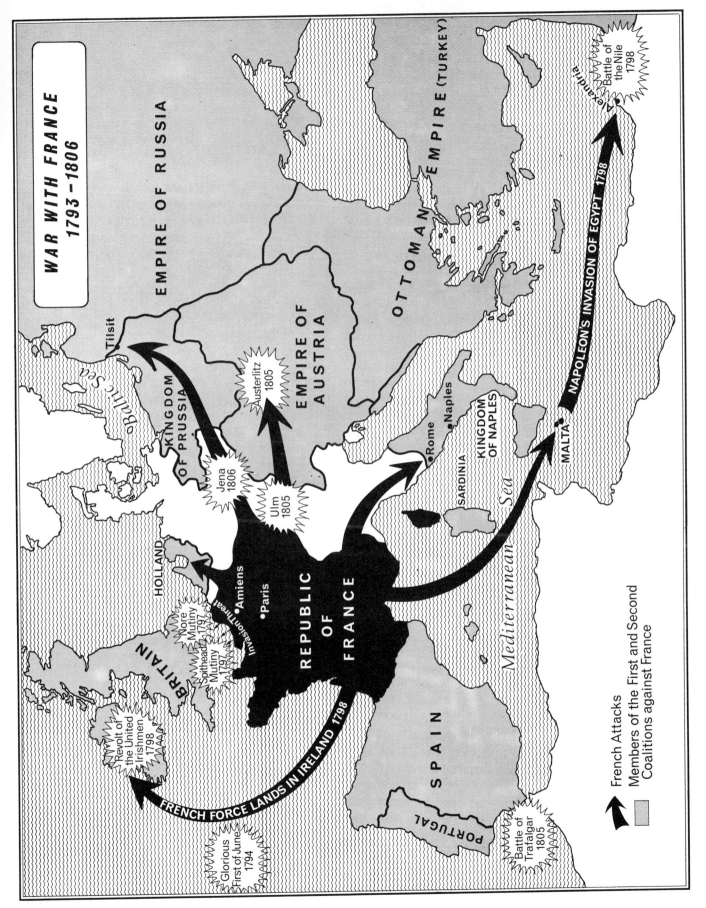

WAR WITH FRANCE
1793 –1806

EMPIRE OF RUSSIA

OTTOMAN EMPIRE (TURKEY)

Battle of the Nile 1798

Alexandria

NAPOLEON'S INVASION OF EGYPT 1798

EMPIRE OF AUSTRIA

Tilsit

KINGDOM OF PRUSSIA

Austerlitz 1805

Jena 1806

Ulm 1805

Baltic Sea

Rome

Naples

SARDINIA

KINGDOM OF NAPLES

MALTA

Mediterranean Sea

HOLLAND

Nore Mutiny 1797

Invasion Threat

Amiens

Paris

Spithead Mutiny 1797

BRITAIN

REPUBLIC OF FRANCE

Revolt of the United Irishmen 1798

FRENCH FORCE LANDS IN IRELAND 1798

SPAIN

PORTUGAL

Glorious First of June 1794

Battle of Trafalgar 1805

French Attacks

Members of the First and Second Coalitions against France

25

12: Wartime Britain, 1793–1806

The nation's security

Pitt was well aware that a number of Englishmen, particularly members of the Corresponding Societies, looked forward to the day when a republic might be set up in Britain, just as it had been in France. These political extremists or 'radicals' might be willing to give aid to the French and were therefore, in Pitt's estimation, a source of danger. So he was willing, for the time being, to sacrifice the liberty of the individual in the national interest. This was why Parliament suspended *Habeas Corpus* between 1794 and 1802; it meant that Englishmen could now be jailed without being brought to trial. A hundred suspects were detained in this way. In 1795 Parliament went on to pass the much-criticized 'Two Acts': the *Treason Act* prohibited any expression of contempt towards the King (who had been attacked in his coach just before this), government or constitution; the *Seditious Meetings Act* declared any meeting of fifty persons or more to be illegal unless they had a magistrate's permission to assemble. Finally, Parliament declared all Trade Union activity illegal by the *Combination Acts* 1799–1800.*

Pitt was equally anxious about another French landing in Ireland. He insisted on uniting England and Ireland under one imperial parliament and the Act of Union took place at the end of 1800. The king refused to let Catholic M.P.s come to Westminster; Pitt resigned and was out of office 1801–4. To defend England, the government built a number of Martello towers along the southeast coast and cut the Royal Military Canal between Shorncliffe and Winchelsea. It also constructed the Caledonian Canal so that warships could cross from coast to coast quickly. By 1803, the government was requisitioning all kinds of transport as Napoleon massed his troops at Boulogne. Pickfords, the well known carriers, offered the loan of 50 wagons, 28 canal boats and 400 horses—but an invasion was one crisis the government did not have to face.

Food crisis

It was sad that this long war coincided with a run of bad harvests and a population explosion. 'Hard times' was on everybody's lips at first, but few thought the war would last for long. Most were optimistic about the future—as the Norwich trade token opposite shows. But the war dragged on and the hard times got worse.

*The acts also abolished the Corresponding Societies.

The basic reason for this was the perennial food shortage which caused prices to rise and wages to lag behind. Britain depended for most of the war on imported grain—there were so many mouths to feed—and this pushed up food prices which in turn led to a general increase in the cost of living. For the rural population—and most people still lived in the countryside—the harvests were crucial. When they failed in 1795 there was a food crisis in southern England; for here wages were low and jobs scarce. Dreadful weather conditions prevailed during 1796–1800—crops of turnip, wheat and barley often failed and extensive foot-rot in sheep reduced supplies of cheap mutton.

Speenhamland, 1795

These events prompted the Poor Law officials at Speenhamland (Berkshire) to deal with the distress in their area. They modified the Poor Law arrangements by supplementing wages out of the Poor Rate. They thought that each family man ought to be able to buy up to three gallon loaves each week. Their idea was adopted or modified by other farming counties so that what had begun as a genuine *local* effort to help a *few* distressed families now developed into a widespread system of 'supplementary allowances' geared to current food prices and the number of children in a family. Each child could be worth up to 30 pence per week—and this had considerable purchasing power in 1795. It would have been better if there had been an agreed minimum wage, because some farmers paid low wages in the knowledge that the Poor Rate would boost their workers' incomes. The 'Speenhamland System' persisted for years and had important results. It reduced the mobility of labour, it excluded unmarried men and thus encouraged early marriages, it forced far too many to 'go on the parish'. But it also saved thousands of lives in a period of food shortage.

Life in the towns

In contrast, wages in many of the new manufacturing towns were on the increase, though living conditions were on the decline. In Manchester, for example, back-to-back houses were common by 1800. Personal hygiene was difficult: there were very few efficient water cisterns and wells were often contaminated. Back yards and gardens were rare and by an act of 1792 clothes lines could not be strung across Manchester's unpaved streets. The industrial slums had arrived.

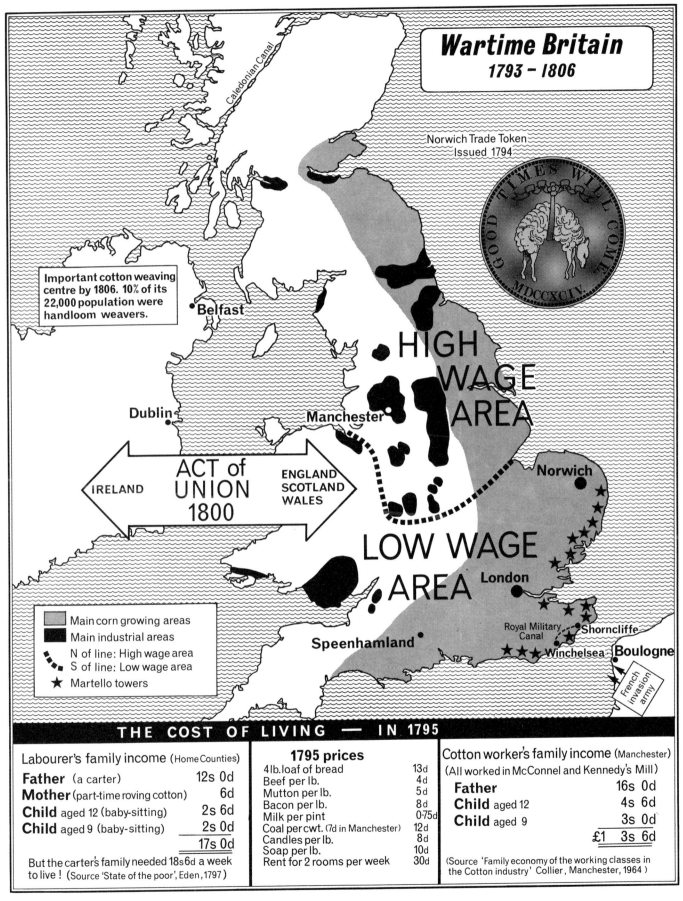

Wartime Britain 1793 – 1806

Caledonian Canal

Norwich Trade Token Issued 1794

GOOD TIMES WILL COME MDCCXCIV.

Important cotton weaving centre by 1806. 10% of its 22,000 population were handloom weavers.

Belfast

Dublin

Manchester

HIGH WAGE AREA

ACT of UNION 1800

IRELAND

ENGLAND SCOTLAND WALES

Norwich

LOW WAGE AREA

London

Royal Military Canal

Shorncliffe

Speenhamland

Winchelsea

Boulogne

French invasion army

Legend
- Main corn growing areas
- Main industrial areas
- N of line: High wage area
- S of line: Low wage area
- ★ Martello towers

THE COST OF LIVING — IN 1795

Labourer's family income (Home Counties)

Father (a carter)	12s 0d
Mother (part-time roving cotton)	6d
Child aged 12 (baby-sitting)	2s 6d
Child aged 9 (baby-sitting)	2s 0d
	17s 0d

But the carter's family needed 18s 6d a week to live! (Source 'State of the poor', Eden, 1797)

1795 prices

4 lb. loaf of bread	13d
Beef per lb.	4d
Mutton per lb.	5d
Bacon per lb.	8d
Milk per pint	0·75d
Coal per cwt. (7d in Manchester)	12d
Candles per lb.	8d
Soap per lb.	10d
Rent for 2 rooms per week	30d

Cotton worker's family income (Manchester)
(All worked in McConnel and Kennedy's Mill)

Father	16s 0d
Child aged 12	4s 6d
Child aged 9	3s 0d
	£1 3s 6d

(Source 'Family economy of the working classes in the Cotton industry' Collier, Manchester, 1964)

27

13: The revolutionary and Napoleonic Wars, (b) To the defeat of Napoleon in 1815

Economic warfare

During 1806, Napoleon rounded off his European conquests by beating the Prussians at the Battle of Jena. Unchallenged on the Continent, he devised a scheme to counter British naval supremacy *par la puissance de la terre*—by defeating sea power with land power. He reasoned that, as master of most of Europe, he could surely control Europe's trade. He would forbid all open commerce between European seaports and the English, but he would condone *smuggling*. This would force the English to pay high cash prices for smuggled goods; and this would mean that their gold reserves would dwindle. And if they tried to pay by smuggling their own manufactured goods into Europe, Napoleon would confiscate them and use them for his own war effort. Such was the substance of Napoleon's Continental System announced in the Berlin Decrees (1806). Britain retaliated with her Orders in Council (1807) and prohibited all trade between one French-occupied port and another. Quite deliberately, the two warring nations upset the whole economy of Western Europe and unwittingly escalated the war throughout the Western Hemisphere.

The Peninsular War 1808–14

The Berlin Decrees turned the whole European coastline into a target for the Royal Navy which soon searched out weak links in the Continental Blockade. The Navy struck first at the Danish fleet based at Copenhagen, opened the Baltic approaches and occupied Heligoland as a base for future smuggling operations. Then, in 1808, the Spanish nationalist revolt against Napoleon allowed the Navy to land a British force on the Iberian Peninsula. Here, for the next six years, Wellesley's redcoats fought the French invaders in the bitter Peninsular War. Year after year Wellesley (created Duke of Wellington in 1810) sallied forth from his heavily defended base at Torres Vedras to tempt a French attack. Year after year the French tried desperately to drive him out of Portugal; in the process they exposed their long lines of communication to merciless attack by Spanish guerrillas. Both sides suffered miserably; the British government was reluctant to spend much money on a 'sideshow' which could not in itself win the war. So Wellington's troops were usually short of food, clothing, medical supplies and weapons. Thousands died from fever and exposure before the victories at Talavera (1809), Fuentes de Onoro (1811), Salamanca (1812) and Vittoria (1813) enabled the British to cross the Pyrenees into France.

The Anglo-American War 1812–14

This conflict arose ostensibly from the zealous manner in which the Royal Navy searched neutral American vessels for contraband and deserters. In fact, President Madison declared war on the assumption that the moment was ripe for clearing all European colonial powers out of North America. Most of the combat was along the Canadian-American border: the Americans attacked and burnt Toronto twice; the British set fire to the President's residence (later known as the White House because of the whitewash used to cover up the repairs!); while there were several firefights around Niagara Falls and on the Great Lakes. One British force attacked New Orleans—disastrously; and on the sea American frigates often outclassed the Royal Navy in ship-to-ship fights. Neither side gained from the conflict; only Napoleon was delighted to see Britain's attention diverted from the other war theatres. Most British and American people desired to exchange goods, not bullets, with one another. They were thankful when the war ended at the Peace of Ghent 1814.

The invasion of Russia and the defeat of Napoleon 1812–15

Napoleon's obsession with his Continental Blockade led him into his catastrophic invasion of Russia. In order to force the Czar to implement the blockade more thoroughly, Napoleon led a quarter of a million first-class troops into Russia in June 1812. After the 'bloodbath of Borodino' (58,000 Russian casualties—30,000 French casualties), they battled towards Moscow and, on 14 September 1812, entered the deserted city. By the following evening, irresponsible French looters had set fire to the city and Napoleon had to abandon his prize. And when snow fell in October, he ordered his men to retreat. 100,000 soldiers, burdened with plunder, set off on the terrifying journey which would destroy them. Napoleon managed to escape and arrived in Paris on 18 December—apparently unmoved by the loss of most of his troops.

These allied successes in Spain and in Russia heartened the old enemies of Napoleon. In 1813 yet another coalition pushed the French back to France after the great 'Battle of the Nations' fought at Leipzig in October. From Spain and Germany, the allies advanced until Paris fell on 31 March 1814. Napoleon abdicated and was confined to the island of Elba. From here he escaped in March 1815, landed in France and raised his last army. At Waterloo it fought and lost its last battle.

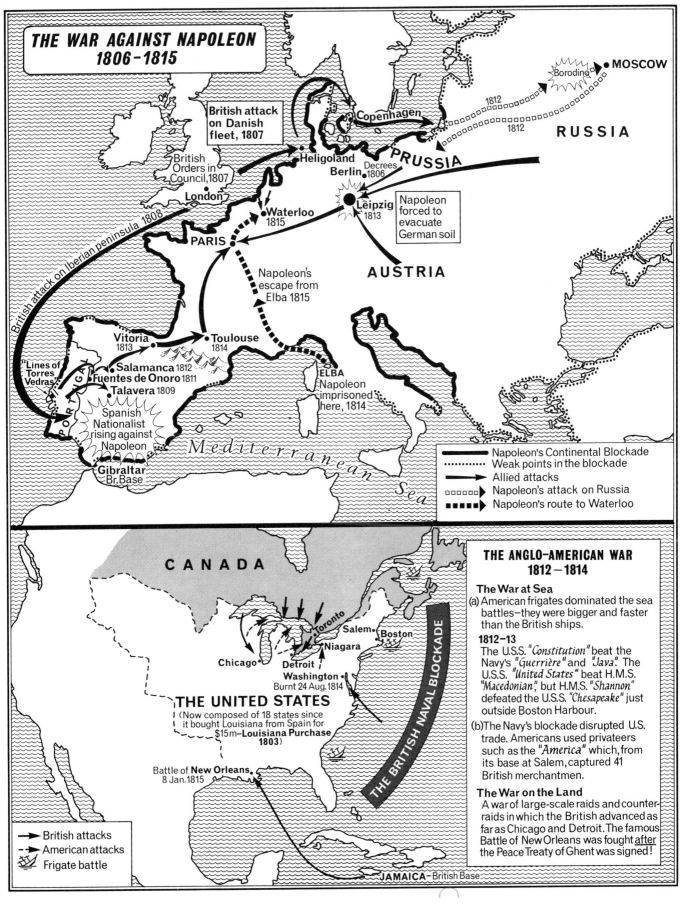

THE WAR AGAINST NAPOLEON 1806-1815

MOSCOW

Borodino

1812
1812

RUSSIA

British attack on Danish fleet, 1807

Copenhagen

Heligoland

PRUSSIA

British Orders in Council, 1807

Berlin
Decrees 1806

London

Waterloo 1815

Leipzig 1813

Napoleon forced to evacuate German soil

PARIS

AUSTRIA

British attack on Iberian peninsula 1808

Napoleon's escape from Elba 1815

Vitoria 1813

Toulouse 1814

"Lines of Torres Vedras"

Salamanca 1812
Fuentes de Onoro 1811

ELBA Napoleon imprisoned here, 1814

Talavera 1809

Spanish Nationalist rising against Napoleon

P O R T U G A L

Mediterranean Sea

Gibraltar Br. Base

	Napoleon's Continental Blockade
·······	Weak points in the blockade
→	Allied attacks
▢▢▢▢▢▶	Napoleon's attack on Russia
■■■■■▶	Napoleon's route to Waterloo

CANADA

Toronto

Salem

Boston

Chicago

Detroit

Niagara

Washington Burnt 24 Aug. 1814

THE UNITED STATES
(Now composed of 18 states since it bought Louisiana from Spain for $15m–**Louisiana Purchase 1803**)

Battle of **New Orleans** 8 Jan. 1815

THE BRITISH NAVAL BLOCKADE

THE ANGLO-AMERICAN WAR 1812 – 1814

The War at Sea

(a) American frigates dominated the sea battles–they were bigger and faster than the British ships.

1812–13
The U.S.S. *"Constitution"* beat the Navy's *"Guerrière"* and *"Java".* The U.S.S. *"United States"* beat H.M.S. *"Macedonian",* but H.M.S. *"Shannon"* defeated the U.S.S. *"Chesapeake"* just outside Boston Harbour.

(b) The Navy's blockade disrupted U.S. trade. Americans used privateers such as the *"America"* which, from its base at Salem, captured 41 British merchantmen.

The War on the Land
A war of large-scale raids and counter-raids in which the British advanced as far as Chicago and Detroit. The famous Battle of New Orleans was fought <u>after</u> the Peace Treaty of Ghent was signed!

→	British attacks
⇢	American attacks
⛵	Frigate battle

JAMAICA–British Base

14: Wartime Britain, 1806–1815

War and the means of production

War made unprecedented demands upon industry and acted as a great spur to production. A man could gain and lose a fortune by speculating in wartime industry. Typical was Samuel Fereday who made huge profits from his blast furnaces at Priestfield and Bradley. When he heard the news of Wellington's victory at Waterloo, he laid on a banquet for his 1500 employees; but he went bankrupt after the war ended. It was also an age of mechanization: Birmingham manufacturers applied steam power to wire-drawing in 1808; to iron forges in 1810; to nail-cutting in 1813. They turned out 3 million gun barrels between 1806 and 1815—this was more than the entire French production for the same period. British coalowners doubled their production—it took seven tons of coal to process one ton of iron. By 1815 they were mining nearly 16 million tons annually. The mill-owners won plenty of government contracts; in Leeds, Ben Gott's firm made uniforms not only for the British army, but for the soldiers of Prussia and Russia also. Farmers did well throughout the war. During bad harvests they could always exact high prices for small crops; while the constant cry for food encouraged them to enclose more common and waste land. Some even ploughed up parts of Dartmoor in the hope of a good crop! After 1806, however, industrialists who depended on export markets and overseas sources of raw materials found that 'economic warfare' hindered trade. Some sought new markets in Spain and Latin America: one optimist tried to sell ice-skates in Rio de Janeiro! Then the American War of 1812 removed that market. Meanwhile, poor harvests aggravated unemployment problems. Had it not been for Napoleon's extraordinary decision to let French farmers sell their grain surplus to Britain in 1810 there would have been nation-wide distress and disorder. As it was, certain sections of the British people suffered excessively.

War and the workers

The hand nailers: the American war was a disaster for them; more than half their production went to the U.S.A. Now the ironmongers were laying off workers, most of whom had no alternative employment other than the army. Those who kept their jobs suffered longer hours and lower piece-rates. In 1812–13 a nailer was lucky to pick up 2/- a day. If his wife and children worked at the nail forge they could earn 10d. per day. It was not unknown for some large families to bring home £2 a week.

The handloom weavers: Their fortunes fluctuated after 1806. The Berlin Decrees cut off the European markets; the Orders in Council and the Royal Navy's searches of neutral ships infuriated the Americans, many of whom cancelled cotton orders. Parliament rejected all the weavers' petitions to end the war with France; so in 1808 the Manchester weavers went on strike for a month. They removed all the shuttles from the looms. When troops arrived to keep order they killed a striker—and the conscience-stricken soldiers handed over a day's pay to the weaver's widow. 1808–9 saw a bad winter and the *Manchester Mercury* commented: 'There was never any period . . . when the distresses of the poorer classes were greater' (3.1.1809). Had it not been for local charity, many weavers would have died that winter. Things looked up in the summer when the weavers were making cloth for Spain and Latin America, but hard times returned during 1810–12. For many textile workers it was the worst period of the war and it led to the Luddite Revolt in many parts of industrial England.

The Luddites, 1811–12: Luddites were militant textile workers who challenged their masters' right to install machinery in factories and reduce wages. For over a year the Luddite rebels in the Midlands terrorized the manufacturers by launching well-organized attacks on the mills, where stocking frames and shearing frames were the main target. Most of the Nottingham and Derbyshire hosiers surrendered to the Luddites' demands and the first stage of the revolt ended in February 1812. Then the government moved in troops and decreed that frame-breaking carried the death penalty. This did not deter the Lancashire and Yorkshire Luddites who began a very effective campaign which culminated in the famous attack upon William Cartwright's mill at Rawfolds (March 1812) and the murder of William Horsfall, a hated mill-owner, in April. The troops—there were 12,000 stationed to keep law and order in the North, exceeding the number Wellington had to fight the Peninsular War!—managed to arrest some of the Luddites and seventeen died on the scaffold at York in 1813. Luddism virtually disappeared for the rest of the war.

Such events underlined the violence of the age; violence caused by the economic hardships of the war, the problem of feeding under difficult conditions an *ever-increasing* population and by the resentment of workers who were compelled to adjust to the gradual mechanization of industry. It was significant that at this moment in history a maniac chose to assassinate Spencer Perceval, Prime Minister of England.

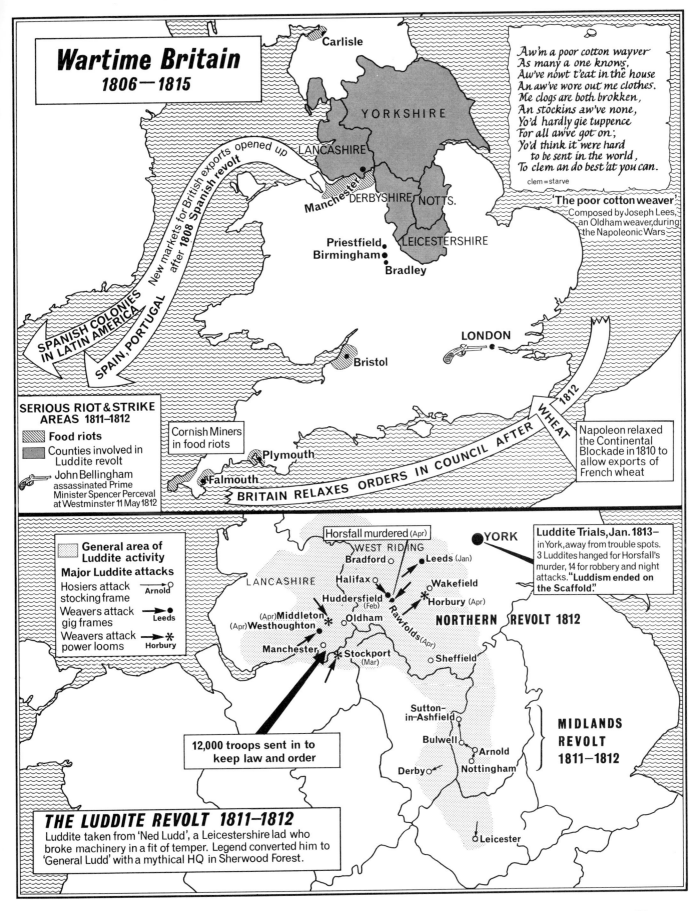

Wartime Britain 1806–1815

New markets for British exports opened up after 1808 Spanish revolt

SPANISH COLONIES IN LATIN AMERICA

SPAIN, PORTUGAL

Carlisle

YORKSHIRE

LANCASHIRE

Manchester

DERBYSHIRE NOTTS.

LEICESTERSHIRE

Priestfield
Birmingham
Bradley

LONDON

Bristol

BRITAIN RELAXES ORDERS IN COUNCIL AFTER

WHEAT 1812

Aw'm a poor cotton wayver
As many a one knows,
Aw've nowt t'eat in th'e house
An aw've wore out me clothes.
Me clogs are both brokken,
An stockins aw've none,
Yo'd hardly gie tuppence
For all aw've got on';
Yo'd think it were hard
to be sent in th'e world,
To clem an do best'at you can.

clem = starve

'The poor cotton weaver'
Composed by Joseph Lees,
an Oldham weaver, during
the Napoleonic Wars

Napoleon relaxed
the Continental
Blockade in 1810 to
allow exports of
French wheat

SERIOUS RIOT & STRIKE AREAS 1811–1812

- ▨ **Food riots**
- ▨ Counties involved in Luddite revolt
- 🔫 John Bellingham assassinated Prime Minister Spencer Perceval at Westminster 11 May 1812

Cornish Miners
in food riots

Plymouth

Falmouth

- ▨ **General area of Luddite activity**

Major Luddite attacks

- Hosiers attack stocking frame → Arnold ○
- Weavers attack gig frames → Leeds ●
- Weavers attack power looms → Horbury ✳

Horsfall murdered (Apr)

WEST RIDING
Bradford ○
Halifax ○
Huddersfield (Feb) ●
Rawfolds (Apr)

Leeds (Jan) ●
Wakefield ○
Horbury (Apr) ✳

YORK

Luddite Trials, Jan. 1813–
in York, away from trouble spots.
3 Luddites hanged for Horsfall's
murder, 14 for robbery and night
attacks. "**Luddism ended on
the Scaffold**."

NORTHERN REVOLT 1812

LANCASHIRE

(Apr) Middleton ✳
(Apr) Westhoughton

Oldham ○

Manchester ○

Stockport (Mar) ✳

Sheffield ○

**12,000 troops sent in to
keep law and order**

Sutton-in-Ashfield ○
Bulwell ○
Derby ○
Arnold ○
Nottingham ○

MIDLANDS
REVOLT
1811–1812

Leicester ○

THE LUDDITE REVOLT 1811–1812

Luddite taken from 'Ned Ludd', a Leicestershire lad who
broke machinery in a fit of temper. Legend converted him to
'General Ludd' with a mythical HQ in Sherwood Forest.

15: The aftermath of war

Peace—but no prosperity

With export orders flooding in from abroad, 1814–15 was a good year for the British. Migrants came flocking into the 'boom towns' and the stage seemed set for industrial growth and full employment. Then distress returned to town and countryside with terrifying suddenness. Overseas orders tailed off, there were bad harvests everywhere and, between January and December 1816, the price of bread, barley and beans doubled. It seemed as though victory in the French wars had made matters worse, not better, and the British people looked resentfully for the cause of their distress. Most identified it with Parliament's selfish legislation during 1815: abolishing Income Tax (a wartime expedient) and replacing it with new taxes on food and consumer goods; passing the new Corn Law which decreed that no foreign wheat would be sold in Britain until home-grown supplies were fetching at least £4 a quarter.* Both of these measures were against the best interests of the British people.

Reaction

Only a tiny fraction of the British people had the right to vote in 1815; Parliament did not represent the people in a democratic sense. Clearly, the system ought to be reformed. The 'Reform of Parliament' was no new idea. In 1780, radicals had urged 'an equal representation of the people . . . annual elections and the universal right of suffrage . . .' Reform had been one of the main aims of the Corresponding Societies before their demise in 1799. But governments had always fended off the idea (Lord Liverpool's government in 1815 was no exception) because they equated 'reform' with 'revolution'. This was why rotten boroughs such as Old Sarum (a deserted hill) and Dunwich (largely eroded by the sea) still sent M.P.s to Westminster; why the new industrial towns such as Birmingham, Manchester and Leeds did not. Popular radical leaders such as William Cobbett and Henry 'Orator' Hunt clamoured for reform and made an immense appeal to the people because the logic of their propaganda was irresistible.

Riot

Between 1816 and 1819 protests and demonstrations became common. In 1816 East Anglian farm-workers destroyed cornstacks in 'Bread or Blood!' riots; huge meetings in Manchester demanded the right to elect M.P.s so that England, as they hopefully put it, 'will become what it once was and what it ought to be—a land of Roast Beef and Plum Pudding'. In London a crowd rioted at Spa Fields in 1816 and broke into a gun-

*Minimum price for oats was 27/-; for barley £2.

smith's shop. Parliament promptly suspended Habeas Corpus (1817) and passed the 'Gagging Act' to restrain 'seditious assemblies'. Manchester workers retorted with the 'March of the Blanketeers'—destination Westminster—but the blanket-laden demonstrators did not manage to get any further than Ashbourne. In June more demonstrators from Pentrich marched on Nottingham, but disbanded when regular troops arrived. Restlessness in the North was not helped by the government's use of secret agents to infiltrate workers' organizations.

Peterloo 16 August 1819

That day about 50,000 people marched to St Peter's Field, Manchester, to hear 'Orator' Hunt demand Parliamentary Reform. The local magistrate, William Hulton, intended to arrest Hunt and disperse the meeting. Unfortunately, he chose the hated local Yeomanry to do the job. These part-time cavalrymen were jeered and jostled as they rode through the huge crowd towards Hunt. They arrested him and then turned their horses to deal with a group of Stockport militants. A fight began and Hulton ordered his reserve of regular soldiers, the Fifteenth Hussars, to charge. Hundreds of people were hurt as the crowd stampeded for safety; ten died, some from sabre cuts. Parliament hurried through the Six Acts to prevent further mass demonstrations and riots; but this did not prevent Arthur Thistlewood, a convinced Republican, from planning the murder of the entire Cabinet in his famous 'Cato Street Conspiracy' 1820. A secret agent betrayed him and he and four accomplices were executed for treason. After this, there was little disorder:

> to the Acts of 1819 we must in no small degree ascribe the quiet state of the country in 1820 (*The Annual Register*, 1820).

1821–2 were economically prosperous—and therefore peaceful—years.

Conclusions

Though the war had given incentive to industry and agriculture, it also distorted the economy. There were no more demands for armament programmes or high-priced corn after 1815. Manufacturers and farmers had to survive in the competitive atmosphere of a peacetime economy, when one year might bring prosperity, the next disaster. For most people, a poor harvest could mean famine prices while the iniquitous Corn Law inflated food prices at the best of times. So the economic pattern of the world's first industrial society was beginning to establish itself in the form of a series of slumps and booms. At the time men had no high opinion of it.

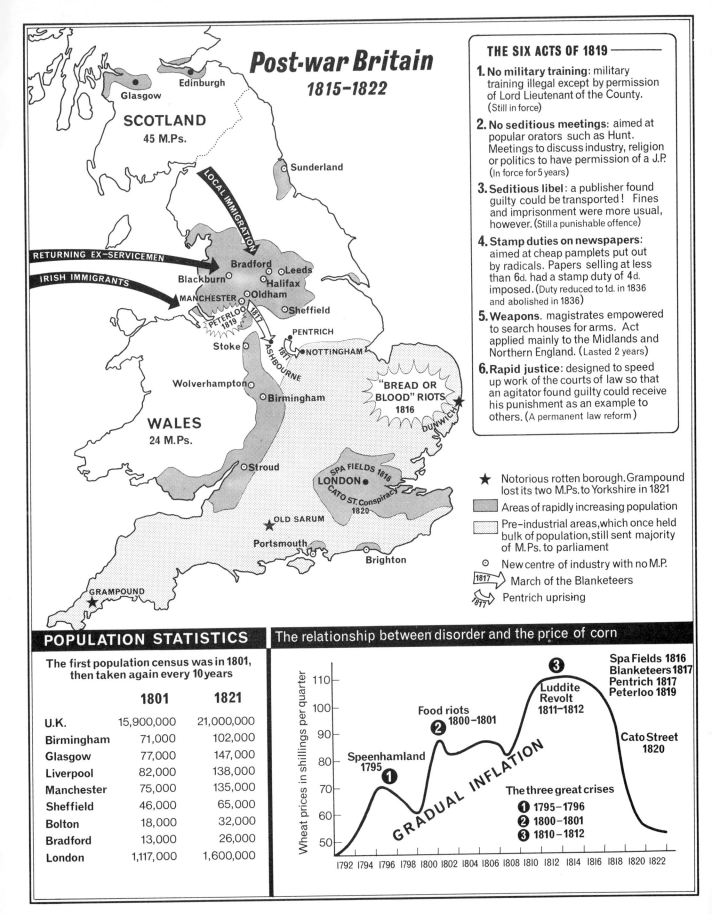

Post-war Britain
1815-1822

SCOTLAND
45 M.Ps.

Edinburgh
Glasgow

Sunderland

LOCAL IMMIGRATION

RETURNING EX-SERVICEMEN

IRISH IMMIGRANTS

Bradford
Blackburn
MANCHESTER
PETERLOO 1819
1817
Stoke

Leeds
Halifax
Oldham
Sheffield

PENTRICH
ASHBOURNE
NOTTINGHAM

Wolverhampton
Birmingham

WALES
24 M.Ps.

"BREAD OR
BLOOD" RIOTS
1816

DUNWICH

Stroud

SPA FIELDS 1816
LONDON
CATO ST. Conspiracy
1820

OLD SARUM

Portsmouth

Brighton

GRAMPOUND

THE SIX ACTS OF 1819

1. **No military training**: military training illegal except by permission of Lord Lieutenant of the County. (Still in force)

2. **No seditious meetings**: aimed at popular orators such as Hunt. Meetings to discuss industry, religion or politics to have permission of a J.P. (In force for 5 years)

3. **Seditious libel**: a publisher found guilty could be transported! Fines and imprisonment were more usual, however. (Still a punishable offence)

4. **Stamp duties on newspapers**: aimed at cheap pamplets put out by radicals. Papers selling at less than 6d. had a stamp duty of 4d. imposed. (Duty reduced to 1d. in 1836 and abolished in 1836)

5. **Weapons**. magistrates empowered to search houses for arms. Act applied mainly to the Midlands and Northern England. (Lasted 2 years)

6. **Rapid justice**: designed to speed up work of the courts of law so that an agitator found guilty could receive his punishment as an example to others. (A permanent law reform)

★ Notorious rotten borough. Grampound lost its two M.Ps. to Yorkshire in 1821

▨ Areas of rapidly increasing population

▢ Pre-industrial areas, which once held bulk of population, still sent majority of M.Ps. to parliament

⊙ New centre of industry with no M.P.

⇨ March of the Blanketeers 1817

↪ Pentrich uprising 1817

POPULATION STATISTICS

The first population census was in 1801, then taken again every 10 years

	1801	1821
U.K.	15,900,000	21,000,000
Birmingham	71,000	102,000
Glasgow	77,000	147,000
Liverpool	82,000	138,000
Manchester	75,000	135,000
Sheffield	46,000	65,000
Bolton	18,000	32,000
Bradford	13,000	26,000
London	1,117,000	1,600,000

The relationship between disorder and the price of corn

Wheat prices in shillings per quarter

Speenhamland 1795 ❶

Food riots 1800-1801 ❷

Luddite Revolt 1811-1812 ❸

GRADUAL INFLATION

Spa Fields 1816
Blanketeers 1817
Pentrich 1817
Peterloo 1819

Cato Street 1820

The three great crises
❶ 1795-1796
❷ 1800-1801
❸ 1810-1812

1792 1794 1796 1798 1800 1802 1804 1806 1808 1810 1812 1814 1816 1818 1820 1822

Part 2 – The impact of war 1793–1822

Spread

11. *The Years of Endurance*** ***	Arthur Bryant	Collins
Nelson	Carola Oman	World Books
12. *Making of the English Working*		
*Class***	E. Thompson	Pelican
13. *Napoleon***	Maurice Hutt	OUP
14. *Making of the English Working*		
*Class***	E. Thompson	Pelican
15. *Peterloo 1819*	G. R. Kesteven	Chatto & Windus

**Especially useful for project and topic work

PART 3

The Clamour for Improvement 1823–1851

Throughout the 1820s, the radical leaders persisted in their campaign to get a large number of working class representatives into Parliament. One can understand their frustration when the 1832 Reform Act gave the vote not to the working classes but to the middle classes. As the middle-class electors were only too ready to vote for 'their betters' it meant that the same aristocratic interests carried on ruling the country. Nevertheless, the 'reformed parliament' did some useful work. It passed the 1833 Factory Act, the 1834 Poor Law Amendment Act and the 1835 Municipal Reform Act. Unfortunately, these proved inadequate to meet the social needs of the day. Plenty of discontent existed and it flared up whenever an economic crisis brought misery to a large section of the population.

As a result, government had to face up to two different kinds of 'pressure groups'. One was the Anti-Corn Law League led by men such as Richard Cobden. He believed that improvement would come as a result of economic change. Government must set out to provide a national system of education plus a higher standard of living for the British people. It must free international trade from the clutter of Corn Laws and Navigation Acts. Then a thrifty, educated people would advance their material comforts; moreover, argued Cobden, if every nation adopted these policies there would be a very good chance of permanent peace in the world. When people reached this condition they were ready to exercise their political rights responsibly. But, he warned, there were very real dangers if one reversed the process. Give an ignorant, discontented people the vote and there was the risk that they would be manipulated by political demagogues who would bring advantages to no-one.

Contemporary with and to some extent in competition with this group were the Chartists. They disagreed with the League and put their faith in political reform first and foremost. If you have representatives of the working class in Parliament then you will get reform in the interests of the working class—this was the basis of their argument summarized in the Six Points of their Charter. However, their methods were far from sophisticated and frequently violent. They suffered from a lack of unity among their leaders. And they were no match for the League's propagandists who were able to turn events in England and Ireland to their own advantage. The League's success culminated in the Repeal of the Corn Laws in 1846.

By the middle of the nineteenth century conditions at last began to show signs of improvement for the majority of people. Agitation died away and during 1851, the year of the Great Exhibition in London, it was clear that most working men had accepted that Britain was committed to an industrial future. More important, there was a general belief that everyone had a fair chance of sharing in some of the resultant prosperity.

16:   The effects of mechanisation, 1823–1830

On industry

By 1830 several industries had passed through the first stage of their industrial revolution. Glass-making and chemicals, for example, were now organized in large factory units. Charles Tennant's famous chemical works at St Rollox, Glasgow produced large quantities of soap, soda and sulphuric acid and covered 30 acres by 1830. Iron and steel also lent themselves to factory organization. Some 33 blast-furnaces, mainly in South Wales and Staffordshire, produced 0.75 million tons annually to meet the growing demand for iron plating, girders and railway track. And now that ironmasters had adopted the puddling and rolling techniques developed during the previous century, wrought iron for heavy duty chains and cables was generally available.

But it was in Lancashire that the most advanced industrial area in the world could be found during the 1820's. Manchester was its centre; nearby Stockport and Blackburn were already 'factory towns'. Yorkshire boasted Rawfold's mill, the first factory to be fully mechanized. In Scotland Robert Owen (1771–1858) had already turned the New Lanark mills into a model estate. Such rapid changes had, however, by-passed the great army of handloom weavers who were reluctant to move from rural areas into the smoky factory towns. They were unskilled workers and they had no hope of competing against the machines. Nevertheless, 240,000 of them tried—and suffered appallingly in the process. Their wages never recovered from the slump which hit the cotton industry in 1826; by 1830 they had no place in the industry. By then the typical economic unit was the small powered factory employing around 200 people. At least two Manchester mills had 1000 workers on their payroll. The resulting degradation of the handloom weavers provided 'the biggest blot on the whole history of the industrial revolution' and helped to open many people's eyes to the urgent need for social reform.

On trade and business

Factory workers were still relatively few in number; most town workers still made their living in the traditional manner. Shoemakers and tailors, shopkeepers and builders were hardly touched by mechanization—although if they lived in big cities such as London, Manchester and Edinburgh they may have worked by gaslight, the product of a brand-new industry. In the towns the biggest group of workers were 670,000 women domestic servants—more than the *combined* totals of factory and handloom workers in the cotton industry.

On agriculture

Although some groups of manual workers had suffered because they chose to compete with rather than adapt to industrial change, others firmly resisted any form of technical innovation. This was certainly true of farmworkers in the 'low wage' areas of Southern England. Their weekly pay—sometimes as low as 7/- in the worst areas—was not enough to provide food for their families who would have starved without the Speenhamland version of Poor Relief. Farmworkers often tried to supplement their food supplies by poaching and pilfering. Both crimes carried severe penalties: a labourer caught netting a rabbit might be transported to the convict settlements of Australia for seven years; he also ran the risk of serious injury from camouflaged 'spring-guns' which were not banned until 1827. Understandably, many labourers resented unsympathetic landowners; had no time for Irish immigrants who were prepared to work on the land for even lower wages; and were intolerant of cheap, portable threshing machines made by firms such as Ransomes of Ipswich. The labourers usually threshed the corn by hand in the barns during the winter months. It was exhausting, but also their best source of income during the winter. Threshing machines took this away from them; and as farmers were always seeking to cut down costs and trying to put their grain on the market quickly these machines were increasingly common by 1830.

In 1830, after a poor harvest and a hard winter, the labourers' anger flared into revolt. Just as the weavers twenty years before had followed *General Ludd* so the labourers supported *Captain Swing*. Many a parson and country squire received threatening 'Swing letters' demanding better wages and the abolition of threshing machines. Militant rebels burnt cornstacks; others destroyed more than 300 threshing machines. Landowners formed private 'police forces', magistrates enrolled special constables and called out the troops. 1,976 rebels found themselves in jail; 19 were hanged and 505 sailed as 'Prisoners of the Motherland' to Australia and Tasmania. Though their revolt was crushed they had made their point. There was hardly any mechanization on the farms for a decade; wages crept up a fraction. And in the words of one anonymous labourer: '...them there riots and burnings did the poor a terrible deal of good...'*

Captain Swing by E. Hobsbawm and G. Rudé, p. 298 (Lawrence & Wishart 1969).

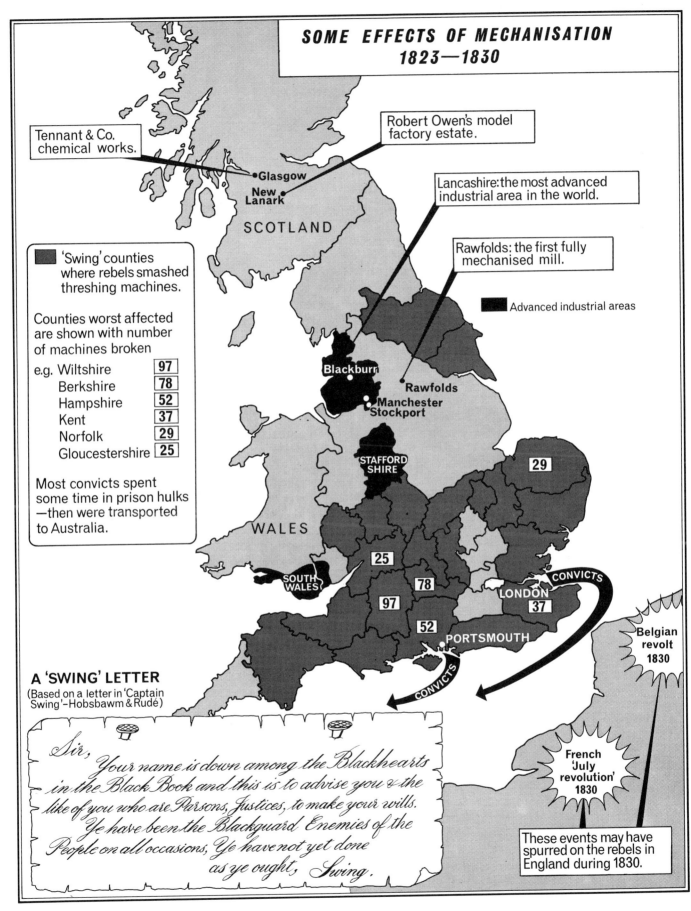

SOME EFFECTS OF MECHANISATION
1823—1830

Tennant & Co. chemical works.

Robert Owen's model factory estate.

Lancashire: the most advanced industrial area in the world.

Rawfolds: the first fully mechanised mill.

Advanced industrial areas

•Glasgow
New Lanark•
SCOTLAND

'Swing' counties where rebels smashed threshing machines.

Counties worst affected are shown with number of machines broken

e.g. Wiltshire   97
       Berkshire   78
       Hampshire   52
       Kent   37
       Norfolk   29
       Gloucestershire 25

Most convicts spent some time in prison hulks —then were transported to Australia.

Blackburn
Rawfolds
Manchester
Stockport

STAFFORD SHIRE

WALES

29

SOUTH WALES

25

78

97

52

LONDON
37

PORTSMOUTH

CONVICTS

CONVICTS

Belgian revolt 1830

French 'July revolution' 1830

These events may have spurred on the rebels in England during 1830.

A 'SWING' LETTER
(Based on a letter in 'Captain Swing'-Hobsbawm & Rudé)

Sir,
Your name is down among the Blackhearts in the Black Book and this is to advise you & the like of you who are Parsons, Justices, to make your wills.
Ye have been the Blackguard Enemies of the People on all occasions, Ye have not yet done
as ye ought, Swing.

17: The First Reform Act, 1832

The voters before 1832

The fourth population census taken in 1831 revealed that the population of Britain had rocketed to 24 million people. But of these a mere 440,000 men had the right to vote in an electoral system whose rules had barely changed for a century. The propertied classes monopolized the vote in the counties, where all who owned land worth forty shillings a year had the vote. In the boroughs, the rules depended on custom: councillors and freemen usually had the vote; sometimes 'potwallopers', 'burgage-holders' and those who paid 'scot and lot' possessed voting rights. However, there was no justice in the system which allowed industrial cities to be without an M.P. and yet permitted a handful of voters in a 'rotten borough' to send *two* M.P.s to Westminster.

Corrupt elections

Voters were quite prepared to accept cash bribes, free drink, travel and accommodation at election times when the hustings would be open for a fortnight and the votes were cast in public. In a 'pocket borough' such as Westbury, The Earl of Abingdon's family controlled all thirteen electors; in a 'rotten borough' such as Old Sarum, the owner of a hill elected two M.P.s. Where voters were more numerous, candidates frequently hired strong-arm gangs to intimidate electors and break up meetings. In the famous Westminster Borough election (1784) King George III was so afraid that Charles James Fox, whom he detested, would win a seat that he ordered all his palace guards and servants down to the hustings to vote against Fox. At the notorious York election (1807) one aristocratic candidate, Lascelles, spent £100,000 on 10,000 electors—and he lost the election.

The Reform Movement

Many British people were appalled by this state of affairs. Until they had honest representatives of the people in Parliament, there did not seem to be any *constitutional* means of helping the discontented farmworkers, or of improving the Poor Law, or of educating children and making their working conditions in factories and mines a great deal better. For fifty years there had been a clamour for reform. In 1780 the Westminster Committee had demanded '... an equal representation of the people in the great council of the nation, annual elections and the universal right of suffrage ...' To many people these seemed reasonable enough demands and by 1830 the belief was widespread that, once the composition of Parliament had been reformed, the gateway to a better life would be opened. This was the message of the 'political unions' which mushroomed at this time. Best known was the Birmingham Political Union which Thomas Attwood, helped by popular Radicals such as William Cobbett, set up in December 1829.

The Reform Crisis

In March 1831 the Whig Prime Minister, Lord Grey, yielded to the mounting pressure and brought in a bill for the reform of Parliament. It scraped through the Commons by a single vote so Grey decided to test the opinion of the electorate by holding a general election. He was returned to office and brought in a second reform bill which the Commons passed in September; but when it went up to the House of Lords they rejected it in October. Spontaneous riots and demonstrations broke out all over the country. In Bristol, where the local M.P. was hostile to reform, the mob burnt public buildings and released prisoners from jail. Grey now brought in a third bill which the Commons passed in March 1832. He then asked King William IV to create enough Whig peers in order to outvote his opponents in the Lords—or otherwise accept his resignation. The king accepted his resignation! For nine days there was no effective government in Britain; the Birmingham Political Union talked of a march on London; soldiers in the Scots Greys had orders to 'rough sharpen swords' and stop the demonstration. The fear of revolt was very real on Sunday 13 May 1832. However, on the following day the king agreed to create as many 'Whig peers' as Grey needed. Under the threat of an influx of ready-made peers, the Lords surrendered and passed the bill on 4 June 1832. It received the Royal Assent three days later and thus became the Reform Act.

The Reform Act 1832

There were two main changes: in the boroughs, every man owning property worth £10 a year gained the vote; in the counties the forty-shilling freeholders kept the vote but lost their monopoly—£10 copyholders and £50 leaseholders won the franchise. It all added up to an additional 217,000 voters. There was no universal suffrage, no secret ballot, no annual parliaments—the aristocrats had simply absorbed the more prosperous middle-class shopkeepers and manufacturers. The working class, quite rightly, felt betrayed. So there were plenty of shortcomings in the new, reformed parliament which assembled in 1833. Nevertheless, its members (which no longer included any from rotten boroughs but had Radicals such as Cobbett representing industrial Oldham) had the chance of improving the appalling conditions in which so many British people lived.

THE REFORM CRISIS 1831-1832

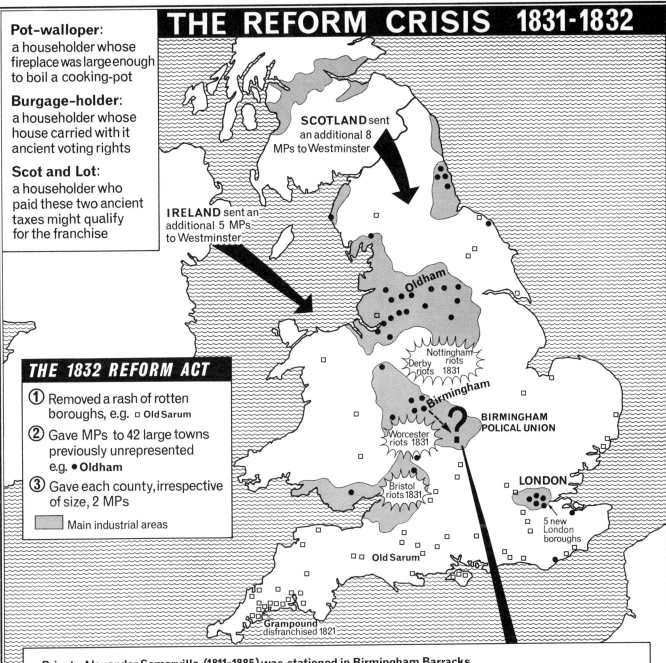

Pot-walloper:
a householder whose fireplace was large enough to boil a cooking-pot

Burgage-holder:
a householder whose house carried with it ancient voting rights

Scot and Lot:
a householder who paid these two ancient taxes might qualify for the franchise

SCOTLAND sent an additional 8 MPs to Westminster

IRELAND sent an additional 5 MPs to Westminster

THE 1832 REFORM ACT

① Removed a rash of rotten boroughs, e.g. □ Old Sarum

② Gave MPs to 42 large towns previously unrepresented e.g. ● Oldham

③ Gave each county, irrespective of size, 2 MPs

□ Main industrial areas

Oldham

Nottingham riots 1831
Derby riots

Birmingham

BIRMINGHAM POLICAL UNION

Worcester riots 1831

Bristol riots 1831

LONDON

5 new London boroughs

Old Sarum

Grampound disfranchised 1821

Private Alexander Somerville (1811-1885) was stationed in Birmingham Barracks at the height of the reform crisis. He later wrote in his autobiography;

"It was rumoured that the Birmingham Political Union was to march for London that night (Sunday 13 May, 1832); and that we were there to stop it on the road .... We had been daily booted and saddled, with ball cartridge in each man's possession for three days .... But until this day we had rough-sharpened no swords. The purpose of so roughening their edges was to make them inflict a ragged wound. Not since the Battle of Waterloo had the swords of the Greys undergone the same process. Old soldiers spoke of it and told the young ones ...."

Somerville was later arrested for his radical opinions and for stating publicly that he dreaded having to cut down his own people. He was lashed one hundred times with the cat o'nine tails.

Extract from **The autobiography of a Working Man** first published in 1848.

18: The reformed parliament at work

Its methods of enquiry

Before parliament met in 1833, its leaders had already decided that the problems of the British people were to be tackled in a thorough and scientific fashion, along the lines recommended by the philosopher Jeremy Bentham (who had died in 1832). The Whigs made use of Royal Commissions charged to enquire into contemporary social problems. They reported back in 'Blue Books' read not only by M.P.s but by many people outside Parliament.

The Poor Law Amendment Act 1834

Although this was not the first act passed by the new parliament, it was nevertheless the one which had the most immediate and important effect upon the British people. The existing system of poor relief based on parish rates was notoriously uneconomic. It absorbed about 20% of the nation's income—in Wiltshire the Poor Rate of 1831 was 16/6 a head, in Suffolk it was 18/3. Enquiries into the Poor Law began in 1832 and the leading 'commissioners' made their report in 1834. They printed 20,000 copies, so it was widely read. They defined the main problem as one of helping the able-bodied poor who did not earn enough to feed and house their families. The best way of helping them was to abolish the *system of parish allowances* and replace it with a *system of workhouses*; these workhouses must offer a strict, grim way of life—so that people would only enter them if they were truly desperate for relief. They suggested that parishes should combine together to form unions which could build the workhouses; these could be run by Boards of Guardians elected by local rate-payers. A Central Board of three commissioners would co-ordinate this work. The report impressed the government who passed a *Poor Law Amendment Act in 1834*. However, there was one important difference between the report and the act, which are sometimes confused. Left-wing historians* have claimed that 'there have been few more inhuman statutes than the Poor Law Act of 1834, which made all relief "less eligible" than the lowest wage outside, confined to the jail-like work-house.' Certainly, there was a lot to deplore in the act; but it never abolished out-door relief. Five years after the act, while nearly 100,000 paupers lived in workhouses, more than half a million received out-door relief. Why did relatively few paupers enter workhouses?

The Anti-Poor Law Movement

There was not much resistance to the act in the southern agricultural counties where the Swing Riots had flared up in 1830. But in the north of England employers and workers resented London bureaucrats telling them how to conduct their local affairs. Lancashire thought it had managed very well—the Poor Rate was only 4/4 a head. So when the Poor Law Commissioners tried in 1836 to introduce the unions north of the Trent they ran into 'a rebellion in embryo'. Most of the textile towns demonstrated against the act; on Hartshead Moor outside Bradford (1837) a huge meeting petitioned parliament to repeal the act. Noisy newspapers, particularly a new one called the *Northern Star*, produced exaggerated tales of the horror of life in the workhouse. Thus the old system of poor relief persisted in the north for several years. However, by 1839 opposition to the act declined; the new workhouses were built and were not quite so bad as rumour made out.

Municipal Reform Act 1835

The growth of the towns had been phenomenal and, because of the absence of building regulations, accommodation in them was usually appalling. In Manchester during the 1830's where, it has been said, 'we see the Industrial Revolution at its ugliest't, workers had filthy cottages and usually suffered from malnutrition. Housewives had no idea of how to cope with a large family in cramped, unventilated rooms where an absence of pure water and sanitation made life squalid. The Municipal Reform Act (1835) created 179 boroughs which were to be governed by municipal councils elected by rate-payers; rates were to be used for improving amenities in the borough.

Factory and School legislation

The 1833 Factory Regulation Act reduced the working hours of children under 13 to 9 per day. It also suggested that children working a 48-hour week should 'attend some school'. Unfortunately, the government did not provide any; instead it made an annual grant of, at first, £20,000 to the non-conformist British and National Foreign School Society and the Church of England's National Society. For many years children who were lucky enough to attend such schools, before there was a state system of education, were known as the 'Brits' and the 'Nats'.

---

*See E. J. Hobsbawm, *Industry and Empire, an economic history of Britain since 1750*, pp. 69–70 and again p. 194 (Weidenfeld and Nicolson 1968).
†Frances Collier, *Family Economy of the working classes in the cotton industry 1784–1833*, (Manchester University Press 1964).

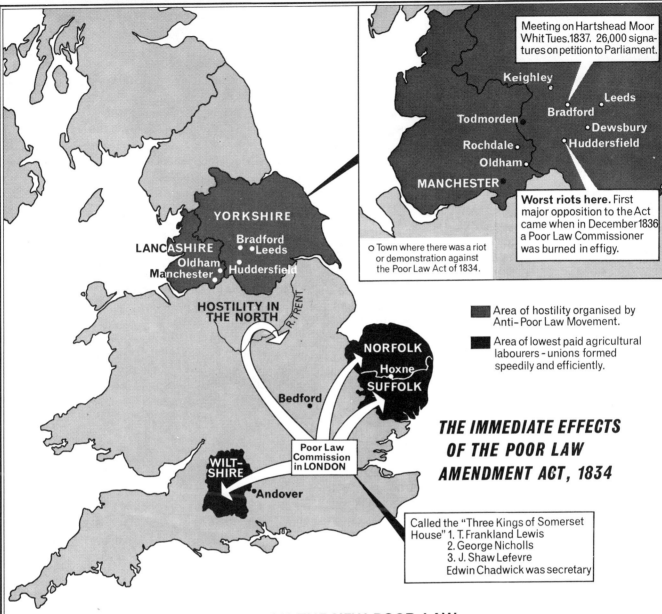

THE IMMEDIATE EFFECTS OF THE POOR LAW AMENDMENT ACT, 1834

Meeting on Hartshead Moor Whit Tues. 1837. 26,000 signatures on petition to Parliament.

Keighley
Leeds
Bradford
Todmorden
Dewsbury
Rochdale
Huddersfield
Oldham
MANCHESTER

Worst riots here. First major opposition to the Act came when in December 1836 a Poor Law Commissioner was burned in effigy.

o Town where there was a riot or demonstration against the Poor Law Act of 1834.

YORKSHIRE
LANCASHIRE
Bradford
Leeds
Oldham
Manchester
Huddersfield

HOSTILITY IN THE NORTH

R. TRENT

NORFOLK
Hoxne
SUFFOLK

Bedford

WILT-SHIRE

Poor Law Commission in LONDON

Andover

Area of hostility organised by Anti-Poor Law Movement.

Area of lowest paid agricultural labourers - unions formed speedily and efficiently.

Called the "Three Kings of Somerset House" 1. T. Frankland Lewis
2. George Nicholls
3. J. Shaw Lefevre
Edwin Chadwick was secretary

SOME REPORTS ON THE NEW POOR LAW

1. The enquiry into the Andover Scandal 1845:
The administration of the workhouse at Andover was scandalous. The workhouse masters ordered paupers to break up rotting bones for manure. It was alleged that paupers had eaten marrow and gristle because they had inadequate food.

2. Extracts from **The Farmer's Magazine** 1837:

(a) ..... when one pauper was sent to prison the Vice-Chairman of the Hoxne Union discovered that he had 17 sovereigns sewed into the lining of his waistcoat.....

(b) Another pauper had pawned 10 'charity blankets.'

(c) The Bedford Union formed in 1835 had cut its expenses (compared with the Old Poor Law) by 70%..... we express our hope that the Legislature will not listen to the gross misrepresentation and idle clamours raised about the Poor Law Amendment Act.....

(d) Several unions reported in 1836 that parishes had raised special funds to pay for migration of labourers to the north of England and to the Canadas.....

19: The Chartists

'A knife and fork question'

The reformed Parliament was powerless to remedy the unstable economy which constantly jeopardized the jobs and living standards of thousands of British workers. So after 1832 the clamour for reform intensified, growing loudest in the years of slump and widespread economic hardship. As early as 1833 a weavers' meeting at Padiham petitioned Parliament for 'universal suffrage, annual parliaments, vote by ballot and the abolition of the property qualification for M.P.s'. At first no organization existed to whip up support for these ideas; then in 1838 William Lovett published his *People's Charter* which repeated the demands of the old Westminster Committee (1780) and the Padiham Petition (1833). Men who supported the Charter and its Six Points became Chartists. They sought through universal suffrage to solve the eternal 'knife and fork question'*; how could every working man secure his right to 'a good coat on his back, a good dinner on his table, no more work than will keep him in health while at it, and as much wages as will keep him in enjoyment of plenty . . .'

Who were the Chartists?

Chartism flourished in the textile areas of Britain, particularly where old industries were in decay or where handweavers had increased in number in response to the mechanization of spinning. Chartism also appealed to workers in trades which had not passed through an 'industrial revolution'. So most Chartists were nailmakers, frame-knitters, miners and handloom weavers; men who during the appalling trade depression of 1837–42 (the so-called 'Hungry Forties') spoke of rebellion and *'physical force'*. In contrast, many factory workers opposed violence and favoured *'moral force'*. They used Chartism as a means of bringing pressure on employers who refused wage increases.

The Chartists in action

The best known Chartist leader was Feargus O'Connor, who published the radical Leeds newspaper *Northern Star*. After the Anti-Poor Law Movement lost its impetus, O'Connor gave a lot of space to Chartism and spoke at inaugural meetings in Northern England. In 1839 delegates assembled, first in London and then in Birmingham, for a Chartist National Convention. They disagreed on future policy, rejected a General Strike and finally decided on a petition to Parliament—who

*The words of J. R. Stephens, a prominent member of the Anti-Poor Law Movement.

†See the Book of Genesis xxiv 60.

rejected it. Drama was provided by a group of misguided Monmouthshire miners who tried to release a Chartist leader named Vincent from Newport Jail. Led by John Frost, the miners entered the town and fought a gun battle with the Mayor and troops barricaded in the Westgate Hotel. About 24 miners died; Frost was transported. In 1842 a second Chartist petition went to Parliament—who again rejected it. Lancashire workers went on strike and knocked out the plugs in factory boilers—the famous 'Plug Riots'. In Wales, protest took the form of the Rebecca Riots, a series of attacks on tollgates led by a man dressed in woman's clothing†. Such activities bore little relation to the Chartists' true aims; they usually ended in death or imprisonment. After 1843, O'Connor decided to meet the problems of an industrialized society by finding 'self-sufficiency' on the land. Accordingly, he formed the National Land Company in which workers could invest. He promised that his smallholdings 'would make a paradise of England in five years'. He founded settlements at Lowbands, Snig's End, Dodford, Charterville and O'Connorville. A few of the original Dodford settlers remained in 1900.

1848

1848 was the 'Year of Revolution' in Europe, marked by revolts in Berlin, Vienna and Paris. In Britain, the slump returned in 1847 and inspired the Chartists to attempt a third petition to Parliament. On 10 April 1848 they assembled on Kennington Common in South London. The government regarded it as a revolutionary threat; *The Times* warned the Chartists that they would find 'every street a rampart and every house a castle against them'. The Duke of Wellington took control and treated the matter as a major military exercise. He stationed the Brigade of Guards as discreetly as possible within the city, while on the Thames rivercraft were fitted with artillery from the Tower in case mobs tried to capture the bridges. O'Connor brought the petition to Westminster in pouring rain; it filled three cabs. He claimed he had 6 million signatures; in fact there were less than 2 million and some of these were forgeries such as 'Queen Victoria' and the 'Duke of Wellington'. These hilarious revelations damaged the Chartist movement as a serious political force while a general revival of trade and prosperity in the autumn of 1848 cost the movement its mass support. Gradually, the movement withered away: its aims, which had their roots in the eighteenth century, were largely won in the nineteenth—but not as a direct result of the work of men such as Lovett, Frost and O'Connor.

THE SIX POINTS

1. **Every man over 21 to have a vote if he is of sound mind and not a criminal serving sentence.**
2. **Votes to be cast by ballot, to prevent corruption.**
3. **No property qualifications for MPs — so that working men may enter parliament.**
4. **MPs must be paid so that honest men may leave their trades to serve as members.**
5. **Constituencies must be of equal size.**
6. **There must be annual parliaments.*** *This was primarily to defeat corruption-nobody could afford to bribe an electorate **every** year.

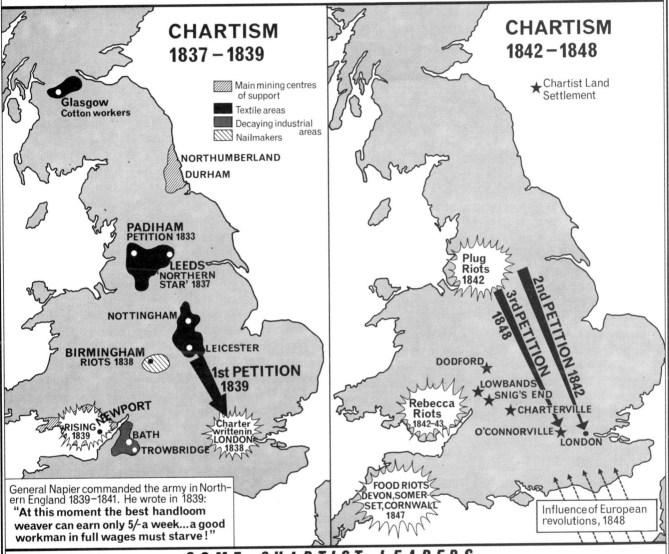

CHARTISM 1837 – 1839

Main mining centres of support

Textile areas

Decaying industrial areas

Nailmakers

Glasgow Cotton workers

NORTHUMBERLAND
DURHAM

PADIHAM PETITION 1833

LEEDS 'NORTHERN STAR' 1837

NOTTINGHAM

LEICESTER

BIRMINGHAM RIOTS 1838

NEWPORT RISING 1839

1st PETITION 1839

BATH
TROWBRIDGE

Charter written in LONDON 1838

General Napier commanded the army in Northern England 1839–1841. He wrote in 1839:
"At this moment the best handloom weaver can earn only 5/- a week...a good workman in full wages must starve!"

CHARTISM 1842 – 1848

★ Chartist Land Settlement

Plug Riots 1842

2nd PETITION 1842

3rd PETITION 1848

DODFORD

LOWBANDS
SNIG'S END

CHARTERVILLE

Rebecca Riots 1842–43

O'CONNORVILLE

LONDON

FOOD RIOTS DEVON, SOMERSET, CORNWALL 1847

Influence of European revolutions, 1848

SOME CHARTIST LEADERS

Feargus O'Connor 1796–1855
An Irishman, Protestant, but a champion of the cause of Roman Catholic peasants in Ireland.
His paper 'Northern Star' made considerable profits, but he could not handle financial affairs–one cause of the failure of his land settlement scheme.
A sick man between 1839–42 and 1848-52. He went insane in 1852 while MP for Nottingham, was arrested and sent to Chiswick Asylum.

John Frost 1784–1877
Born in Newport; dismissed when a JP because of his Chartist beliefs. Disliked violence but agreed to lead the miners in 1839. Sentenced to death, but transported to Tasmania. Released and became a teacher. He returned to Britain on a full pardon and lectured on Chartism and convict life in Australia.

William Lovett 1800–1876
Born in Cornwall. Believed in a national trade union for workers. Quiet but effective speaker–a great contrast to O'Connor.
Jailed for his views; in prison wrote a book in which he said that people should be educated first **before** they received the vote.
Eventually he left politics for teaching.

20: The Anti-Corn Law League, 1838–1846

The Corn Laws

In 1815 a Parliament dominated by country gentlemen passed a Corn Law which prevented the sale of imported wheat before home grown supplies were fetching 80/– a quarter. The aim was to maintain an assured profit for British farmers and to keep Britain independent of foreign food supplies. In 1828. William Huskisson, President of the Board of Trade, modified this arrangment by introducing a 'sliding scale' of import duties which would fall as the price of British wheat rose. However, most people were concerned not with government regulations, but with whether the annual harvest would feed the expanding population. When there were good harvests, there was little protest against the Corn Laws; but when times were bad, there was plenty of agitation. Even then it was usually in the form of localized food riots. The first effective campaign against the Corn Laws was begun by manufacturers who deplored high food costs as a waste of the nation's wealth when there was plenty of foreign food available. Britain should buy it in exchange for her manufactured goods. The workers would have spare cash to buy consumer goods and thus improve their standard of living. This was the advantage of free trade, they said. And when critics said that the manufacturers simply wanted cheap food so they could cut down wages, the free traders pointed to countries such as Holland and said that where there were no Corn Laws the people enjoyed the highest wages of all. But because it was still difficult to get into Parliament, these arguments were barely heard at first. When Richard Cobden, the calico manufacturer, managed it in 1841, he told his brother 'I am looked on as a Gothic invader . . . nothing seems to be considered so decided a stigma as to brand a man as a millowner . . .'

The formation of the League

When the trade depression arrived in 1838 there was the usual widespread suffering and protests against the Corn Laws. A London Radical, Francis Place, wrote to the Chartist leader Lovett urging resistance to the Laws—'the crops being so short and bread dear'. Chartists, however, were more interested in winning the vote. In September 1838 several Manchester manufacturers met to discuss the possibility of repealing the Laws. Led by J. B. Smith and John Bright, the Rochdale manufacturer, they set up the Anti-Corn Law League which Cobden, who was abroad at the time, joined later. They organized some lectures in Manchester, but soon ran into competition from the Anti-Poor Law Movement and the Chartists; but the Leaguers proved more lasting than their rivals and soon their 'missionaries' were setting out on the new railway routes to convert farmers to the virtues of free-trade.

The League's propaganda

The League was the first pressure group in British history to mobilize public opinion at grass-root level in favour of a political cause. Lecturers had to run the gamut of hostile audiences; one came under physical attack from Cambridge students; several others, failing to appreciate that large numbers of tenant farmers were loyal to their Tory landlords, finished up in village duckponds. During the 1840 Walsall by-election the League hired 'two rather disreputable election specialists . . . who seem to have been adept at the impersonation of electors and the polling of dead men'. The fact that the League had raised the question of repeal on the hustings made the Corn Laws into a national election issue; while during 1841 the Leaguers managed to persuade a meeting of 700 clergymen to condemn the Laws and thus transformed 'repeal' into a religious and humanitarian cause. However, the Tories led by Sir Robert Peel, won the general election so Cobden and his friends concentrated on winning the next one, seven years distant. Cobden recommended his supporters to claim a county vote by buying up freeholds; he also hinted to wealthy followers that a forty-shilling freehold made an excellent 21st birthday present. And all the time the League sent out tons of pamphlets, exploiting the new postal services introduced by Rowland Hill in 1839. The Leaguers held jumble sales, distributed posters, sold 'anti-corn law tea and breakfast sets'. They ran their own newspaper—*The League*—and bought the support of others. Their most important contribution to political journalism was to found *The Economist* in 1843.

The Repeal of the Corn Laws 1846

Repeal was destined to be won, not on the hustings or in the popular press, but in the House of Commons. Prime Minister Peel grew more and more convinced of the wisdom of Cobden's arguments; but his final conversion, largely on humanitarian grounds, arose from the disastrous Irish potato famine (1845–6). Peel had to admit cheap foreign food; he told a horrified Tory party that he planned to end import duties on corn. He forced this through the Commons and split the Tory party in the process. The Repeal received the royal assent on 26 June 1846. Peel resigned three days later. He gave the credit for repeal to Cobden; now, he said, the labouring classes could 'recruit their strength with abundant and untaxed food'. The Duke of Wellington gave the credit to rotten potatoes: 'rotten potatoes have done it all; they put Peel in his damned fright'. But they did more than this; they caused the death of a million Irish.

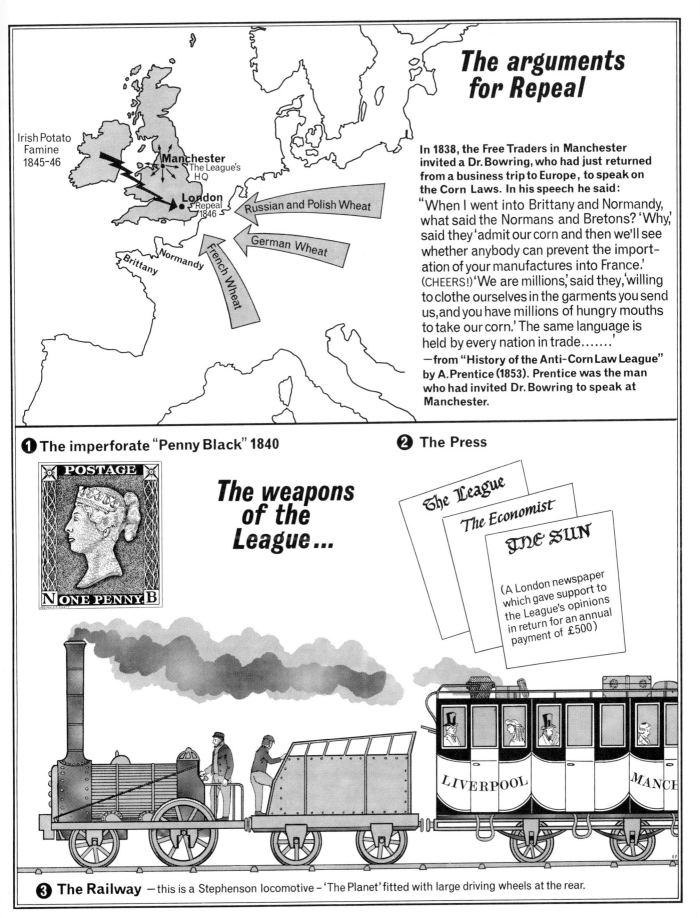

The arguments for Repeal

Irish Potato Famine 1845-46

Manchester — The League's HQ

London — Repeal 1846

Russian and Polish Wheat

German Wheat

French Wheat

Brittany

Normandy

In 1838, the Free Traders in Manchester invited a Dr. Bowring, who had just returned from a business trip to Europe, to speak on the Corn Laws. In his speech he said:

"When I went into Brittany and Normandy, what said the Normans and Bretons? 'Why,' said they 'admit our corn and then we'll see whether anybody can prevent the importation of your manufactures into France.' (CHEERS!) 'We are millions,' said they, 'willing to clothe ourselves in the garments you send us, and you have millions of hungry mouths to take our corn.' The same language is held by every nation in trade.......'

—from "History of the Anti-Corn Law League" by A. Prentice (1853). Prentice was the man who had invited Dr. Bowring to speak at Manchester.

❶ The imperforate "Penny Black" 1840

POSTAGE
N ONE PENNY B

The weapons of the League...

❷ The Press

The League

The Economist

THE SUN

(A London newspaper which gave support to the League's opinions in return for an annual payment of £500)

LIVERPOOL   MANCH

❸ **The Railway** — this is a Stephenson locomotive – 'The Planet' fitted with large driving wheels at the rear.

21: The misery of the Irish

The Penal Laws

Since the end of the seventeenth century, the Catholic population of Ireland (about 75% of the population) had suffered from a set of English *Penal Laws* which Edmund Burke once described 'as well fitted for the oppression, impoverishment and degradation of a people . . . as ever proceeded from the perverted ingenuity of man'. No Roman Catholic could *legally* practise his faith, educate his children, vote, purchase land or seek a career in parliament or the armed services. Understandably, Irish Catholics never regarded themselves as 'British people'— despite the fact that since 1 January 1801 they had been governed by Parliament at Westminster by authority of the Act of Union (1800).

The Repeal Movement 1828–43

One remarkable Irishman, Daniel O'Connell, tried to fight the system. He sought to destroy the Penal Laws, get Catholic M.P.s into parliament and there repeal the Act of Union. In 1828 he contested the County Clare by-election as a Catholic candidate—and won; but as the law then stood, he could not enter Parliament. Rather than risk an Irish rebellion, Peel and Wellington decided to *emancipate* the Irish to the extent of repealing the seventeenth-century *Test* and *Corporation Acts* in 1828; and in 1829 they pushed through a Catholic Relief Act which gave the vote to all Irish £10 freeholders—there were very few of these! O'Connell took his seat and organized the Repeal Movement in Ireland. He was not seeking independence but, after the accession of Victoria in 1837, 'self-rule under the Queen'. He rejected violence and advocated peaceful protest. His biggest demonstration was scheduled for 1843 at Clontarf Field where the British assumed a major riot would develop. They brought in troops and when thousands of Irish assembled there was a serious risk of blood-shed. Fortunately, O'Connell managed to disperse his people; a week later he was jailed.

The condition of the Irish

The root of all Ireland's troubles was the land problem. Dominated by absentee English landlords, the Irish were usually 'tenants at will'; that is, they had no security of tenure and could be ejected from their windowless mud cabins the moment they were in arrears of rent. Due to the population explosion between 1780 and 1840 there was never enough arable land available; rents rocketed and bailiffs had no qualms about ejecting families who fell on hard times. So there was always a large number of homeless, penniless Irish living under conditions rarely found elsewhere in Western Europe. Those who had a smallholding grew grain to sell for cash in order to raise the rent. There was a saying in Ireland: no man dared to eat his rent. Instead the Irish lived on a cheap but nutritious diet of buttermilk and potatoes. Potatoes are easy to grow but subject to failure; so the Irish were accustomed to regular shortages and localized starvation. There were never enough potatoes in July and August—when the 'old potatoes' had gone and the new crop was not ready for lifting. But there was never a total failure—until the arrival of the potato blight in 1845.

The blight and its effects 1845–51

Potato blight is caused by the fungus *Phytophthora infestans*. It flourishes in warm, wet conditions— such as Ireland. The fungus spores devour potato leaves and invade the tubers underground. It can be controlled by spraying plants with a 'Bordeaux mixture' of copper compounds. Regrettably, nobody possessed this information in 1845. The blight destroyed most of the crop that year and within six months of the potato harvest being lifted people were starving. In London, Peel acted with speed and determination, he repealed the Corn Laws and organized an aid programme of local relief, public works and imports of cheap 'Indian corn'— maize. But these efforts were wrecked when the 1846 crop was a total failure—an unprecedented experience. This began the 'great hunger' which forced thousands of starving peasants to wander in search of food. Gifts of money poured in from England, the U.S.A. and India. Wealthy families such as the Barings headed subscriptions lists— the Queen donated £2000. But it was not enough to provide food. Famine brought in its wake several fever epidemics—mainly typhus and cholera—together with scurvy. In terror, thousands of penniless, diseased Irish abandoned their homeland and set sail for America and various parts of Britain. This mass exodus went on for most of 1847 and spread disease in cities as far apart as Manchester and New York. 1848 saw a half-hearted Irish attempt at rebellion—and then *another* total crop failure. By the beginning of 1849 the Irish were ready to swear that 'the land is cursed', for now the problem was quite beyond any nineteenth-century relief organization—nature had to be allowed to take its course. Between 1846 and 1851 more than a million Irish died from starvation, typhus, dysentery and cholera. More than two million emigrated. This was the greatest disaster in modern British history. It left a legacy of permanent Irish hatred for the British people; and condemned Ireland to dismally slow economic growth for the next hundred years.

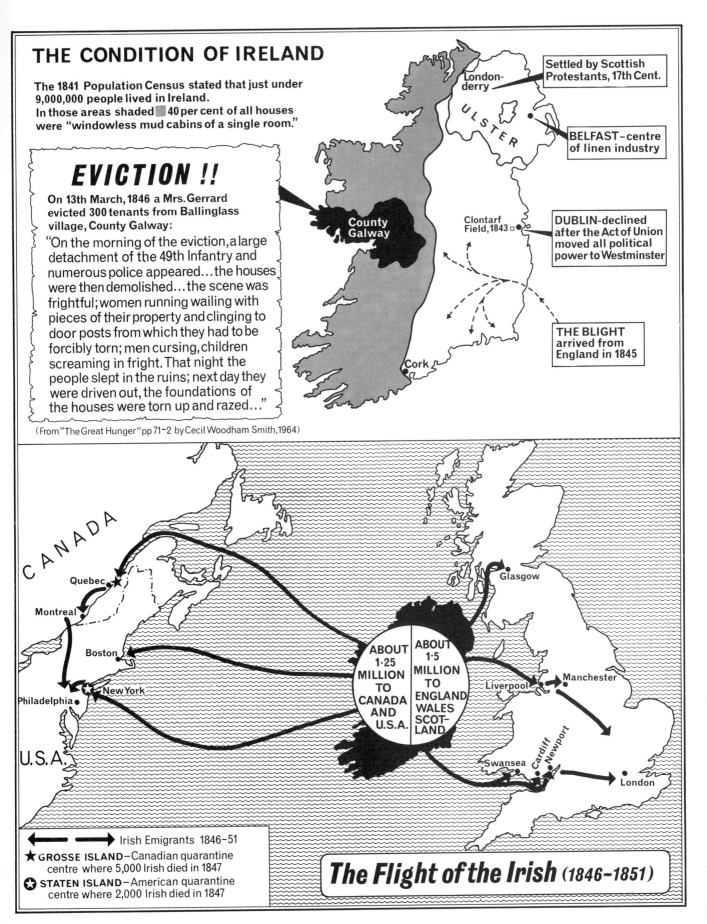

THE CONDITION OF IRELAND

The 1841 Population Census stated that just under 9,000,000 people lived in Ireland.
In those areas shaded ▨ 40 per cent of all houses were "windowless mud cabins of a single room."

EVICTION !!

On 13th March, 1846 a Mrs. Gerrard evicted 300 tenants from Ballinglass village, County Galway:

"On the morning of the eviction, a large detachment of the 49th Infantry and numerous police appeared...the houses were then demolished...the scene was frightful; women running wailing with pieces of their property and clinging to door posts from which they had to be forcibly torn; men cursing, children screaming in fright. That night the people slept in the ruins; next day they were driven out, the foundations of the houses were torn up and razed..."

(From "The Great Hunger" pp 71-2 by Cecil Woodham Smith, 1964)

Settled by Scottish Protestants, 17th Cent.

Londonderry

ULSTER

BELFAST—centre of linen industry

County Galway

Clontarf Field, 1843

DUBLIN—declined after the Act of Union moved all political power to Westminster

THE BLIGHT arrived from England in 1845

Cork

CANADA

Quebec ★

Montreal

Boston

Philadelphia

New York ✪

U.S.A.

Glasgow

ABOUT 1·25 MILLION TO CANADA AND U.S.A.

ABOUT 1·5 MILLION TO ENGLAND WALES SCOTLAND

Liverpool

Manchester

Swansea Cardiff Newport

London

◄——— ———► Irish Emigrants 1846–51
★ GROSSE ISLAND—Canadian quarantine centre where 5,000 Irish died in 1847
✪ STATEN ISLAND—American quarantine centre where 2,000 Irish died in 1847

The Flight of the Irish (1846–1851)

47

22: The early railways

George and Robert Stephenson

'The locomotive of Mr Stephenson,' enthused a contemporary in 1821, 'is superior beyond compare to all other engines I have seen'. George Stephenson (1781–1848), a natural mechanical genius, had built an *efficient* locomotive before the end of the Napoleonic Wars. In 1825 the directors of the Stockton & Darlington colliery railway chose his *Locomotion* to open their line. His son, Robert (1805–59), was equally talented. His famous *Rocket* won the 1829 Rainhill locomotive trials and became the prototype for the engines used on the Liverpool and Manchester railway (1830). Soon Stephenson's engines were hauling thousands of passengers annually and earning handsome dividends for the company's shareholders. Within a couple of years other railway companies mushroomed. The railway age had begun.

The railway builders

Railway construction required organization, money and labour—all on a scale hitherto unknown. Men such as Thomas Brassey, Samuel Peto, Isambard Kingdom Brunel, supervized the building of miles of level railroad which soon radiated from London. The money was raised by private investors who bought shares by the million. These deals were sometimes crooked; even brilliant financiers such as George Hudson, the 'Railway King', who at one time controlled a third of the railways, was not above misusing company funds. However, the most remarkable feature of all this frantic railway building was that it was carried out almost entirely by human muscle-power. In fact, the railways may be credited with siphoning off thousands of unemployed men at a time when social discontent was reaching danger level. The railway *navvies* (a corruption of 'navigators'—canal builders) were tough, hard-drinking, well-paid manual workers who tunnelled, banked and blasted the first railways in the world. The strongest moved huge barrowloads of soil, 'making the running' in hair-raising fashion. The bravest tackled the tunnelling: when they built the Woodhead tunnels between 1838 and 1849 they lost 3% killed and 14% injured in accidents—higher casualty rates than in some of the Peninsular War battles! Then the 1847–49 cholera outbreak carried off another 28 Woodhead navvies. Such were the risks run by the navvies, men who constructed not only Britain's railways but who put up the Crystal Palace in 1851 and built the first French, Canadian and Australian railways.

The railway revolution

Parliament authorized but did not control the early railways. They were all private ventures built with no thought of a 'national railway plan'. Poor connections, unreliable timetables and lots of open coaches made travelling uncomfortable and dangerous. During 1841 alone 24 people died and 71 suffered injury in rail accidents. Gradually, the state took a hand. The 1844 Railway Act ordered all companies to run at least one train per day at a penny a mile on *each* route; it had to average at least 12 m.p.h. and provide *covered* third class accommodation. In 1846, parliament standardized the rail gauge at 4′ 8½″. By 1848 the railway was a part of the British way of life. Although existing mail coach services and turnpike trusts suffered from competition, the nation as a whole prospered. 30 million passengers used the trains each year; industry, which had created the railways in the first place, derived instant benefits from their construction. There was an ever increasing demand for iron and steel, bricks and cement, coal and gunpowder; there were new jobs for drivers, guards, porters, and firemen. Even new towns sprang up out of the railway revolution as places such as Crewe concentrated on building and servicing the locomotives and rolling stock.

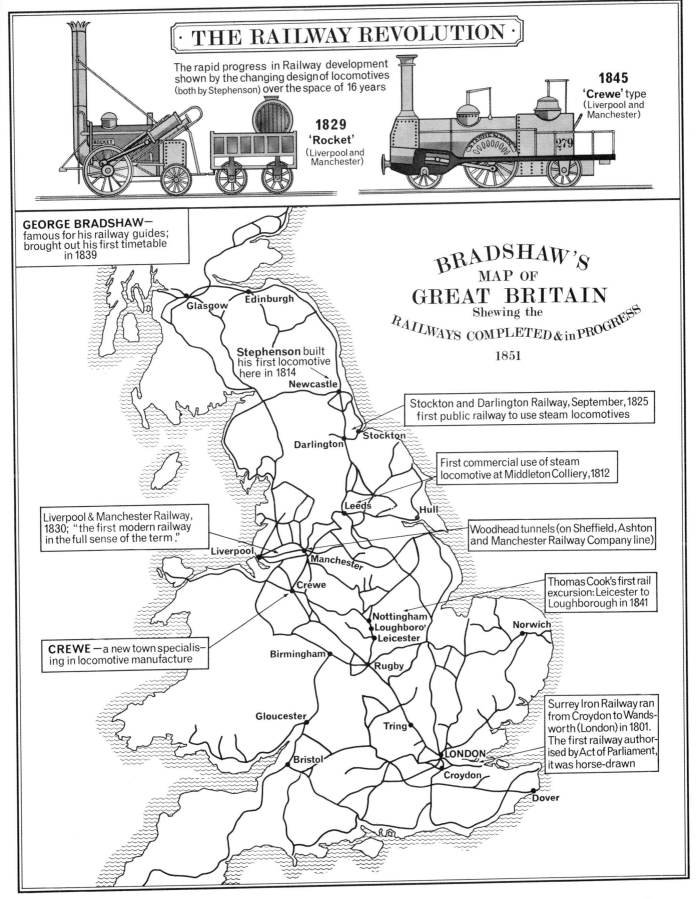

· THE RAILWAY REVOLUTION ·

The rapid progress in Railway development shown by the changing design of locomotives (both by Stephenson) over the space of 16 years

1829 'Rocket' (Liverpool and Manchester)

1845 'Crewe' type (Liverpool and Manchester)

GEORGE BRADSHAW— famous for his railway guides; brought out his first timetable in 1839

BRADSHAW'S MAP OF GREAT BRITAIN Shewing the RAILWAYS COMPLETED & in PROGRESS 1851

Stephenson built his first locomotive here in 1814

Stockton and Darlington Railway, September, 1825 first public railway to use steam locomotives

First commercial use of steam locomotive at Middleton Colliery, 1812

Liverpool & Manchester Railway, 1830; "the first modern railway in the full sense of the term."

Woodhead tunnels (on Sheffield, Ashton and Manchester Railway Company line)

Thomas Cook's first rail excursion: Leicester to Loughborough in 1841

CREWE — a new town specialising in locomotive manufacture

Surrey Iron Railway ran from Croydon to Wandsworth (London) in 1801. The first railway authorised by Act of Parliament, it was horse-drawn

Glasgow · Edinburgh · Newcastle · Darlington · Stockton · Leeds · Hull · Liverpool · Manchester · Crewe · Nottingham · Loughboro' · Leicester · Norwich · Birmingham · Rugby · Gloucester · Tring · Bristol · LONDON · Croydon · Dover

49

23: Law and order, 1822–1851

Crime and the police

An absurd number of crimes carried the death penalty in 1822; a man could be hanged for impersonating a Chelsea Pensioner. In that year, however, Robert Peel became Home Secretary and began to reform the criminal code. He abolished the death penalty for more than a hundred offences, replacing it with imprisonment or transportation. Realizing that the *detection* and *prevention* of crime were more important than the scale of punishments, Peel formed the Metropolitan Police Force in 1829. With one hand clutching a truncheon and the other free to catch the crook, the white-trousered, top-hatted 'bobby' was Peel's answer to the problem of maintaining law and order. The first 'bobbies' were moderately successful and soon they were being lent to other large towns with a crime problem on their hands. The counties showed far less interest so in 1839 parliament passed the Rural Constabulary Act which authorized County Constabularies. Very slowly, a system of civilian police forces under Home Office control developed at the very moment when, in view of all the current Poor Law and Chartist protest, a *military* style police force might have provoked rebellion.

The plight of trade unions

According to the law of the land, trade unionism was a crime against the state. This was expressed in the 1799–1800 Combination Acts which made combinations (unions) of workmen illegal. The governing classes repudiated any right on the part of the workers to dispute poor pay and working conditions. There was a brief respite in 1824 when the radical Francis Place, aided by Joseph Hume M.P., managed to persuade an unwary Parliament to repeal the Combination Acts; but a rash of strikes in 1825 made Parliament hurriedly reduce a working man's right to one of simply *joining* a union. There was no tolerance of strike action as Tommy Hepburn, leader of a miners' union in Newcastle soon discovered. His mass meetings held on the moors around Newcastle encouraged strike action; but every strike he started was broken by the pit-owners who used the police to evict miners' families from tied cottages and also resorted to bringing in 'blackleg' miners from other areas. Then Robert Owen made his ambitious attempt to mobilize British workers by means of a *Grand National Consolidated Trades Union* made up of district lodges. Scores of these lodges sprang up during 1834 and Owen soon claimed the support of half a million workers. Employers countered such moves with 'lock-outs' and prevented strikers from resuming their old jobs; while the government resorted to an act which dated from the Nore Mutiny of 1797 and prohibited the use of 'illegal

oaths'. The classic example of this method of destroying trade unionism was the case of the Tolpuddle Martyrs in 1834.

The Tolpuddle Martyrs 1834

In an effort to save their wages from further cuts, a group of farm labourers formed a branch of the GNCTU in their Dorset village of Tolpuddle. They were typical of thousands of labourers who, after tasting defeat during the 1830 Swing Riots, were now turning to non-violent means of improving their standard of living. But governments were always hyper-sensitive to any hint of agitation in the counties; so when the Duke of Wellington told the Home Secretary, Lord Melbourne, that rural workers were forming unions and agitating for a weekly wage of ten shillings, there was a quick response. In Tolpuddle, where wages were down to 7/– a week, the six founder members of the GNCTU branch were unwise enough to commission a large painting of Death, to add atmosphere to their branch initiation ceremonies. They were all arrested and found guilty of administering illegal oaths. The sentence was seven years transportation:

> I am not sentencing you for any crime you have committed, or that it could be proved that you were about to commit, but as an example to the working classes of this country.
> *Judge John Williams, Dorchester Assizes, 19 March 1834*

The New Model Unions

This sort of barbaric treatment had a catastrophic effect on the early unions. The GNCTU lost its nation-wide support and disbanded in August 1834. Most workers now abandoned trade union activity as a means of raising their standard of living. The short-lived Northumbrian Miners' Association, for example, gained absolutely nothing by striking in 1844. Workers therefore turned to education, to 'self-help', to 'Friendly Societies' in an effort to better themselves and protect their families against adversity. They were seeking security. An age of insurance began—the Prudential Assurance Company dates from 1848—and so did a new chapter in the history of trade unions. In 1851 the Amalgamated Society of Engineers formed their 'New Model' union. Its members, all highly skilled mechanics and specialists in the manufacture of the new steam-engines and industrial machinery, commanded some of the highest wages paid to early Victorian workers. They could afford the relatively high 'union sub' of a shilling a week. But it explains why the New Model was the first union capable of building up large reserves of cash—an essential feature of any union which wanted to help its members who were sick, injured, or on strike.

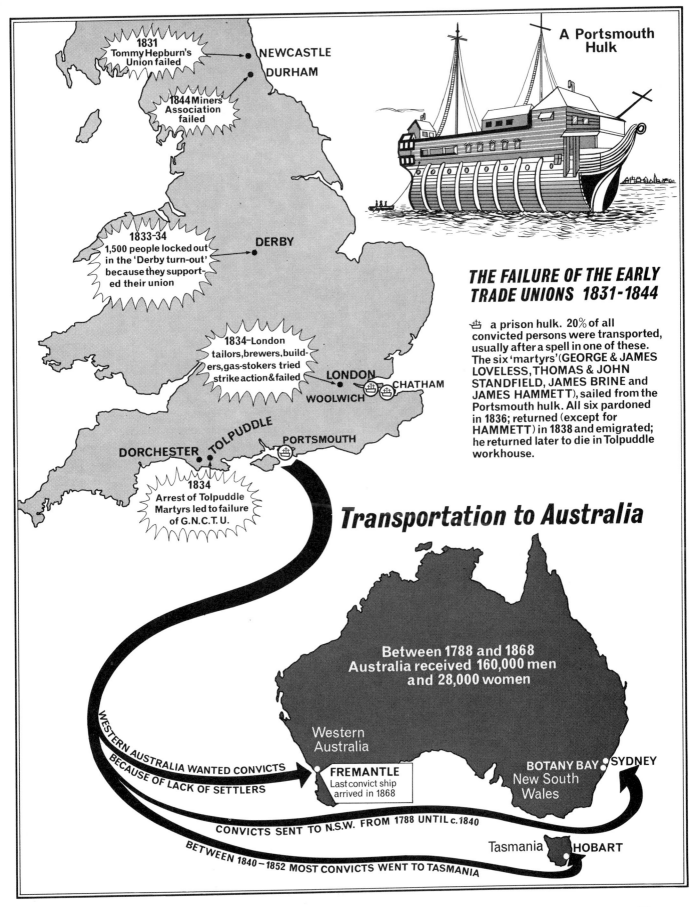

1831
Tommy Hepburn's Union failed

NEWCASTLE
DURHAM

1844 Miners Association failed

A Portsmouth Hulk

DERBY

1833-34
1,500 people locked out in the 'Derby turn-out' because they supported their union

1834–London tailors, brewers, builders, gas-stokers tried strike action & failed

LONDON
WOOLWICH
CHATHAM

DORCHESTER TOLPUDDLE
PORTSMOUTH

1834
Arrest of Tolpuddle Martyrs led to failure of G.N.C.T.U.

THE FAILURE OF THE EARLY TRADE UNIONS 1831-1844

⛴ a prison hulk. 20% of all convicted persons were transported, usually after a spell in one of these. The six 'martyrs'(GEORGE & JAMES LOVELESS, THOMAS & JOHN STANDFIELD, JAMES BRINE and JAMES HAMMETT), sailed from the Portsmouth hulk. All six pardoned in 1836; returned (except for HAMMETT) in 1838 and emigrated; he returned later to die in Tolpuddle workhouse.

Transportation to Australia

Between 1788 and 1868 Australia received 160,000 men and 28,000 women

WESTERN AUSTRALIA WANTED CONVICTS
BECAUSE OF LACK OF SETTLERS

Western Australia

FREMANTLE
Last convict ship arrived in 1868

BOTANY BAY SYDNEY
New South Wales

CONVICTS SENT TO N.S.W. FROM 1788 UNTIL c.1840

Tasmania HOBART

BETWEEN 1840-1852 MOST CONVICTS WENT TO TASMANIA

24: A time of slow improvement, 1823–1851

Working in the textile factories

Once the factories adopted steam power they either concentrated in existing towns or formed the nucleus of new ones. Men, women and children poured into the cotton trade to work long hours at dull, routine jobs. A spinner went to work at 6 a.m. and put in two hours before breakfast. Then he worked until the dinner-hour at noon. The hardest part of the day then followed; many spinners worked through until 8 p.m. For this the worker received around 12/- a week—small return for sweating in a temperature of 80° for 12 hours a day, six days a week. One group of spinners, out on strike during 1823, complained bitterly about being fined a shilling if they were found dirty at work; and then if they were caught having a wash without permission they were fined another shilling! Such was the harsh discipline common in the small textile factories at the beginning of the century.

Gradual improvements for children

Children were bound to suffer in the early period of factory development. Some parents were only too ready to put them to work and industrialists tended to exploit this source of cheap labour. As early as 1802 Parliament concerned itself with cutting down children's working hours. First it tried to protect *apprentices* by insisting on a maximum of 12 hours work a day with some time allowed for basic education—to be provided by the mill-owner. Many industrialists wriggled out of this responsibility by ending apprenticeships and taking on children as casual labourers. Parliament retaliated with the 1819 Factory Act which forbade the employment of children under nine and limited the working day for *all* children under sixteen to 12 hours. But there were not enough inspectors to enforce these early industrial regulations. Harsh conditions and exploitation persisted, especially in the worsted mills around Bradford. In 1832 a Select Committee enquired into the use of child labour and reported the next year—at the same moment as a nation-wide movement for a 'Ten Hour Day' was gaining support. The government promptly introduced the *1833 Factory Act* which reduced the working day for all children under thirteen to 9 hours. But it was not until 1847 that women and young people under eighteen were restricted to a 10 hour day. Then in 1850 another Factory Act limited the number of hours a factory could stay open—and it was this that established the English tradition of a Saturday half-day for factory workers.

Conditions in the mines

Conditions here were far worse than in most textile factories—yet they received very little publicity. It was common knowledge in Lancashire during the 1830s that parents put their children down the mines because they were *too young* to get a factory job! Five and six year olds spent hours in cold, dark pits as 'trappers'—operating the ventilation doors. Ten year olds were bent double, 'hurrying' heavy coal barrows along the narrow shafts. Another Commission enquired into the employment of children in mines. Its report, which contained drawings of children working in appalling conditions, horrified the House of Commons so much that the 1842 Mines and Collieries Act soon followed. After that no children under ten were to work underground.

Living in the towns

For tens of thousands of people, rapid industrialization brought with it the completely new experience of living in close-packed urban communities. Factory hands had to live within walking distance of their jobs; they urgently needed accommodation which had to be cheap to rent. So the 'jerry builders' erected cheap houses which soon degenerated into slums. The factory workers had no organized sanitation, no piped water—hardly a house in the land boasted this sort of amenity and even Queen Victoria lacked a bathroom in Buckingham Palace when she became Queen in 1837. Understandably, conditions in workers' homes were grim. Uneducated, overworked women could not cope with husbands and children in cramped, filthy, back-to-back dwellings, especially when money was short. The British people paid a heavy price for their industrial development. Disease was soon rife; tuberculosis, bronchitis, typhoid and cholera flourished and attacked the rich as well as the poor. Men racked their brains for a solution. Edwin Chadwick, famous for his operation of the New Poor Law, was sure (though he couldn't prove it) that cholera originated in the uncollected refuse which polluted industrial communities. His famous *Report on the Sanitary Condition of the Labouring Poor* (1842) urged the government to attack this problem. In 1848 Parliament approved a *Health of Towns Act* and set up a Board of Health—on which Chadwick served—to advise local Boards of Guardians on ways of improving public health and of coping with the wave of cholera which was causing terror in Britain towards the end of the eighteen-forties.

PROBLEMS OF AN INDUSTRIAL SOCIETY: 1823-1851

GIRL SHACKLED TO COAL BARROW

She wears a wide leather strap **"to which is attached a ring and about four feet of chain terminating in a hook"**
(Extract from the 1842 Report on the employment of children in mines.)

Conditions such as this were common in Scotland and the North East coalfields

MR. SHEPPARD edited a "Handbook to Hull" in 1922. In it he wrote:

"I can just remember the days of defective water supply, and of bad sanitation, in the late 'forties, and the consequent cholera and other epidemics, sought to be averted or abated by tar barrels burning weirdly in the public streets .... I saw LISTER STREET thus illuminated in 1849."

This sort of development was typical of mid-19th Century Lancashire towns such as Preston

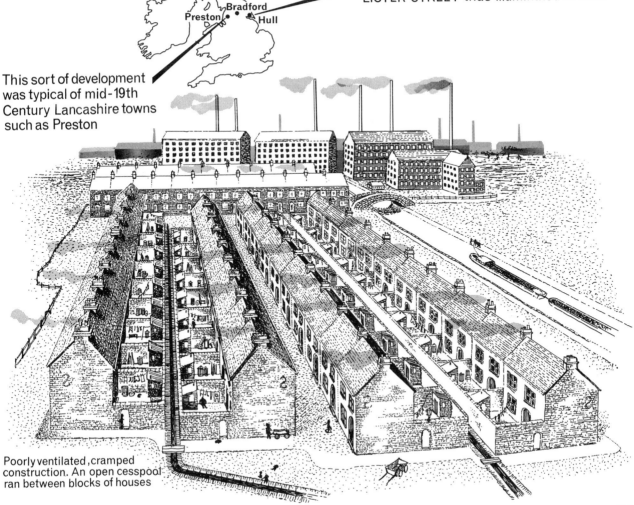

Preston   Bradford   Hull

Poorly ventilated, cramped construction. An open cesspool ran between blocks of houses

25: The year of the Great Exhibition, 1851

The idea

While some men such as Chadwick were determined to solve the problems of Britain's industrial society, others were equally concerned with promoting the quality of Britain's industrial products. Such a man was Henry Cole, civil servant and member of the Royal Society of Arts—the President of which was Prince Albert, consort of Queen Victoria. Cole wanted the Prince to back a national industrial exhibition, along the lines of one he had seen in Paris during 1849. Albert agreed, so long as it would be an *international* exhibition—'The Great Exhibition of the Works and Industries of all Nations'.

The 'Crystal Palace'

A Royal Commission, presided over by the Prince, began planning the Exhibition in 1850. It selected a talented horticulturist, Joseph Paxton, to design the exhibition hall which would be sited in Hyde Park. Paxton had prepared a revolutionary glass structure, supported by pre-fabricated metal units; *Punch* magazine soon labelled it the 'Crystal Palace'. The builders had a mere 22 weeks to complete the project—yet when the Queen drove across Hyde Park on 1 May 1851 to open the Great Exhibition only a few touches of paint were lacking. Huge glass-roofed halls enclosed exhibits from all over the world—Paxton had created a spectacle such as the early Victorians had never seen before. They swarmed into London—literally in their millions. Railway excursions (5 shillings from Yorkshire to London) gave many people their first train ride *and* their first trip to the capital where, for a shilling, a visitor could see some of the wonders of mid-nineteenth century technology. Whitworth's latest machine tools, accurate to one ten-thousandth of an inch, were rivalled by a sewing machine from America. Warsaw sent a calculating machine; Australia sent tinned mutton. And though the Exhibition was dedicated to international peace, German field-guns and Samuel Colt's 'six-shooter' attracted plenty of interest.

Effects of the Exhibition

The Great Exhibition closed in October 1851. Navvies dismantled the Crystal Palace and then re-built it at Sydenham, where it remained until fire destroyed it in 1936. In its short life, the Exhibition made an enormous impact. International trade exhibitions were now frequently held in Paris, Brussels and New York. Many branded products—some still do it in the 1970's—proudly flaunted facsimiles of gold and silver medals won in this way. The Exhibition therefore certainly succeeded, as Albert and many others had hoped, in the promotion of international trade. But it did not usher in an era of peace. The Crimean War began in 1854 and before long Europe was involved in a series of conflicts which preceded the unification of Italy and Germany. However, the Exhibition had one important and perhaps unexpected effect on British society. Many workers saw in the Exhibition the promise of increased wages and a higher standard of comfort based upon the expansion of British industry. The factory, only a few years before rejected by the Chartists, now offered a hope for the future. Certainly, after 1851, the riotous clamour for improvement died away as most people received the first benefits of industrial progress in the form of a steady increase in real wages.

Navvies during the re-construction of the Crystal Palace at Sydenham

1851 The Year of the GREAT EXHIBITION

It was also the year of the sixth population census which defined the main occupations of the British people, who now numbered 27,000,000. The main industries and products are listed below, and <u>one</u> example of each is shown on the map. The largest industry of all was AGRICULTURE which employed 17% of the male population.

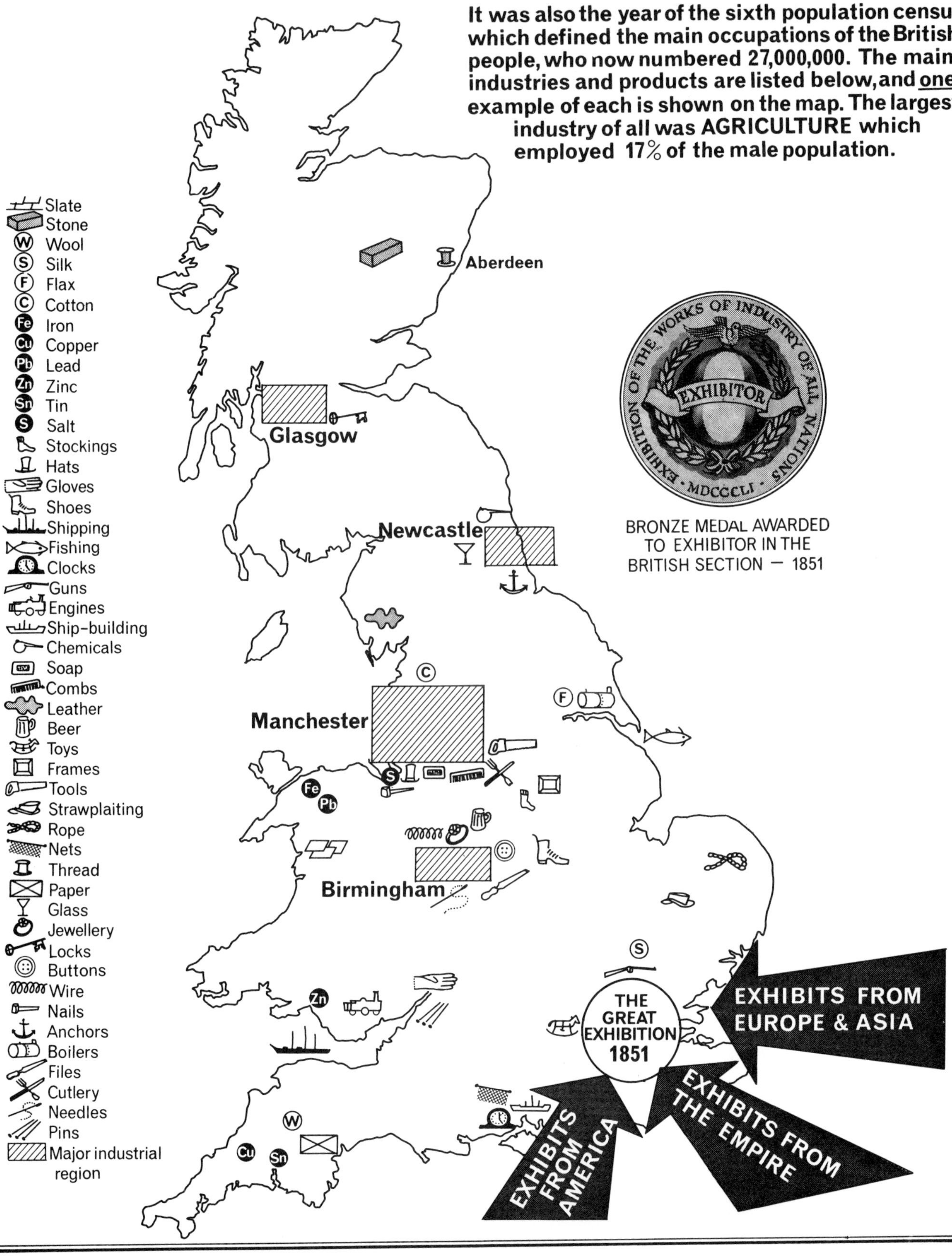

Legend:
- Slate
- Stone
- (W) Wool
- (S) Silk
- (F) Flax
- (C) Cotton
- (Fe) Iron
- (Cu) Copper
- (Pb) Lead
- (Zn) Zinc
- (Sn) Tin
- (S) Salt
- Stockings
- Hats
- Gloves
- Shoes
- Shipping
- Fishing
- Clocks
- Guns
- Engines
- Ship-building
- Chemicals
- Soap
- Combs
- Leather
- Beer
- Toys
- Frames
- Tools
- Strawplaiting
- Rope
- Nets
- Thread
- Paper
- Glass
- Jewellery
- Locks
- Buttons
- Wire
- Nails
- Anchors
- Boilers
- Files
- Cutlery
- Needles
- Pins
- Major industrial region

Map labels: Aberdeen, Glasgow, Newcastle, Manchester, Birmingham

THE GREAT EXHIBITION 1851

EXHIBITS FROM EUROPE & ASIA

EXHIBITS FROM THE EMPIRE

EXHIBITS FROM AMERICA

EXHIBITION OF THE WORKS OF INDUSTRY OF ALL NATIONS · MDCCCLI ·
EXHIBITOR

BRONZE MEDAL AWARDED TO EXHIBITOR IN THE BRITISH SECTION — 1851

Part 3 – The Clamour for Improvement 1823–1851

Spread

16.	*Captain Swing***	Hobsbawm and Rudé	Lawrence & Wishart
17.	*William Cobbett***	Asa Briggs	OUP
	*Parliamentary Elections and Reform***	J. Addy	Longmans
	The Autobiography of a Working Man	Alexander Somerville	McGibbon and Kee
18.	*Edwin Chadwick, Poor Law and Public Health***	R. Watson	Longmans
19.	*Chartism*	Historical Association Pamphlet	
	*The Chartists***	P. Searby	Longmans
20.	*Cobden and Bright*	D. Read	Arnold
21.	*The Great Hunger***	Cecil Woodham-Smith	Hamish Hamitton
22.	*Railways and Life in Britain***	S. Gregory	Ginn
	*The Railway Navvies***	T. Coleman	Hutchinson
23.	*The Early Trade Unions***	Jackdaw Publication	
24.	*Factory Reform***	Dawson and Wall	OUP
25.	*Victorian People*	Asa Briggs	Odhams
	*Joseph Paxton and the Crystal Palace***	J. Kamm	Methuen
	*The Great Exhibition***	Jackdaw Publication	

**Especially useful for project and topic work

PART 4

Fifty Years of Progress 1851–1901

The Victorians were great believers in progress and during these fifty years they brought to themselves and to the world at large the fruits of their invention and technical achievement. Railways and bridges, factories and mines dominated, and often devastated, the landscape at home and abroad. Smoke, steam and exhaust gases polluted the atmosphere. What a pity this was; but, as the Victorians were always saying, such was the price of progress. This was how you paid for the benefits of gas, electricity, faster forms of travel and a generally higher standard of living. Unfortunately, the price wasn't always measured in financial terms. Industrial progress was at the price of malnutrition for millions of working people. Imperial progress cost thousands of natives their lives.

Though society was class-ridden throughout this period, it remained fairly tolerable partly because the ruling aristocracy and upper middle class kept a sense of duty towards their social inferiors. They did their best to make working conditions more bearable in mines and factories; they safeguarded the welfare of women and children in employment; they gave the vote to workers thrifty enough to keep a roof over their heads; and after 1870 they provided British children with an elementary education. Admittedly, they tended to ignore the plight of the poorest people, assuming that those who were in a parlous condition were lazy and immoral and had only themselves to blame. It was not until the very end of the century that investigation showed that many basic assumptions about poverty were pretty wide of the mark.

Fortunately, many people cared for their fellow men, no matter what their circumstances might be. Dr Barnardo, a 'ragged school' teacher in London's East End, cared about destitute children. Samuel Plimsoll, M.P. for Derby, cared about the hazards that sailors faced when they went to sea in leaky, overloaded merchant vessels. Both names became household words: Barnardo for the children's homes he founded after 1866; Plimsoll for the load line all ships had to carry after the passing of the Merchant Shipping Act in 1876.

1901 was the year in which Queen Victoria died. The Victorians themselves regarded her reign (1837–1901—the longest in British history) with something approaching awe. They were very conscious of the giant strides made in their lifetime and very much aware that 1901 marked the end of an era. It was not just a matter of pure technical achievement, although the Victorians could still thrill in the knowledge that their trains could touch 75 m.p.h., that they could send a telegram to New York, take a photo, watch the moving pictures and listen to the phonograph. By then the Victorians had lost their complacence. They appreciated that many beliefs previously taken for granted were now under serious attack.

26: Religion and good works in Mid-Victorian Britain

The religion of the people

While the mid-Victorian period was a time of deep religious feeling for the few, it was also a time of nominal Christianity for the many. By no means everybody went to Church or received any form of religious instruction. Out of 18 million people in England and Wales on Sunday 30 March 1851 (the day of the Church Attendance Census) only 7.25 million went to a service. And only half of these went to a Church of England service; the rest attended either mass or chapel. This sort of statistical information came as a great shock to the upper and middle classes who, as pillars of society, were unfailing churchgoers. Did it mean, they asked, that the Church could not cope with the challenge of a rapidly expanding industrial society? At first, the Church of England hotly denied the validity of the figures; then it admitted it had been working under difficult conditions for years. Thousands of industrial workers now lived in what had been *rural* parishes. Local ministers could not—or would not—deal with such numbers. Bradford's parish church, for example, had a potential congregation of 78,000 people but, if one excluded the pews reserved for *regular* churchgoers, it had room for a mere *200* worshippers. Of course, the churches spent money on buildings and teacher-training programmes, but these alone were not the key to success. They needed men who, fired with missionary zeal, could go out to win the hearts and minds of the masses. A few men of this calibre emerged. The Rev. Spurgeon began his remarkable Baptist mission in 1854. A. C. Tait, who became Bishop of London in 1856, preached to gypsies and costermongers. But despite this religious revival, the churches made little impact upon the workers, their wives and children, who lived in the industrial slums. And it was somehow ironic that, at this very moment, many fine missionary teachers should turn their backs on their own people in order to convert the teeming millions of Africa and Asia.

The missionaries

It was usual for the churches to allocate some funds for missionary work overseas. One reason for this was the genuine desire to eradicate forever the trade in human beings. British Parliaments had abolished the slave trade (1807) and the institution of slavery within the Empire (1833), but there were still plenty of slave markets in the world. Many missionaries wanted to end this evil and give care and protection to the freed slaves. The London Missionary Society, the United Methodists and the Universities' Mission to Central Africa did a great deal of good work in remote areas of the world. Most famous of all the missionary explorers was David Livingstone (1813–73). He started work in a textile mill but studied to be a doctor. As a member of the London Missionary Society, he went out to Africa in 1841. From his mission stations in Bechuanaland (modern Botswana), Livingstone explored likely trade routes to the coast so that his backward African followers could create trade links and thus raise their standards of living. Livingstone was simply trying to make the slave-trade unprofitable for those who were running it. His work resulted in the three great expeditions: 1853–56, which led to the discovery of Victoria Falls; 1858–63, during which he found Lake Nyasa (modern Lake Malawi); 1866–73, when he unsuccessfully searched for the source of the Nile. He died in 1873, to be revered by many Africans ever since.

Shaftesbury (1801–85)

One of the many Victorians to devote a career to good works was Antony Ashley Cooper, Earl of Shaftesbury. A God-fearing, humane man, he was also narrow-minded and bigoted in matters of religion. He was convinced that his beliefs, in the eyes of God, were the correct beliefs. Therefore, all men must conform to those beliefs. He was a man of his times, tireless in his efforts to prevent the exploitation of children, but totally opposed to free and liberal forms of education! State schools, he said, might not heed the Bible; better to keep the 'Ragged Schools' which did. Ragged schools were charitable schools designed to provide street urchins with a chance of bettering themselves. But he was best known for his campaigns against the use of children in mines—the 1842 Mines and Collieries Act had resulted from his efforts—and in chimney sweeping. Though he bombarded Parliament with horrifying tales of youngsters employed as 'climbing boys' in the huge chimneys favoured by Victorian builders, it was not until 1875 that the Commons heeded his agitation. Only then did it declare that the practice of employing climbing boys, who could be suffocated or burnt whilst at work, was illegal. We can gauge Shaftesbury's contemporary reputation for good works from the 200 odd deputations which attended his Memorial Service in Westminster Abbey:

> The Ragged School Union, Sunday School Union, Dr. Barnardo's Homes, Society for the Prevention of Cruelty to Children, Missions to Seamen, One Tun Ragged School, the Home for Little Boys . . .
> *(The list of deputations is printed in the appendix to Hodder's 'Life and Work of Shaftesbury', Cassell, 1890)*

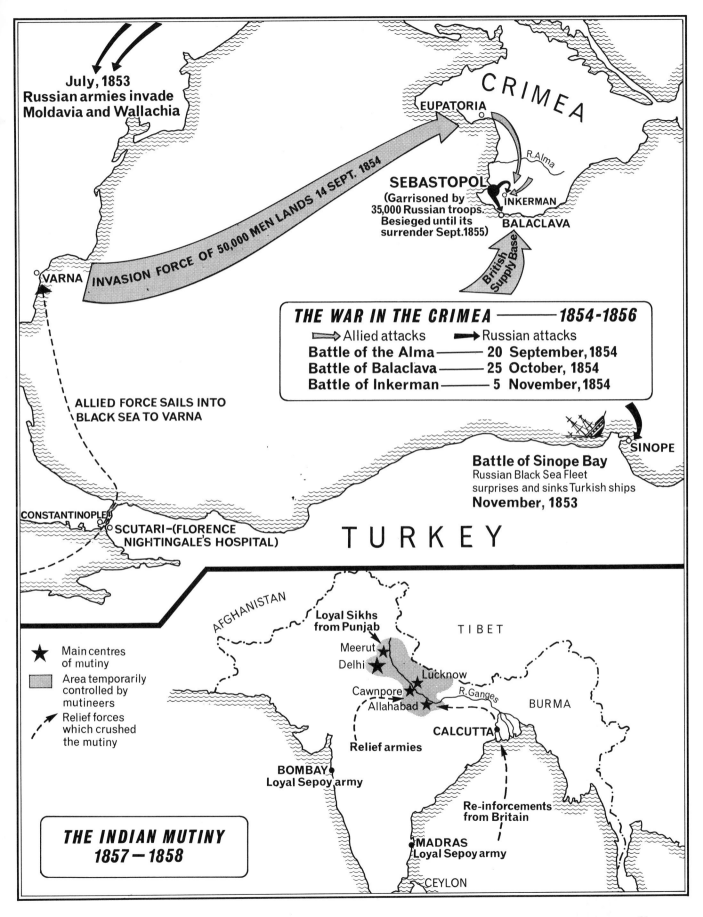

July, 1853
Russian armies invade
Moldavia and Wallachia

C R I M E A

EUPATORIA

R.Alma

SEBASTOPOL
(Garrisoned by
35,000 Russian troops.
Besieged until its
surrender Sept.1855)

INKERMAN

BALACLAVA

British Supply Base

INVASION FORCE OF 50,000 MEN LANDS 14 SEPT. 1854

VARNA

ALLIED FORCE SAILS INTO
BLACK SEA TO VARNA

THE WAR IN THE CRIMEA ———— **1854-1856**

⇨ Allied attacks   ➤ Russian attacks

Battle of the Alma ———— 20 September, 1854
Battle of Balaclava ———— 25 October, 1854
Battle of Inkerman ———— 5 November, 1854

SINOPE

Battle of Sinope Bay
Russian Black Sea Fleet
surprises and sinks Turkish ships
November, 1853

CONSTANTINOPLE
SCUTARI–(FLORENCE
NIGHTINGALE'S HOSPITAL)

T U R K E Y

AFGHANISTAN

**Loyal Sikhs
from Punjab**

Meerut
Delhi

T I B E T

Lucknow

Cawnpore

Allahabad

R.Ganges

BURMA

CALCUTTA

★ Main centres
of mutiny

Area temporarily
controlled by
mutineers

Relief forces
which crushed
the mutiny

Relief armies

BOMBAY
Loyal Sepoy army

**Re-inforcements
from Britain**

**THE INDIAN MUTINY
1857 – 1858**

MADRAS
Loyal Sepoy army

CEYLON

28: Science: discovery and controversy

The voyage of the 'Beagle' 1831–6

On 27 December 1831 HMS *Beagle* left Devonport on a round the world voyage with orders to carry out a series of scientific surveys. On board was a young naturalist, Charles Darwin. When the Beagle reached the Galapagos Archipelago, Darwin discovered species of animal life quite unknown in any part of the world. For example he found 25 new kinds of birds and some remarkable lizards—'hideous reptiles may oftentimes be seen on the black rocks, basking in the sun with outstretched legs ...' Even more remarkable was his discovery that each small island had its own set of species. The turtles on one island were quite different from those on another. Darwin reasoned that all living things must have evolved, by the process of natural selection, into the variety of life to be seen on earth. By 'natural selection', Darwin meant that all living organisms have to struggle for survival; the weakest of the species go under, the strongest go on evolving. He published these ideas in two books: *The Origin of Species by Natural Selection* (1859) and *The Descent of Man* (1871).

Evolution

Darwin's theories implied that life had taken millions of years to evolve, an idea previously suggested by geologists who had found many examples of fossilized prehistoric animals. However, the Book of Genesis said that the earth and all things on it had been created in six days—an event which took place, according to learned clerics, in the year 4004 B.C. For years, the controversy went on. Eminent scientists such as Thomas Huxley backed Darwin's theories. 'It is quite certain', wrote Huxley, 'that the Ape which most nearly approaches man, in the totality of its organization, is either the Chimpanzee or the Gorilla ...'* Later on, however, he was careful to say '... no-one is more strongly convinced than I am of the vastness of the gulf between civilized man and the brutes; or is more certain that whether *from* them or not, he is assuredly not *of* them.'† Un-

Man's Place in Nature by T. Huxley, p. 86, 1959 edition published by University of Michigan Press.
†*Man's Place in Nature* by T. Huxley, pp. 129–30, 1959 edition published by University of Michigan Press.

fortunately, the controversy caused many people to over-simplify the argument and assume, quite wrongly, that man was descended from monkeys! For many years there was a futile search for the 'missing link'. Sure enough, 'he' appeared. A man called Dawson produced a skull found on Piltdown Common, near Lewes. It had the cranium of a man and the jawbone of an ape. 'Piltdown man' was an embarrassment to the experts for 40 years; it was not until the 1950s that he was shown to be a clever fake. All in all, the research and writings by men such as Darwin and Huxley caused many people to doubt their beliefs, especially in the literal truth of the Bible.

Lister and surgery

After the Crimean war, Florence Nightingale returned to England to found her School of Nursing in 1860. At St Thomas' Hospital in London, she set the high standards for which the nursing profession has since become renowned. Equally important, by her example she had opened the door of a professional career for women— though women doctors such as Elizabeth Garrett Anderson, Edith Pechey and Sophia Jex-Blake had to fight for many years before Victorian society would accept them. New ideas in the medical profession aroused controversy automatically. This was certainly true for Joseph Lister, a brilliant surgeon. He worked in Glasgow and was deeply troubled by the high mortality rate in surgical operations. He knew that the basic unit of human tissue was the cell—Rudolf Virchow had discovered this in Germany during 1858—and that the task was to prevent infection of the cells during an operation. He also knew, from the work of Louis Pasteur in France, that infection was due to germs which could multiply with astonishing rapidity. So Lister argued that if he could keep germs away from the scene of an operation then the patient would have a much better chance of survival. Lister used diluted carbolic acid as an *antiseptic* and carried out a successful operation in 1865. Soon pump-operated carbolic sprays were common in Scottish hospitals, though English doctors remained suspicious of Lister, carbolic acid and germs. After all, you couldn't *see* germs floating in the air! However, medical science advanced and by the 1880s most surgeons had adopted Lister's methods.

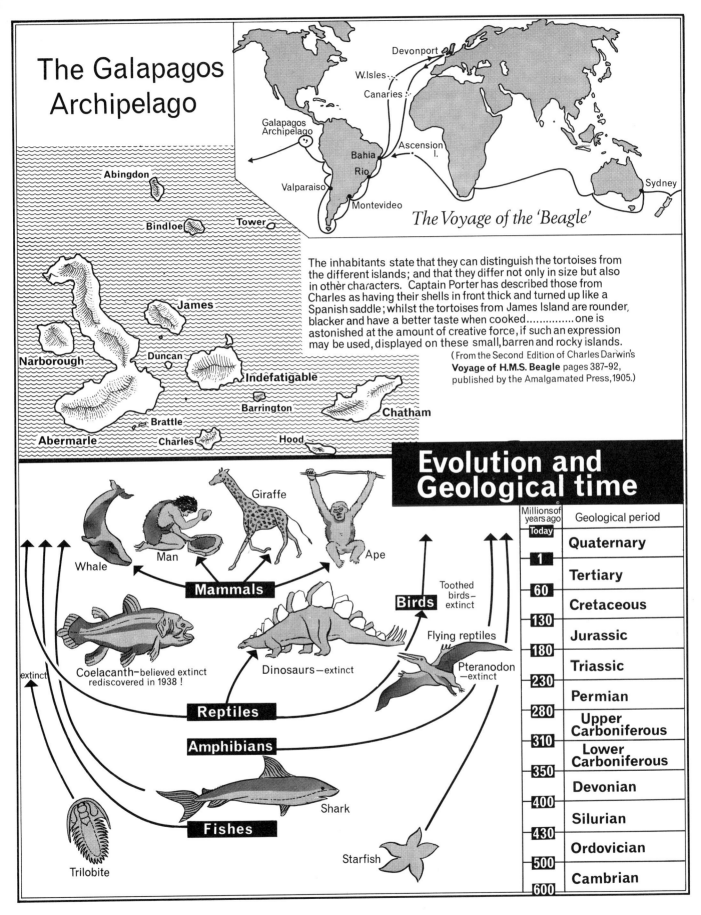

The Galapagos Archipelago

The Voyage of the 'Beagle'

Devonport
W. Isles
Canaries
Galapagos Archipelago
Ascension I.
Bahia
Rio
Valparaiso
Montevideo
Sydney

Abingdon
Bindloe
Tower
James
Narborough
Duncan
Indefatigable
Barrington
Brattle
Chatham
Abermarle
Charles
Hood

The inhabitants state that they can distinguish the tortoises from the different islands; and that they differ not only in size but also in other characters. Captain Porter has described those from Charles as having their shells in front thick and turned up like a Spanish saddle; whilst the tortoises from James Island are rounder, blacker and have a better taste when cooked...............one is astonished at the amount of creative force, if such an expression may be used, displayed on these small, barren and rocky islands.

(From the Second Edition of Charles Darwin's **Voyage of H.M.S. Beagle** pages 387-92, published by the Amalgamated Press, 1905.)

Evolution and Geological time

Giraffe
Man
Ape
Whale

Mammals

Toothed birds—extinct
Birds
Flying reptiles
Pteranodon—extinct

Coelacanth—believed extinct rediscovered in 1938!
Dinosaurs—extinct

extinct

Reptiles

Amphibians

Shark

Fishes

Trilobite
Starfish

Millions of years ago	Geological period
Today	Quaternary
1	Tertiary
60	Cretaceous
130	Jurassic
180	Triassic
230	Permian
280	Upper Carboniferous
310	Lower Carboniferous
350	Devonian
400	Silurian
430	Ordovician
500	Cambrian
600	

29: The advance of technology

Technological breakthroughs came fast and furious towards the end of the nineteenth century as pure and applied science combined to meet the growing needs of a complex, industrial society.

The age of steel

Henry Bessemer, inventor and businessman, revolutionized the metallurgical industries by his discovery of mild steel in 1856. In his tiny St Pancras factory, he had blown cold air through molten iron, with quite startling effects on his 7 cwt. crucible. Flames, sparks, slag and molten metal poured out of its mouth and when Bessemer's workmen cast the metal into ingots they found they had made mild steel. Bessemer promptly patented the process and persuaded the Ebbw Vale ironmasters to try out one of his converters. They did—and the process didn't work! An embarrassed Bessemer discovered that the iron works had used *phosphoric ore* (iron ore with a high phosphorus content). The phosphorus had stayed in the metal and made the ingots brittle. Bessemer's steel-converter worked as long as foundries used non-phosphoric ores—most of which had to be imported. Inevitably, other metallurgists experimented with the cheaper phosphoric-ores. By 1878 Sidney Gilchrist-Thomas had made a lining which, when used inside a Bessemer converter, absorbed the unwanted phosphorus. Now any industrial nation with iron-ore reserves could make high-grade steel. Today the Manhattan skyscrapers and the Eiffel Tower in Paris are tributes to the use of high-grade steel in the 1880s.

Refrigeration and steam-turbines.

Steam had many new and exciting applications for marine engineering. Clydeside engineers designed the sailing-ship *Strathleven* complete with a steam-operated refrigeration plant; in 1880 it arrived from Australia with a cargo of frozen mutton. In 1882 the *Dunedin* sailed in from New Zealand with a similar cargo. At the same time, Sir Charles Parsons was working on a new marine propulsion unit—the steam turbine. He forced high-pressure steam against 'turbine blades' fitted to a propeller shaft and incorporated the unit into a small craft called the *Turbinia*. Then, in 1897, he treated an astonished Royal Navy (drawn up for review at Spithead) to a show of speed with which no destroyer could compete—it persuaded the Navy to fit steam-turbines into their fastest ships. These technological advances brought many ironworks and engineering firms into marine construction and for the next 40 years Britain was to be the greatest shipbuilding country in the world.

Electricity and motor cars

Though at first railways had a monopoly of the electric telegraph, by 1866 the *Great Eastern* had laid the Atlantic cable. Ten years later Graham Bell, a Scotsman living in America, invented the telephone. Around 1878 Edison, an American, and Swan, an Englishman, invented the electric filament lamp quite independently of one another. In the last year of Queen Victoria's reign, Marconi managed to transmit radio signals from Cornwall to Newfoundland. There was, however, one area of technology where Britain lagged behind. Germans led the development of the four stroke internal combustion engine which was to revolutionize life in the twentieth century. While Nikolaus Otto was making his gas-air engine in Deutz, the Americans were bringing up petroleum from deep rock strata in Titusville. It took the genius of Otto's technical manager, Gottlieb Daimler, to use petrol in the 'gas' engine and thus create an efficient power unit; and it also took the genius of Carl Benz to devise the *motor-car*—the product, not of one man's brains, but the result of scientific research and technical development and co-operation.

X-Rays and radium

Professor Röntgen, a German physicist, discovered *X-Rays* in 1895; next year Henri Becquerel, a French professor, discovered the *radio-active properties* of uranium. His assistant, Marie Curie, investigated the phenomenon of radio-activity and discovered the existence of *radium*. Thus even before the end of the Victorian age, many scientific discoveries of crucial importance to life today had already been made.

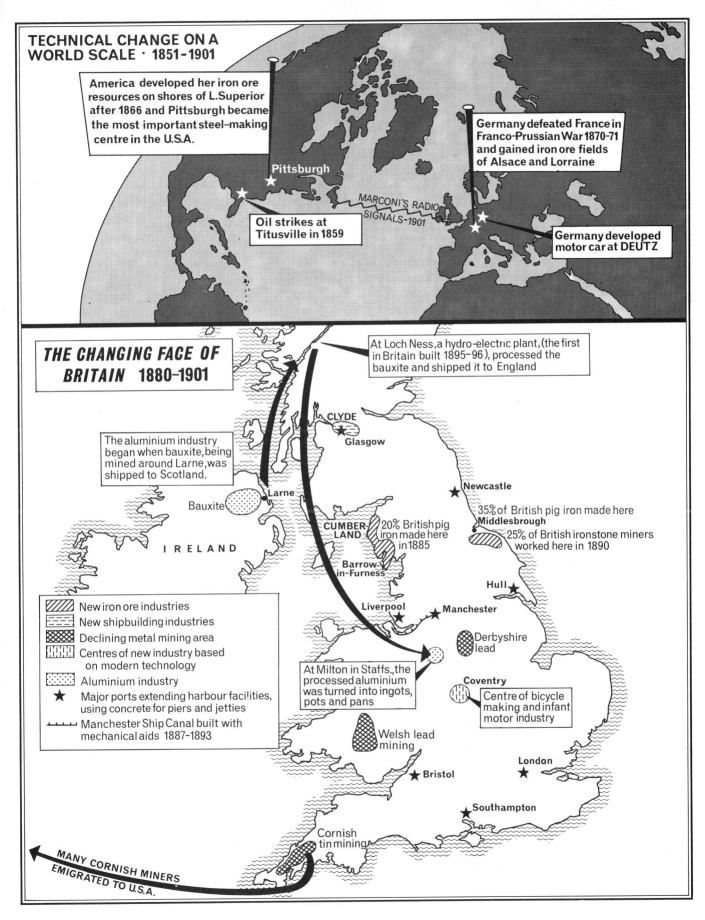

TECHNICAL CHANGE ON A WORLD SCALE · 1851-1901

America developed her iron ore resources on shores of L.Superior after 1866 and Pittsburgh became the most important steel-making centre in the U.S.A.

Germany defeated France in Franco-Prussian War 1870-71 and gained iron ore fields of Alsace and Lorraine

Pittsburgh

MARCONI'S RADIO SIGNALS-1901

Oil strikes at Titusville in 1859

Germany developed motor car at DEUTZ

THE CHANGING FACE OF BRITAIN 1880-1901

At Loch Ness, a hydro-electric plant, (the first in Britain built 1895-96), processed the bauxite and shipped it to England

CLYDE
★ Glasgow

The aluminium industry began when bauxite, being mined around Larne, was shipped to Scotland.

Bauxite

Larne

Newcastle

35% of British pig iron made here
Middlesbrough
25% of British ironstone miners worked here in 1890

CUMBER-LAND
20% British pig iron made here in 1885

IRELAND

Barrow-in-Furness

Hull

Liverpool
★ Manchester

Derbyshire lead

New iron ore industries
New shipbuilding industries
Declining metal mining area
Centres of new industry based on modern technology
Aluminium industry
★ Major ports extending harbour facilities, using concrete for piers and jetties
Manchester Ship Canal built with mechanical aids 1887-1893

At Milton in Staffs., the processed aluminium was turned into ingots, pots and pans

Coventry
Centre of bicycle making and infant motor industry

Welsh lead mining

London

★ Bristol

Southampton

Cornish tin mining

MANY CORNISH MINERS EMIGRATED TO U.S.A.

30: Trade and the economy, 1851–1901

Workshop of the world 1851–75

British manufacturers were now convinced free-traders, rejecting any attempt at government control. *Laissez-faire*—leave things to take their course—had become their motto, as well it might be for they had little foreign competition to worry about. They could produce more steel, more pig-iron, more coal *more cheaply* than any continental manufacturer and this meant that the British had a monopoly of what the world most dearly wanted: locomotives, railway track, pots and pans and cotton goods. These were the boom years for Britain's exports, when manufacturers and all who invested in industry enjoyed handsome dividends. But the British working class, though its wages tended to increase, never earned enough to create a 'consumer society'. Most money still went on food, clothing and rent. Sometimes a family managed to put a bit away in a Friendly Society or in the Post Office Savings Bank which opened in 1861, but more often than not any extra cash went on beer and tobacco. The people took their pleasures when they could—there was always the chance of a slump and unemployment round the corner.

The Lancashire cotton crisis 1861–5

By 1861, Lancashire's mechanized textile industries manufactured half the world's cotton products. 500,000 workers toiled in 2000 factories to produce exports worth £45 million annually. For raw materials they depended on the slave-owning cotton plantations in the southern states of the U.S.A. When these states formed a breakaway Confederacy in 1861, there was Civil War in America. Union warships blockaded the Confederate ports and Lancashire lost its supply of raw cotton. By 1862, half the county's textile workers were on Poor Relief; Parliament passed the 1863 Public Works Act and poured money into the stricken area; private relief funds raised a million pounds for the unemployed. Yet there was barely any disorder; the unemployed *understood* the situation and accepted that their suffering was in the cause of freedom for the

American negro slaves. When the Civil War ended in 1865, so did the crisis; by 1867 Lancashire's workers were enjoying another boom.

The 'Great Depression'

This term is used to describe the falling prices and declining dividends characteristic of the period 1875–96. It was the time when Britain first felt the backwash of her previously unchallenged industrial supremacy. She had built most of the world's locomotives and railway tracks; now the world was using them to open up undeveloped areas such as the North American prairies and the Ukrainian steppelands. Foreign wheat and foreign beef appeared on the open market in abundance. Prices fell and the British people got the benefit of plenty of cheap food during the 1870s and 1880s. Farmers thought this was disastrous; manufacturers deplored their shrinking profits. Of course, the world was simply beginning to follow in Britain's industrial footsteps. Americans, Germans, Russians, Frenchmen and Japanese were manufacturing goods to sell on their home markets. It became harder to sell British goods. Obviously, this was the moment for Britain to streamline her industries, to introduce new machinery and manufacturing techniques. After all, she was irrevocably committed to an economy based on *exports*—her free trade policies, and the rising population in her industrial towns made this essential. Yet Britain did not modernize. Instead, her manufacturers opened up much of the remaining 'undeveloped' world: Latin America, India, China, Africa, South East Asia, Australia and New Zealand. By organizing trade in these areas, Britain survived the 'Great Depression'; but when it ended around 1896 a very different world economy had come into existence. Two industrial giants—Germany and the U.S.A.—dominated the scene. Britain, the first of the industrial nations and therefore the one with the oldest and least efficient industrial plant, now had to face serious competition.

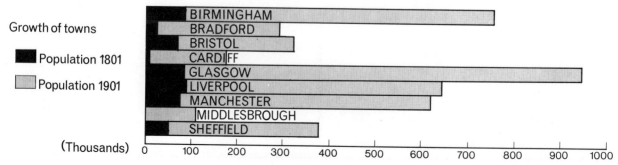

Growth of towns

■ Population 1801

□ Population 1901

BIRMINGHAM
BRADFORD
BRISTOL
CARDIFF
GLASGOW
LIVERPOOL
MANCHESTER
MIDDLESBROUGH
SHEFFIELD

(Thousands) 0 100 200 300 400 500 600 700 800 900 1000

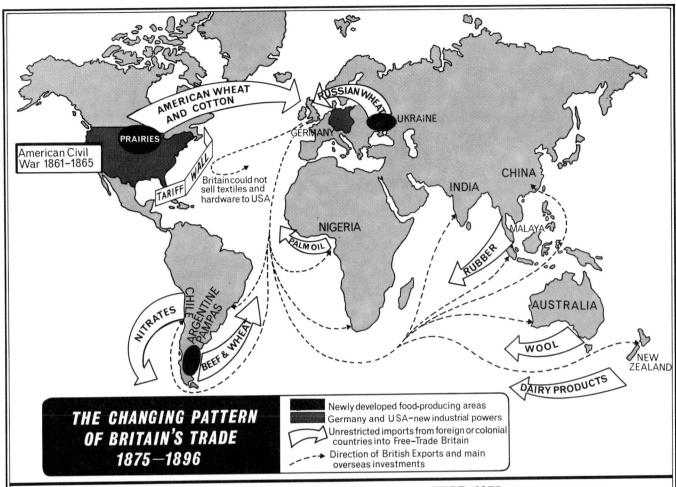

American Civil War 1861–1865

AMERICAN WHEAT AND COTTON

PRAIRIES

TARIFF WALL

Britain could not sell textiles and hardware to USA

RUSSIAN WHEAT

GERMANY

UKRAINE

CHINA

INDIA

NIGERIA

PALM OIL

MALAYA

RUBBER

NITRATES

ARGENTINE PAMPAS

CHILE

BEEF & WHEAT

AUSTRALIA

WOOL

NEW ZEALAND

DAIRY PRODUCTS

THE CHANGING PATTERN OF BRITAIN'S TRADE 1875–1896

■ Newly developed food-producing areas
■ Germany and USA–new industrial powers
⇦ Unrestricted imports from foreign or colonial countries into Free–Trade Britain
- - → Direction of British Exports and main overseas investments

FIVE IMPORTANT FEATURES OF ECONOMIC CHANGE AFTER 1875

1. A great deal of British capital invested (and not always profitably) overseas.
2. Inadequate amounts of money invested in Britain's future, e.g. the pressing problems of housing and poverty.
3. Inadequate amounts of cash spent on modernising British industry.
4. There was no answer to foreign tariffs, e.g. Britain found it increasingly difficult to sell on the American home market.
5. Main advantage for British people:—Cheap food meant that the cost of living went down.

The destination of British cotton exports 1851——1901

	W. Europe and USA took:	Undeveloped world took:	The rest took:
In 1851	25%	70%	5%
In 1880	10%	82%*	8%
In 1901	7%	86%*	7%

✱ Britain exported nearly half of this to India alone! This shows why Britain was so anxious to hold on to the sub–continent.

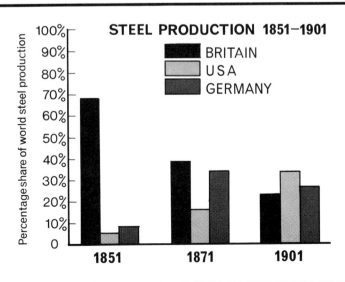

STEEL PRODUCTION 1851–1901

■ BRITAIN
□ USA
▨ GERMANY

Percentage share of world steel production

1851   1871   1901

31: Britain: an urban society, 1851–1901

The 1851 Census had shown that more people were living in the towns than in the countryside. Moreover, as the population was still increasing it meant that the number of towndwellers rose dramatically. At the same time, there was a distinct improvement in living conditions for many people. However, it was quite impossible to solve in this period all the large-scale social problems thrown up by an expanding urban society. Major public health and housing problems persisted well into the twentieth century. Some idea of the kind of problem facing leading Victorian citizens—and some of the answers they came up with—may be grasped by looking at three different urban areas.

London

The capital provided the best example of the widely differing levels of Victorian life. London boasted fine parks, theatres and rows of expensive town houses occupied by the gentry and the successful middle class. This upper-crust of Victorian society lived well away from the smelly riverside with its dirty wharves and factory sites; beyond earshot of the railway termini which had thrust themselves into the centre of London to add their smoke and grime to the already polluted atmosphere. The age of the London 'peasouper' had arrived. Out in the suburbs, builders erected rows of neat terrace houses for shopkeepers, clerks and skilled artisans. They were leaving the slums, the overcrowded tenements where thousands of people lived under appalling conditions. More than 4 million people lived in London by 1880; yet there was still no proper sewage system, no means of bringing untainted drinking water to every household. London and London's health desperately needed reform. It was not until 1888 that the County Councils Act established the famous L.C.C. (London County Council)—together with many other councils up and down the country—to cope with problems such as these.

Glasgow

Glasgow paid a high price for the industrial revolution. Between 1850 and 1870 it was producing the cheapest pig-iron in Britain. Its furnaces and factories provided iron for the railways and the steamships and laid on the Clyde the foundation of one of the world's greatest shipbuilding industries. And they also attracted thousands of immigrants both from abroad and the surrounding countryside. Simultaneously, factories and workers swarmed into those areas which were beyond the control of existing local authorities. Soon industrial chaos grew south of the Clyde as railways, brickyards, ironworks and gasometers engulfed existing residential areas. One industrialist, William Dixon, cared nothing about amenities. He built a truckway from his yards to the quayside—right across the main street! Local property values declined, people moved away, the houses fell into disrepair; and as the rents fell, so the poorest, most ignorant people moved in. Much of Glasgow's centre, together with the village of Gorbals, grew into an industrial slum—typical of the fate of many a city's industrial centre during the second half of the nineteenth century.

Huddersfield

It took a lot of time and money to deal with these problems; nevertheless, lots of towns made the effort. Huddersfield was a typical Victorian 'boom town.' It received its Charter of Incorporation in 1868 and its first Borough Council met that year. It set out to improve the town's water supply and during 1870–75 built a reservoir. It modernized the gasworks and hired out gas cookers to local families. It was the first council to run its own tramway system with steam-trains pulling passenger cars through the streets on rails. When it underwent electrification in 1901, the tramway was making a handsome profit. Huddersfield had a public electricity supply in 1893, when 83 privileged consumers were able to switch on the lights in their homes. By 1901 Huddersfield, in common with many other boroughs, had provided water, gas, electricity, tramways, a Public Library, a Town Hall and, after Parliament passed the 1870 Education Act, some state schools in which to educate the children of the townsfolk.

The Second Reform Act 1867

This act gave the vote to most adult males living in towns—if they were householders or lodgers paying £10 a year they could vote for their M.P.s. Now half the electorate lived in the industrial towns—farmworkers were still excluded, unless they were £12 freeholders or £5 leaseholders, which were the minimum qualifications for rural voters under the 1867 Act. So the workers who had displayed so much calm during the cotton crisis of the 'sixties at last received their political rights. It was, said the politicians, 'a leap in the dark'—a bit of a risk; but it was also a firm, first step towards a democratic Britain.

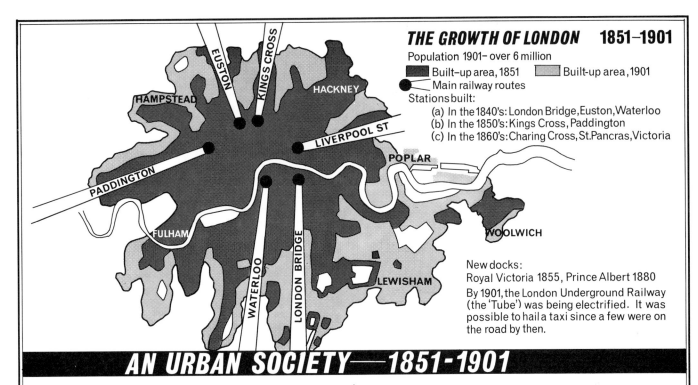

THE GROWTH OF LONDON 1851–1901

Population 1901– over 6 million

◾ Built-up area, 1851   ▨ Built-up area, 1901

● ╱ Main railway routes

Stations built:
- (a) In the 1840's: London Bridge, Euston, Waterloo
- (b) In the 1850's: Kings Cross, Paddington
- (c) In the 1860's: Charing Cross, St. Pancras, Victoria

New docks:
Royal Victoria 1855, Prince Albert 1880

By 1901, the London Underground Railway (the 'Tube') was being electrified. It was possible to hail a taxi since a few were on the road by then.

AN URBAN SOCIETY—1851-1901

PROBLEM OF HOUSING IN GLASGOW

In Glasgow, a 'house' usually means a 'flat'. Also, as J.R.Kellett has pointed out in his book **Glasgow —a concise history** (Blond Educational, 1967), it is possible 'to own not merely the ground itself, as in England, but to own horizontal chunks of air. This ownership of air is as real as landownership in England, so that if, for example, a tenement collapsed completely it would still be possible to own a slice of air twenty or forty feet up, and anyone who bought the site would have to buy the title to it before he could extend the building upwards. As can be imagined, this concept of horizontal ownership has led to intense subdivision of property in Scotland'.

This helps to explain why there is a traditional problem of overcrowding, particularly in the big city of Glasgow.

PROBLEM OF ELECTRICITY SUPPLY IN HUDDERSFIELD

The first generators were worked by steam engines and life was never dull at the local power station.......... 'One engineer, suddenly called to the telephone, returned to find half a hundredweight of debris in the place where he had been sitting. Part of the cylinder and pistons of an engine had gone through the roof...... On another occasion an engineer pulled out what he thought to be a dead plug from the switchboard when it was carrying a full load at 2,200 volts. Half the town was blacked out and the power station was bathed in a sea of yellow fog, while the unfortunate man, almost blinded, made some more mistakes and some blinding flashes before he managed to get the lights on again.......'
From **The Story of Huddersfield** by Roy Brook, published by MacGibbon and Kee, 1968 (p.184).

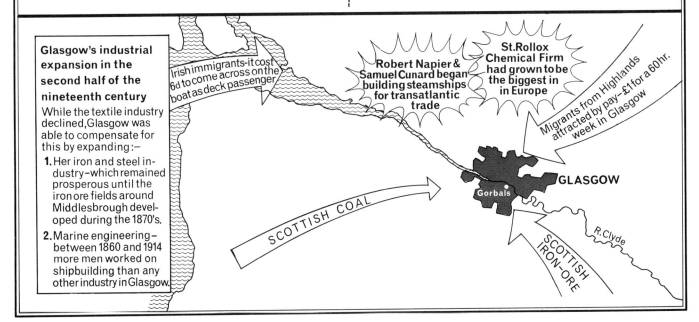

Glasgow's industrial expansion in the second half of the nineteenth century

While the textile industry declined, Glasgow was able to compensate for this by expanding:–

1. Her iron and steel industry–which remained prosperous until the iron ore fields around Middlesbrough developed during the 1870's.

2. Marine engineering– between 1860 and 1914 more men worked on shipbuilding than any other industry in Glasgow.

Irish immigrants-it cost 6d to come across on the boat as deck passenger

Robert Napier & Samuel Cunard began building steamships for transatlantic trade

St. Rollox Chemical Firm had grown to be the biggest in in Europe

Migrants from Highlands attracted by pay-£1 for a 60hr. week in Glasgow

GLASGOW

Gorbals

SCOTTISH COAL

SCOTTISH IRON-ORE

R.Clyde

32: Conditions in the countryside, 1851–1901

The modernization of British farming

Lots of farmers had expected that the Corn Law Repeal of 1846 would lead to a glut of cheap corn imports into Britain. But because no foreign food producers could compete with either British farming methods or with British prices, this didn't happen for twenty years. An expanding population provided an incessant demand for food and as late as 1868, 75% of all food eaten in Britain had been grown in Britain. This explains why farmers tried to make their traditional 'mixed farming' methods more efficient, why they bought the new glazed pipes to drain their fields, why they went in for artificial fertilizers. They were able to meet the demand for food by growing more cereals and rearing more livestock. Unfortunately, they tied up too much capital in cereal farming. The new steam ploughs and traction engines were expensive, slow in operation and difficult to use on soft soil. Investments in agriculture take a long time to show a profit. Nevertheless, the farmers seemed prosperous and the farm-labourers wanted a share in this prosperity.

Condition of the farm-labourer

Already his way of life had begun to improve in many parts of the countryside. Estate owners were beginning to offer better accommodation and allotments at nominal rents. A few cottage hospitals and village schools began to appear. Many families, attracted by relatively high wages in industrial towns, had left the land and thus reduced the hazard of unemployment for those who remained behind. Moreover, as the farm-labourer had also shared in the general rise in real wages there was less need for his wife and children to slave in the work-gangs, planting, thinning and pulling crops. Of course, plenty of misery and poverty existed; the standard of life in the countryside, especially in the south, was a national disgrace. Farm-labourers were right to demand better conditions for themselves and their families.

The 'Revolt of the Field' in the 1870s

Trade unionism among farmworkers began around 1865. There were a few strikes at harvest time—when farmers desperately needed labour. All sorts of men led these unions in the counties but the best known was Joseph Arch, a remarkable Warwickshire labourer who was also a Primitive Methodist preacher. During 1872 he formed not only a union in his own county but also a *National Agricultural Workers' Union*. At first, enthusiasm was enormous. Arch won support in the countryside and factory towns alike and enrolled 150,000 people in the first twelve months. Through union pressure, Arch forced wages up to about 14/6 per week. But when foreign corn flooded into the country in the 1870s the farmers retaliated by 'locking out' the strikers, evicting them from tied cottages and, when necessary, hiring immigrant Irish labour. Enthusiasm for the unions died away and Arch turned his attention to securing the vote for the farmworkers.

The Third Reform Act 1884

This was another step forward in the creation of a democratic electorate. The 1867 Act had excluded farmworkers and most miners from the vote. This unfairness disappeared in 1884 when the Third Reform Act added another 1,800,000 voters to the electorate. If the local squire wanted a seat in Parliament he now had to convince his farmworkers that he was worth a vote! The Act had smashed the traditional forms of county politics—especially since the 1872 Secret Ballott Act ensured that voting went on within the privacy of the voting booth.

Agriculture in 1901

Though there was no general agricultural depression in this period, most arable farmers were hard hit. By the end of the century there was a real shortage of farmworkers and to offset this some farmers introduced new mechanical aids. Better steam engines, windpumps and electric power were available by 1900. But they were too expensive for most farmers who had to recognize they no longer represented the most important British industry. They had had to adjust, sometimes painfully, to the pressure of foreign competition and to the task of supplying large urban communities with more dairy and market gardening products.

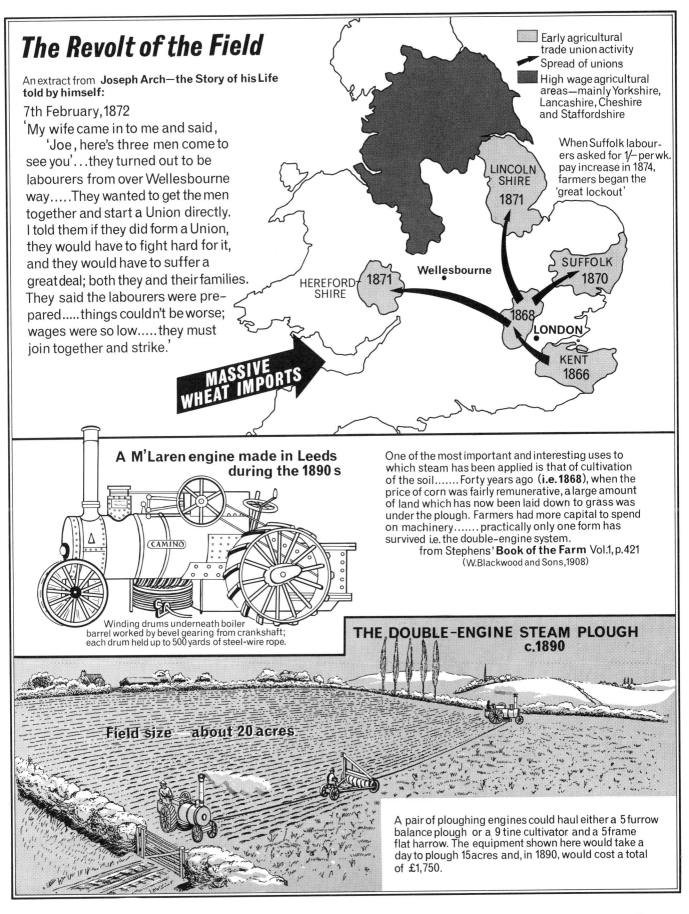

The Revolt of the Field

An extract from **Joseph Arch—the Story of his Life told by himself:**

7th February, 1872

'My wife came in to me and said,
'Joe, here's three men come to see you'…they turned out to be labourers from over Wellesbourne way…..They wanted to get the men together and start a Union directly. I told them if they did form a Union, they would have to fight hard for it, and they would have to suffer a great deal; both they and their families. They said the labourers were pre-pared…..things couldn't be worse; wages were so low…..they must join together and strike.'

Early agricultural trade union activity
→ Spread of unions
High wage agricultural areas—mainly Yorkshire, Lancashire, Cheshire and Staffordshire

When Suffolk labour-ers asked for 1/– per wk. pay increase in 1874, farmers began the 'great lockout'

LINCOLN SHIRE **1871**

HEREFORD SHIRE **1871**

Wellesbourne

1868

SUFFOLK **1870**

LONDON

KENT **1866**

MASSIVE WHEAT IMPORTS

A M'Laren engine made in Leeds during the 1890s

CAMINO

Winding drums underneath boiler barrel worked by bevel gearing from crankshaft; each drum held up to 500 yards of steel-wire rope.

One of the most important and interesting uses to which steam has been applied is that of cultivation of the soil…….Forty years ago (**i.e. 1868**), when the price of corn was fairly remunerative, a large amount of land which has now been laid down to grass was under the plough. Farmers had more capital to spend on machinery…….practically only one form has survived i.e. the double-engine system.
from Stephens' **Book of the Farm** Vol.1, p.421
(W.Blackwood and Sons,1908)

THE DOUBLE-ENGINE STEAM PLOUGH c.1890

Field size   about 20 acres

A pair of ploughing engines could haul either a 5 furrow balance plough or a 9 tine cultivator and a 5 frame flat harrow. The equipment shown here would take a day to plough 15 acres and, in 1890, would cost a total of £1,750.

33:   Law and order: the Trade Unions, 1851–1901

Notoriety

During the 1860s a number of unions representing skilled workers pooled their resources and formed a committee later called the 'Junta.' The Junta's aim was to give trade unions a good public image, but from the beginning everything seemed to be against them. When some Sheffield grinders refused to pay their union 'subs' gunpowder bombs exploded in their homes and while the government investigated these 'Sheffield outrages' a fresh scandal came to light. A union secretary misappropriated union funds and when his society prosecuted him the judge ruled that the union was technically an illegal organization. If its members cared to hand their money over to a secretary, that was their affair; but they couldn't expect any help from the law in enforcing the regulations of an *unlawful* union.

Respectability

Eventually the Junta persuaded parliament to legalize the union by the Trade Union Act (1871). However, Parliament insisted in passing a Criminal Law Amendment Act which made picketing illegal; and when next year seven ladies shouted 'Bah!' at a blacklegger they found themselves in jail. Then parliament relented and in 1875 replaced the Criminal Law Amendment Act with legislation that permitted 'peaceful picketing.'

The rise of the unskilled unions

Already the farmworkers had set an example by forming a union in 1872. In 1887 the London dockers followed suit and in the following year the Bryant & May's match-girls made their remarkable protest. They worked in especially dangerous conditions in the East End; they faced the risk of 'phossie-jaw', a bone deformity due to phosphorus infection. They went on strike for better conditions—and won. They then formed a union, thus setting the pattern for later working-class agitation. Just by threatening a strike in 1888, the gasworkers won an eight-hour day. Their success encouraged the dockers to air their grievances and in 1889 they went on strike for a basic wage of sixpence an hour plus over-time.

The London Dock Strike 1889

The dockers' leaders—Ben Tillett, Tom Mann and John Burns—organized the strike superbly. They never antagonized public opinion, even though they brought the docks to a standstill. Nation-wide subscriptions raised £48,000 for strike pay; Australian dockers sent £30,000 so that the strikers had enough money to pay potential blackleggers. Inevitably, the employers surrendered and the dockers won their famous 'tanner'. Their success caused unions to mushroom all over the country as clerks, teachers, miners and shop-assistants joined in the scramble. Within four years 1.5 million trade-unionists had affiliated themselves to the TUC (Trades Union Congress), formed back in the dark days of union notoriety in 1868.

Socialism

Side by side with this flurry of trade union activity came completely new political movements. Some drew inspiration from the teaching of European socialists such as Karl Marx who had written the Communist Manifesto as early as 1848. For example, the Social Democratic Federation (SDF), founded in 1881, was a progressive socialist movement. It wanted to pay M.P.s and give women the vote; it intended to abolish the House of Lords and nationalize the land. Unlike Marx, the SDF did not insist on a bloodthirsty revolution; a new society could be achieved through parliamentary legislation. So the SDF whipped up public support through protest and demonstrations—and one of these, held in Trafalgar Square on Sunday 13 November 1887, degenerated into a brutal fight. In complete contrast were the intellectuals—people such as George Bernard Shaw and the Webbs—who formed their Fabian Society in 1884. They intended to reconstruct society through reasoned propaganda and by applying intellectual pressure on government committees at national and local level. A third socialist movement sought to elect working-class M.P.s to Parliament. Three working-class candidates won seats in 1892 and one of them, Keir Hardie, formed the Independent Labour Party in 1893. In 1900 the ILP, the Fabians and the SDF met in London and there agreed to join forces in a Labour Representation Committee. Its young secretary, Ramsay MacDonald, was destined to be Britain's first Labour Prime Minister. More immediately, the ILP M.P.s faced a major crisis in trade union history.

The Taff Vale Judgement 1901

A dispute between workers and management on the Taff Vale Railway led to a strike, which in turn caused the employers to prosecute the railway union for loss of receipts. The law held that the unionists were responsible for the employers' losses and required the workers to pay up. This judgement meant that in future trade unions wouldn't be able to afford a strike.

Opposite, Bloody Sunday, 1887, fighting in Trafalgar Square

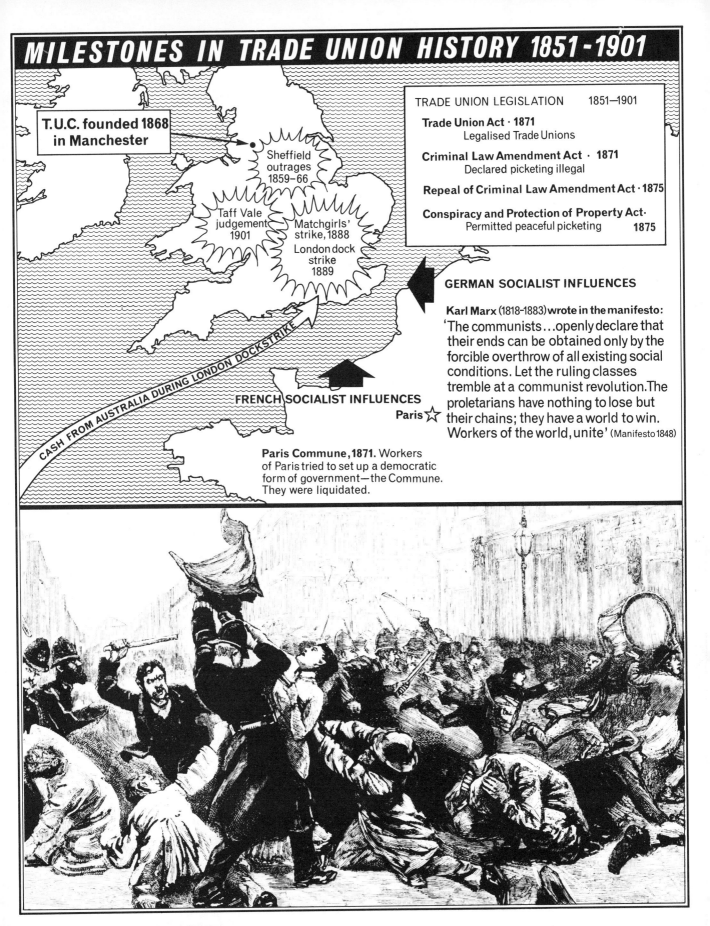

MILESTONES IN TRADE UNION HISTORY 1851-1901

T.U.C. founded 1868 in Manchester

Sheffield outrages 1859–66

Taff Vale judgement 1901

Matchgirls' strike, 1888

London dock strike 1889

CASH FROM AUSTRALIA DURING LONDON DOCKSTRIKE

TRADE UNION LEGISLATION   1851–1901

Trade Union Act · 1871
Legalised Trade Unions

Criminal Law Amendment Act · 1871
Declared picketing illegal

Repeal of Criminal Law Amendment Act · 1875

Conspiracy and Protection of Property Act·
Permitted peaceful picketing   **1875**

GERMAN SOCIALIST INFLUENCES

Karl Marx (1818-1883) **wrote in the manifesto:**
'The communists…openly declare that their ends can be obtained only by the forcible overthrow of all existing social conditions. Let the ruling classes tremble at a communist revolution. The proletarians have nothing to lose but their chains; they have a world to win. Workers of the world, unite' (Manifesto 1848)

FRENCH SOCIALIST INFLUENCES

Paris ☆

Paris Commune, 1871. Workers of Paris tried to set up a democratic form of government—the Commune. They were liquidated.

34: A national system of education

'Payment by results'

Educational systems are strongly rooted in their nation's history: this is certainly true of German, French, American and, more recently, communist forms of education. It also explains why Britain was backward in providing elementary education for its children. For years, the state had relied upon the work of voluntary religious schools. The state's attitude was simple: if Catholics, Anglicans and Non-conformists wanted to build their own schools, if dedicated individuals wanted to run ragged schools, then it was better to leave things alone—another example of *laissez-faire* in operation. Graciously, the state offered voluntary schools a few thousand pounds of grant-aid every year. Any school accepting this help had to suffer an annual examination by government inspectors to see that the money was not being wasted. Schoolchildren had to attain specified standards in the 3 Rs; and unless the children could spell properly and recite their tables, they would not qualify for a grant. This was the system of 'payment by results', forced on the schools in 1862 by a government minister, Robert Lowe. In many ways, it made education a farce. Children who could not (or would not) learn their lessons had to be hurried off to another school whenever an inspector was in the vicinity. Schools dare not risk any failures. 'Payment by results' lasted 30 years and destroyed any love of learning in thousands of children. They were the victims of deliberate government policy, a policy summed up by Robert Lowe himself when he told the House of Commons in 1862: 'We do not profess to give these children an education that will raise them above their station and business in life—that is not our object—but to give them an education that will fit them for that business . . .'

The 1870 Education Act

After the town workers had won their voting rights in 1867, the government accepted its duty to deal with illiteracy. For many years industrialists and intellectuals had clamoured for a national system of education. Now it was the task of another government minister, W. E. Forster, to push an Education Act through parliament. He wasn't going to make education free, just compulsory. He wanted to build schools to co-exist with the voluntary schools—'to fill up gaps', he said, 'not to destroy the existing system in introducing a new one'. His Education Act in 1870 divided England and Wales into school districts; if a district found itself without a school, its local ratepayers had to elect a board and build a school. Once the school was up, the board could compel local children to attend it—at a fee of between a 1d and 3d a week. Lots of parents were hostile to this; an eleven-year-old could earn about 6d a week doing farm work at this time. So this was hardly a *national* system of education but at least it was a major step in the right direction.

The Board Schools

Some of the boards attracted the finest intellects in the country. Thomas Huxley, for example, sat on the London School Board and sponsored the idea of 'junior education' for children between the ages of 7 and 10, and 'senior education' for older children—a pattern that has survived into the 1970s. The London School Board sent its architect to study building methods in Germany; he brought back the novel idea of teaching children in classrooms as an alternative to cramming the whole school into one large hall for instruction. Towering high above the industrial slums, London's Board Schools became a model for the rest of the country. Bradford, Leeds and Nottingham were equally progressive and pioneered specialist science teaching which, towards the end of the century, formed part of the curriculum of the higher grade schools. Slowly, the state system of education began to function. Parliament made education free in 1891; raised the school-leaving age to 11 in 1893 and then 12 in 1899. By 1900, education had overtaken poor relief as the costliest social service in the country—yet there were still more children in voluntary schools than there were in state schools!

Secondary education

Lots of children did not want to leave school at an early age. In fact, during 1895 there were 470,000 children over 12 and 252,000 over 13 staying on in the elementary schools. Less than a thousand of these had any chance of a grammar school place. In London, the Board tried to give its older children secondary education but the law frustrated the attempt. In the famous Cockerton Judgement (1900) the judge ruled that the Board had no right to fritter away ratepayers' money on newfangled subjects such as 'French, German, History and I know not what . . .' Clearly, if the boards could not provide children with secondary education, then the government must. Again, the state accepted its duty to society: in 1902 Parliament passed another Education Act and laid the foundations of secondary education in England and Wales.

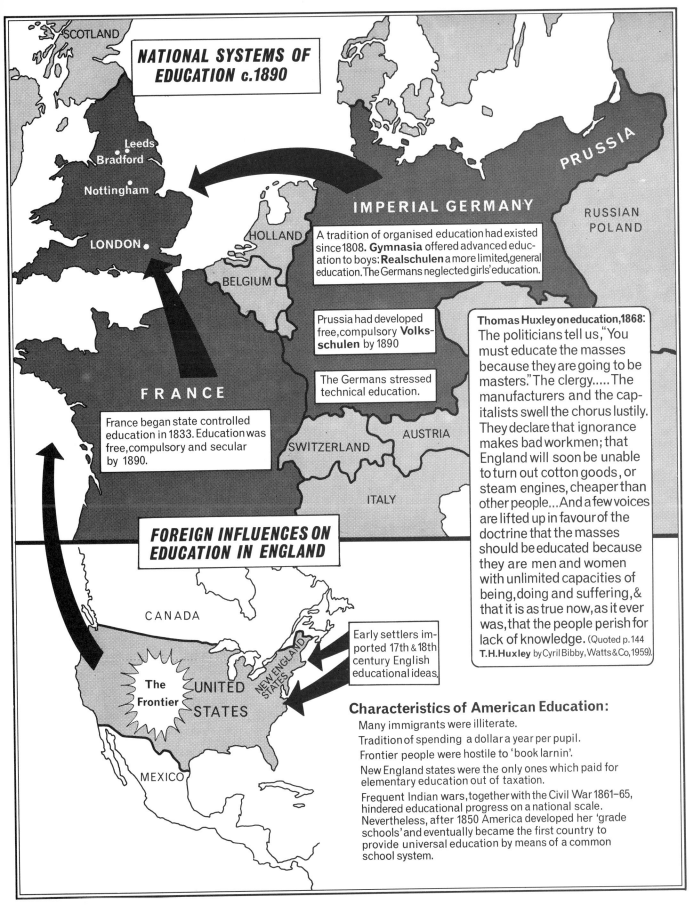

NATIONAL SYSTEMS OF EDUCATION c.1890

SCOTLAND

Leeds
Bradford

Nottingham

LONDON

HOLLAND

BELGIUM

PRUSSIA

RUSSIAN POLAND

IMPERIAL GERMANY

A tradition of organised education had existed since 1808. **Gymnasia** offered advanced education to boys: **Realschulen** a more limited, general education. The Germans neglected girls' education.

Prussia had developed free, compulsory **Volksschulen** by 1890

The Germans stressed technical education.

FRANCE

France began state controlled education in 1833. Education was free, compulsory and secular by 1890.

AUSTRIA

SWITZERLAND

ITALY

FOREIGN INFLUENCES ON EDUCATION IN ENGLAND

Thomas Huxley on education, 1868:
The politicians tell us, "You must educate the masses because they are going to be masters." The clergy..... The manufacturers and the capitalists swell the chorus lustily. They declare that ignorance makes bad workmen; that England will soon be unable to turn out cotton goods, or steam engines, cheaper than other people... And a few voices are lifted up in favour of the doctrine that the masses should be educated because they are men and women with unlimited capacities of being, doing and suffering, & that it is as true now, as it ever was, that the people perish for lack of knowledge. (Quoted p.144 **T.H. Huxley** by Cyril Bibby, Watts & Co, 1959).

CANADA

The Frontier

UNITED STATES

NEW ENGLAND STATES

MEXICO

Early settlers imported 17th & 18th century English educational ideas.

Characteristics of American Education:

Many immigrants were illiterate.

Tradition of spending a dollar a year per pupil.

Frontier people were hostile to 'book larnin'.

New England states were the only ones which paid for elementary education out of taxation.

Frequent Indian wars, together with the Civil War 1861–65, hindered educational progress on a national scale. Nevertheless, after 1850 America developed her 'grade schools' and eventually became the first country to provide universal education by means of a common school system.

35: Features of working class life at the end of the nineteenth century

A consumer society

By the 1890s most people were living either in or very close to large, built-up areas. Gathered in their millions, they formed the beginnings of a new consumer society, constantly demanding more material goods. They wanted proprietary brands of foodstuffs, bottled or canned, patent medicines, boot-polish and toothpaste. They also sought leisure and relaxation; they were prepared to spend some of their wages, travelling to and from work on one of the new electric trams, to save a bit of time. Perhaps the time saved meant an extra hour in bed or an extra hour in the pub; but it could also mean the chance to cheer the local football or cricket club. For the housewife in the towns, it might mean for the first time a chance to become 'house-proud', to make some of the children's clothes on one of the new sewing machines you could buy on hire-purchase.

The shops

More money usually meant more food. And for the Victorian housewife, one of the most dramatic changes was the way in which she now did her shopping. The coming of the retail shop was a boon. It destroyed the *truck-system*, in which an employer paid his workers in tickets which they could exchange for goods—often over-priced—at the firm's truck-shop. It also forced many *cheapjacks* out of business—these were the travelling shopkeepers on whose wares many housewives had depended. Soon shops began to develop into '*multiple*' and '*department*' stores. The Co-operatives, first founded by the Rochdale Pioneers in 1844, were early examples of 'multiple' or 'chain' stores. A co-operative would share out its profits among the customers, the origin of the famous 'co-op divvie'. Side by side with these stores came the privately owned multiples. Thomas Lipton, for example, started his chain with a Glasgow grocery shop in 1872. By 1890 he dominated London's grocery trade and provided 10% of Britain's housewives with their packeted tea. He stocked his shops with 'Lipton products', pre-packed, weighed, priced and trade-marked. His shop assistants simply had to sell the goods. A highly successful businessman, he owned a chain of 245 'Lipton markets' by 1898. Then from France came the 'department store' which offered a wide range of products under one roof. Many firms such as Harrod's the grocers and Debenham's the drapers adopted the idea. One American, Gordon Selfridge, believed that one must appeal to the middle-class customer and organized his London store accordingly. Another American, F. W. Woolworth, disagreed and introduced his 'bazaar' where there was 'nothing over sixpence'. It caught on and a number of towns boasted a 'Woolworth's' by the end of the century, by which time most retailers were exploiting the mass purchasing power of the people. Jesse Boot brought in his first-class chemist shops; Sainsbury's demonstrated to an ignorant public the importance of food hygiene.

Leisure

There wasn't much time—or opportunity—for relaxation during the nineteenth century. Leisure was the privilege of the aristocratic and upper middle classes. For instance, 'high society' muttered fiercely about the dangers of working class idleness when the Shop Hours Act (1886) cut the working week for youngsters under eighteen to 74 hours. In addition, there was not much to do with one's spare time. Sunday observance was strictly enforced. Commercial entertainment was unthinkable on the Sabbath. A family at the end of the century faced a limited choice of activities: Church, Sunday School, the prolonged ritual of Sunday lunch, an afternoon stroll in Sunday best, tea in the parlour. Entertainment had to be provided by the family—apart from the occasional visit to the music-hall, a visit to the fair or a few days each year at one of the expanding seaside towns such as Scarborough, Blackpool and Yarmouth. Saturday, however, was different. In the afternoon there was pigeon flying, dog racing and bicycle competitions. The first Cup Final was in 1871 and by 1880 amateur soccer and rugby football had devoted followings. Rugby League began in earnest in 1895. Cricket, especially when the legendary W. G. Grace was playing, flourished; and athletics attracted plenty of working-class competitors and spectators by 1900. One of the strangest spectator sports, perhaps, was the Boat Race. Once a year thousands of British people would crowd the banks of the Thames, cheering on the crews of universities that they had not a hope of attending.

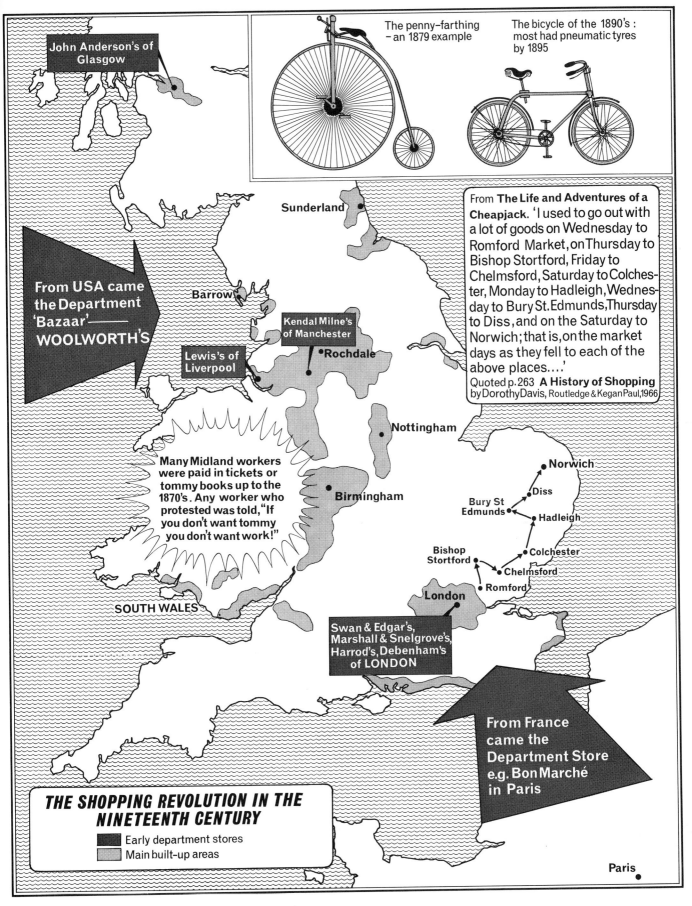

John Anderson's of Glasgow

The penny-farthing – an 1879 example

The bicycle of the 1890's : most had pneumatic tyres by 1895

Sunderland

From USA came the Department 'Bazaar' —— WOOLWORTH'S

Barrow

Kendal Milne's of Manchester

Rochdale

Lewis's of Liverpool

From **The Life and Adventures of a Cheapjack**. 'I used to go out with a lot of goods on Wednesday to Romford Market, on Thursday to Bishop Stortford, Friday to Chelmsford, Saturday to Colchester, Monday to Hadleigh, Wednesday to Bury St. Edmunds, Thursday to Diss, and on the Saturday to Norwich; that is, on the market days as they fell to each of the above places....'
Quoted p. 263 **A History of Shopping** by Dorothy Davis, Routledge & Kegan Paul, 1966

Nottingham

Many Midland workers were paid in tickets or tommy books up to the 1870's. Any worker who protested was told, "If you don't want tommy you don't want work!"

Birmingham

Norwich

Diss

Bury St Edmunds

Hadleigh

Bishop Stortford

Colchester

Chelmsford

Romford

London

SOUTH WALES

Swan & Edgar's, Marshall & Snelgrove's, Harrod's, Debenham's of LONDON

From France came the Department Store e.g. Bon Marché in Paris

THE SHOPPING REVOLUTION IN THE NINETEENTH CENTURY

- Early department stores
- Main built-up areas

Paris

36: The survival of poverty

Despite their remarkable achievements in almost every field of human activity, the Victorians never managed to remove the stain of poverty from their society. Millions of people still lived and worked under humiliating conditions until well into the twentieth century.

The responsibility

As long as society tolerated the idea of casual labour, it was condemning a great many people to a life of poverty. The cities teemed with people leading a 'hand to mouth' existence. Dockers and general labourers, hawkers and porters, dungmen and crossingsweepers, boot-blacks and mudlarks, rat-catchers and ballad-mongers struggled each day for the price of a meal and a night's lodgings. A few remarkable organizations such as General Booth's Salvation Army (founded 1878) tried to help, but the working-men's hostels and prayer-meetings were no answer to this massive social problem. And there was another source of poverty: many workers in full-time jobs did not take home sufficient pay for their families to live on. Some of the small-time, back-street employers were hardhearted, tight-fisted men who exploited their work-people. Yet there was a strong tradition which the Victorians inherited, that workers should be well paid and adequately housed. It was begun by Robert Owen at his mills in New Lanark and continued by such men as Sir Titus Salt in Bradford. Their philosophy was that a contented worker was an efficient worker. This sort of attitude—developed to extremes in nineteenth-century Germany by the Krupp family in Essen—is termed paternalism; it implies that an employer has a duty to take a fatherly interest in the welfare of his workers and their families. In fact, this had long been the custom of many English land-owners who genuinely looked after their estate workers. But it was impossible for the urban employers to take a fatherly interest in the hordes of casual labourers who might be here today and gone tomorrow. They thought it perfectly normal that there should always be a natural reservoir of people seeking work; 'the poor are always with us' was a common enough expression.

An awareness of poverty

In 1888 middle class shoppers in London's West End could hardly believe their eyes when the Bryant & May's matchgirls paraded in protest against their abominable working conditions. They had never seen women in such a wretched condition before. This was part of the problem: it was far too easy in Britain's class-ridden society for people to remain ignorant of the conditions in which others existed. A Victorian businessman, commuting between home and office in the 1880s, might never pass through the smelly, overcrowded industrial areas; if he did, his railway carriage insulated him from the harsh realities of life in the slums. Occasionally, he might read lurid accounts of poverty and squalor—the *Pall Mall Gazette* serialized some sensational working class stories during 1885—but he would not believe all he read. However, one exceptional businessman, Charles Booth, devoted much of his life to the investigation of the nature and causes of poverty. He produced an extensive survey called *The Life and Labour of the People in London* and was amazed to find that no less than 30% of all Londoners lived on the poverty line—which Charles Booth defined as an income of between 18/– and 21/– per week. He also discovered a definite relationship between old age and poverty and after 1892 he was constantly urging governments to provide pensions of 5/– per week to all people over 65. Another investigator, Seebohm Rowntree, confirmed Booth's findings in 1901. He examined the condition of the people of York and found that just under 30% lived in a state of poverty.

The gains and the losses

Due to the work of men such as Booth and Rowntree the government now had some hard statistical facts. It now knew that old age, unemployment and casual labour were prime causes of poverty. The other main cause, the inadequate wages paid to people in full employment, was a national disgrace. It also knew that poverty was far more widespread than people had ever imagined. But even more frightening was the discovery that an increasing number of people were suffering from malnutrition and deformity. The children of the poor were stunted and diseased. Such was the price Britain was paying for industrial and imperial eminence. Certainly many people had seen a very real improvement in their way of life; but a substantial minority, nearly one-third of the population, 'had suffered all the losses, and shared very few of the gains'.*

*P. 247, *The Wealth of Britain*, Pollard and Crossley (Batsford 1968).

Opposite, poor children in the East End of London in the early 1900s.

Rickets is a children's deficiency disease caused by poverty and malnutrition. Here is a comment from the Medical Congress Report 1889:

In some areas, such as the Clyde district, almost every child was found to be affected. A map of its distribution over the whole of England was a map showing the density of the industrial population.

(Quoted p.242 **The Wealth of Britain**)

A minimum weekly bill for a family of five as calculated by Rowntree in 1899

Food for husband and wife	6s – 0d
Food for 3 children	6 – 9
Rent	4 – 0
Adults' clothing	1 – 0
Children's clothing	1 – 3
Fuel	1 – 10
Sundries (to include cost of soap, gas or candles and other household goods	10
TOTAL	£1 – 1s – 8d

This did not include any meat; and therefore this diet was likely to be far less adequate than workhouse meals. This was why children were undernourished and diseased.

Areas with a high incidence of rickets at the end of the 19th century

37: The Boer War: 1899–1902

British imperialism

In the name of Her Majesty the Queen, a handful of colonial officers administered the biggest and most populous empire in the world. They saw nothing morally wrong in this. Joseph Chamberlain, the Colonial Secretary in 1895, assured them that the British were the 'greatest of the governing races the world has ever seen'. Cecil Rhodes, Prime Minister of Cape Colony, went much further. He claimed that to be governed by the British was the best thing that could happen to anybody!

The Jameson Raid 1895–96

After the discovery of gold in the 1880s, thousands of immigrants (Uitlanders) swarmed into the Transvaal where they soon outnumbered the resident Boer farmers. President Kruger forced them to pay heavy taxes, but denied them any political rights. When the disgruntled Uitlanders planned a revolt against Kruger, Rhodes decided to lend assistance by sending in a band of armed raiders under the command of his friend, Dr Jameson. Almost immediately, a Boer commando captured the raiders and in the resulting scandal Rhodes resigned his office. Relations between Britain and the Boers worsened and in October 1899 Chamberlain ordered troop reinforcements to South Africa. Kruger responded with an ultimatum: keep away from Transvaal's frontiers and send the reinforcements home! Britain rejected the ultimatum and hostilities began on 10 October 1899.

Good-bye Dolly Gray

Most people in Britain neither understood nor cared *why* there was a war in South Africa; but they were mostly in favour of it! They liked the look of the Queen's soldiers, now clad in khaki and equipped with magazine loading rifles. The Boers would be no match for such men, backed as they were with armoured trains, artillery and Maxim machine guns. Thousands volunteered for the army, many were rejected medically unfit, a sad comment on poverty in Britain, but the rest went off singing the latest in patriotic songs:

Good-bye Dolly I must leave you, Though it breaks my heart to go,
Something tells me I am needed, At the front to fight the foe,
See, the soldier boys are marching, And I can no longer stay—
Hark! I hear the bugle calling, Good-bye Dolly Gray.

It would all be over by Christmas . . .

The battles

The mobile Boers rapidly attacked across the frontiers. They besieged Mafeking and Kimberley, then in Black Week (December 1899) they defeated the British at the Battles of Stormberg, Magersfontein and Colenso. Clearly, the war was to last. The Queen sent each soldier a tin of chocolates; Messrs Lyons sent 10,000 plum puddings; Boer gunners fired Christmas puddings into besieged Ladysmith. Then in January came the fearful slaughter at Spion Kop followed by a general British advance under Lord Roberts and Lord Kitchener. They relieved all the besieged towns by May 1900 and when the Reuter news service announced the relief of Mafeking (defended by Baden-Powell for seven and a half months) the nation went wild with delight as rioting 'maffickers' made the night of 18 May a memorable one.

Guerrilla war

Though the Boers had in effect now lost the war, they refused to surrender and at the end of 1900 Kitchener had to begin systematic attempts to round up scores of guerrilla units. He covered the veld with barbed wire and blockhouses, deprived the Boers of food and shelter by burning their crops and farmhouses, and concentrated their women and children in large, hurriedly built camps. He was a humane man and had no idea of the effect 'concentration' would have on the civilians. Many people in Britain became concerned at the news of epidemics in the camps and at the general lack of progress in the war. In fact, some of the last words uttered by the Queen before her death on 22 January 1901 were to ask about events in South Africa. The Boers fought on until they were exhausted and then accepted the generous *Treaty of Vereeniging* in May 1902. In financial terms, the war cost Britain £200 million—far more than the Crimean War. In human terms, Britain lost 22,000 soldiers—mostly to disease. The Boers lost 24,000—mostly women and children who died of disease. There were very few gains: the British learnt a few lessons about modern warfare. Twelve years later, in 1914, they had to put those lessons into practice.

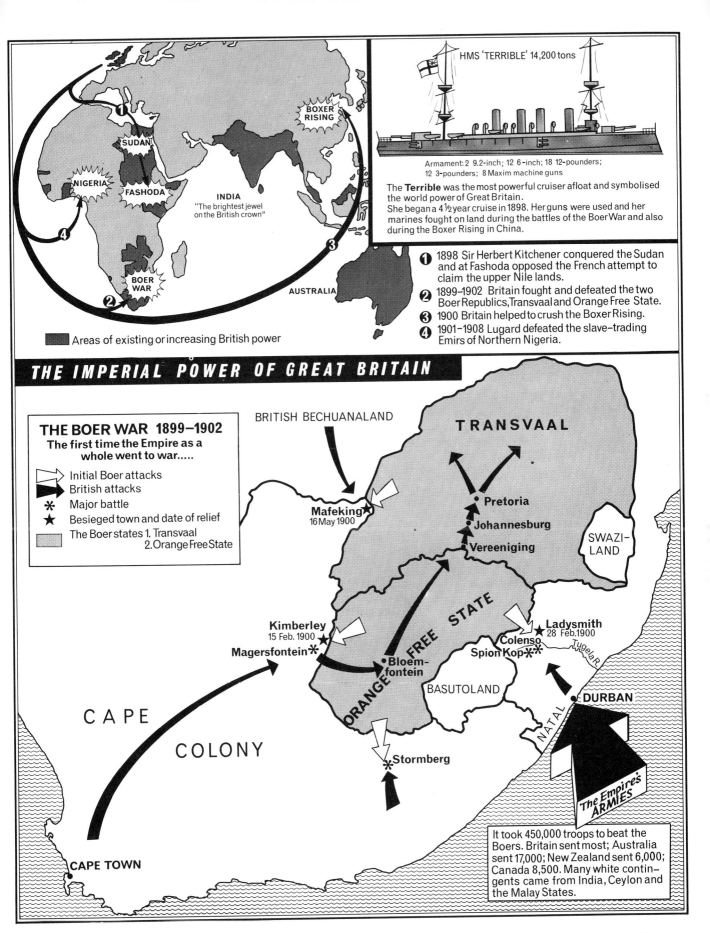

THE IMPERIAL POWER OF GREAT BRITAIN

HMS 'TERRIBLE' 14,200 tons

Armament: 2 9.2-inch; 12 6-inch; 18 12-pounders; 12 3-pounders; 8 Maxim machine guns

The **Terrible** was the most powerful cruiser afloat and symbolised the world power of Great Britain.
She began a 4½ year cruise in 1898. Her guns were used and her marines fought on land during the battles of the Boer War and also during the Boxer Rising in China.

1 1898 Sir Herbert Kitchener conquered the Sudan and at Fashoda opposed the French attempt to claim the upper Nile lands.

2 1899–1902 Britain fought and defeated the two Boer Republics, Transvaal and Orange Free State.

3 1900 Britain helped to crush the Boxer Rising.

4 1901–1908 Lugard defeated the slave-trading Emirs of Northern Nigeria.

SUDAN
NIGERIA
FASHODA
INDIA
"The brightest jewel on the British crown"
BOXER RISING
BOER WAR
AUSTRALIA

■ Areas of existing or increasing British power

THE BOER WAR 1899–1902
The first time the Empire as a whole went to war.....

▷ Initial Boer attacks
▶ British attacks
✶ Major battle
★ Besieged town and date of relief
▦ The Boer states 1. Transvaal
               2. Orange Free State

BRITISH BECHUANALAND

TRANSVAAL

Mafeking ★
16 May 1900

Pretoria
Johannesburg
Vereeniging

SWAZI-LAND

Kimberley ★
15 Feb. 1900
Magersfontein ✶

ORANGE FREE STATE

Bloem-fontein

Ladysmith ★
28 Feb. 1900
Colenso
Spion Kop ✶✶
Tugela R.

BASUTOLAND

NATAL

DURBAN

CAPE COLONY

Stormberg ✶

The Empire's ARMIES

CAPE TOWN

It took 450,000 troops to beat the Boers. Britain sent most; Australia sent 17,000; New Zealand sent 6,000; Canada 8,500. Many white contingents came from India, Ceylon and the Malay States.

Part 4 – Fifty Years of Progress 1851–1901

Spread

26. *The Making of Victorian England*	G. Kitson Clark	Methuen
*David Livingstone***	R. Arnold	Muller
27. *The Reason Why*	Cecil Woodham-Smith	Constable
*The Indian Mutiny***	Jackdaw Publication	
*The Crimean War***	Jackdaw Publication	
28. Darwin and	Alan Moorehead	
the Beagle		Hamish Hamilton
Man's Place in Nature	T. Huxley	Univ. of Michigan
Voyage of H.M.S. Beagle	Charles Darwin	
*Lady-in Chief***	Cecil Woodham-Smith	Methuen
29. *Great Inventors***	N. Wymer	OUP
30. *The Myth of the Great Depression 1873–1896*	S. Saul	Macmillan (Advanced discussion of a complex problem)
31. *Glasgow***	J. R. Kellett	Blond
The Story of Huddersfield	Roy Brook	McGibbon & Kee
32. *Parliamentary Representation***	Dawson and Wall	OUP
A Country Camera	G. Winter	Country Life
33. *Trade Unions***	Dawson and Wall	OUP
34. *Nineteenth Century Education***	E. Midwinter	Longmans
T. H. Huxley	Cyril Bibby	Watts
35. *History of Shopping***	D. Davis	Routledge
*The Seaside Holiday***	A. Hern	Cresset Press
36. *The Wealth of Britain*	Pollard and Crossley	Batsford
*Blood and Fire***	E. Bishop	Longmans (account of General Booth's Salvation Army)
37. *Goodbye, Dolly Gray*	Rayne Kruger	Cassell

**Especially useful for project and topic work

PART 5

Into the Twentieth Century and the First World War

The years between 1902 and 1914 were remarkable not only for a spate of long-overdue social legislation but also a marked tendency among certain groups of society to abandon the usual constitutional channels when they brought pressure to bear on governments.

Conservative and Liberal ministries introduced changes of immense importance in British social history: the 1902 Education Act originated the state control of secondary education; the 1908 Old Age Pensions Act recognized that the state had a duty to care for the aged; the 1908 Coal Mines Act acknowledged that the state must limit the hours a man might work—in this case, eight hours a day—in particularly arduous and dangerous conditions. So it was ironical that, at the very moment when the state tried to remedy the law in favour of underprivileged groups in society, many people should show less and less faith in the established processes of parliamentary government. Trade unionists, influenced by syndicalist ideas from abroad, adopted a new and militant approach to their wage demands. Between 1910 and 1914 the government was quite unsure about the best methods of dealing with the rash of strikes then sweeping the nation. Working-class militancy, on a nation-wide basis, was a new phenomenon. In addition, middle-class suffragettes began their systematic campaign to win votes for women. Their demands were very reasonable; but when the government refused to grant them the women harrassed ministers and committed some outrageous crimes. At the same time, there was the prospect of civil war in Ireland. Protestant Ulster and the Catholic South prepared for open conflict. In the Irish Sea the Royal Navy tried to catch the very well-organized gun-runners to both the North and South. There was thus very little stability in Britain, where millions still lived on and below the poverty line and where emigration to the Dominions and to the U.S.A. was the last resort for thousands of people *every* year.

In one sense, therefore, the experience of the First World War 1914–18 provided the British people with a much-needed sense of unity. The war brought people into hard contact with their responsibilities as citizens and, overnight, they were ready to accept the many government restrictions as part and parcel of the war effort. In the same way they accepted the holocaust of war on the Western Front, of death in the air and on the sea and in the sands and forests of scores of battlefields all over the world. Before Siegfried Sassoon and Wilfred Owen wrote their war poetry there was barely a voice raised in protest against all this useless killing. The sacrifice was supposed to be worthwhile; it was 'the war to end wars'.

38: A fresh start—the foundation of the welfare state, 1902–1914

Between 1902 and 1914 successive British governments passed a mass of social legislation which may be fairly described as the foundation of the welfare state. Most credit went to the remarkable Liberal governments after 1906 but the Conservatives, led by A. J. Balfour, passed one piece of legislation which affected many people's lives profoundly for the next sixty years.

Balfour's Education Act 1902

This abolished the School Boards in England and Wales and required local education authorities (LEAs) to provide secondary education. Most LEAs built or re-surrected 'grammar' schools and charged fees for books and tuition; but they also offered places to children of 'ability'. They measured 'ability' by means of a scholarship examination, an arrangement which offered some working class children the chance to stay on at school, pass examinations and then enter industry, commerce or the professions halfway up the ladder of success. So, despite all their shortcomings, the state grammar schools provided 'the only successful solvent of class conditions which this country evolved during the first half of the twentieth century'.*

Liberal legislation 1906–14

In 1906 the Liberals won the General Election and launched the first major assault on the glaring social evils in Britain. Systematically, they improved the condition of four important groups of people: children, the elderly, the sick and unemployed.

a) *the children*: Robert Morant, a brilliant civil servant, was behind many of the reforms concerning school-children. The *Provision of Meals Act 1906* required LEAs to provide school meals; the *School Medical Services Act 1907* ordered the medical inspection of elementary school children. Morant felt that the 'examination of each child need not, as a rule, occupy more than a few minutes'—so it wouldn't interfere with lessons! By 1911 the system revealed that a third of the school population needed medical treatment. Another set of regulations, called the *Children's Charter, 1907–8*, set up Juvenile Courts in which young offenders might be put on probation or committed to prisons modelled on the Borstal experiment.

b) *the elderly*: 'Thank God for Lloyd George!' These words were on the lips of the very first old age pensioners who, after 1 January 1909, could draw a pension from the state. David Lloyd George, Chancellor of the Exchequer, had guided the *Old Age Pensions Act* through parliament in 1908—at long last the state recognized it had a duty towards elderly. The act helped to remove the threat of poverty from the anxieties of old people over 70 and allowed them, according to their circumstances, to draw a pension of up to 5/– per week.

c) *the sick*: The *Workmen's Compensation Act 1906* compelled employers to compensate workers in a limited number of dangerous trades for accidents incurred at work. Lloyd George felt this wasn't enough—he was very impressed by current insurance schemes operating in Germany. Eventually, in Part I of the *National Insurance Act 1911* every person between 16 and 70 could pay 4d a week into a national fund. The state added 2d; the employer 3d. This would then pay for medical attention—it was 'Ninepence for Fourpence!!'—Lloyd George's famous slogan. Employers and doctors opposed the scheme at first, arguing that there would be a national health hazard if we all licked the back of Lloyd George's National Health stamps!

d) *the unemployed*: The *Labour Exchanges Act 1909* permitted the Board of Trade to set up offices 'for the purpose of collecting and furnishing information ... respecting employers who desire to engage workpeople and workpeople who seek engagement or employment.' The first 80 Labour Exchanges opened in 1910 and, next year in Part II of the *National Insurance Act*, the Liberals introduced compulsory unemployment insurance for workers in the building, engineering, vehicle, iron-founding and shipbuilding industries. In return for contributions, an unemployed worker received benefit up to 7/– a week for a maximum of 15 weeks in a year.

The cost

Obviously, to pay for all these reforms as well as a new re-armament programme, the government had to raise extra revenue from taxation; and when Lloyd George presented his 'People's Budget' in 1909 he was frankly taxing the rich to help the poor. But the rich objected and the peers of the realm blocked the budget in the Lords. This was a major constitutional crisis; it took two General Elections and a threat from King George V that he would create enough Liberal peers to outvote the Conservatives before the Lords would back down in 1911. And when they did, the Commons virtually eliminated the power of the Lords to delay money bills in future, cut the life of parliament from 7 to 5 years and decided to pay M.P.s a salary of £400 a year. It all added up to a triumph for the forces of democracy and social reform.

*pp. 12–13, L. C. B. Seaman, *Post-Victorian Britain 1902–1951* (Methuen 1966).

THE URGE TO REFORM ————— 1906—1914

I should like to see the State embark on various novel and adventurous experiments. I am of the opinion that the State should assume the position of the reserve employer of labour.....We are all agreed that the State must increasingly and earnestly concern itself with the care of the sick and the aged and, above all, of the children. I look forward to the universal establishment of minimum standards of life and labour......

WINSTON CHURCHILL, a speech in Glasgow, 1906

GLASGOW

⊛ Original scheme at Borstal in Kent
★ Boys' Borstal
☆ Girls' Borstal

Lloyd George made a record at His Master's Voice recording studio in 1909 and had his political speeches played on phonographs which were taken round the streets on barrows. But one of his most famous speeches was at Limehouse on 30 July, 1909:

.....The provision for the aged and deserving poor—it was time it was done. It is rather a shame for a rich country like ours- probably the richest in the world, if not the richest the world has ever seen—that it should allow those who have toiled all their days to end in penury and possibly starvation. It is rather hard that an old workman should have to find his way to the gates of the tomb, bleeding and footsore, through the brambles of poverty. We cut a new path through it, an easier one, a pleasanter one, through fields of waving corn. We are raising money to pay for the new road, aye, and to widen it so that 200,000 paupers shall be able to join in the march.....(Cheers!!!)

American Influence:
Z.R.Brockway ran a reform school in New York; copied by Sir Evelyn Ruggles-Brise at Borstal. Home Office impressed—and set up other Borstals elsewhere.

AYLESBURY ☆
LONDON
FELTHAM ★
BORSTAL ⊛

German Influence
Insurance laws against
sickness (1883)
accident (1884)
old age (1889)

PORTLAND ★

THE PROVISIONS OF THE OLD AGE PENSIONS ACT · 1908

Pensioner's income	Weekly pension entitlement
Up to £21 per year	5 shillings
£21—£23.12.6 per year	4 shillings
£23.12.6 —£26. 5.0 per year	3 shillings
£26.5.0 —£28.17.6 per year	2 shillings
£28.17.6 —£31.10.0 per year	1 shilling
Over £31.10.0 per year	Nothing

For a married couple, both over 70, the maximum pension was 7/6 per week— presumably it was officially believed that 'two could live almost as cheaply as one'.

Though the sums involved were small, the Act was of immense importance. The State had at last agreed to relieve poverty in the land by means of direct pension payments.

39: Law and order—the Trade Unions, 1902–1914

The frustration of labour

One might suppose that the Liberal policy of social reform would make the working classes much happier about their living and working conditions. In fact, the reverse was true. Working men were more conscious of the gulf between themselves and the rest of society than they had been for the past fifty years. The reason for this was the decline in the purchasing power of real wages paid to manual workers. Industrial production was up; so were share values and dividends. But so were prices and, as usual, the lower incomes lagged behind. Yet it seemed almost impossible for the manual workers to do much about this because of a series of legal entanglements. First of all, the Amalgamated Society of Railway Servants (*ASRS*) had had to pay the Taff Vale Railway Company £23,000 to compensate for the famous strike of 1900. Admittedly, Parliament reversed this situation in 1906 when the *Trades Disputes Act* decreed that unions would not be held responsible for employers' losses sustained during strikes. Then within a couple of years the *ASRS* were in trouble again. Their Walthamstow branch secretary, W. V. Osborne, challenged their right to use union funds in support of the Labour Party. He argued that a man was not automatically a Labour voter just because he was a railway servant. He took the matter to law and won his case; the 1908 *Osborne Judgement* stopped trade unions from funding political parties. As M.P.s did not receive salaries before 1911, this decision robbed the Labour Party of a great deal of revenue and prevented it from contesting many seats in the important General Elections held in 1910. Eventually, Parliament agreed to pass the *Trades Union Act 1913* which allowed unions to play a role in politics and gave union members the right (which very few exercised) of contracting out of the political levy.

A new militancy

During this period of frustration (1908–13) many workers turned to new *Syndicalist* ideas coming in from France and the United States. Syndicalists sought to establish a new kind of society; a miners' leader named B. C. Roberts described the methods to adopt:

> ...miners' unions should reorganize themselves on industrial lines with a strong central direction of policy. The object of which would be to bring the industry to a standstill, with strike after strike, until the system of private industry collapsed. Then the miners would take over the paralyzed industry....*

*Quoted *The History of the TUC 1868–1968* (published by General Council of the TUC 1968) p. 57.

If the other unions would do the same thing, argued Roberts, then the existing social system would disappear, taking with it all the evils of industrial capitalism. These were dangerous words and threatened the whole structure of law and order. Total strikes would force the government to call out the troops...then there would be bloodshed.

Strike chaos 1910–12

The first widespread strikes, involving many manual workers, went on throughout the summer and autumn of 1910. Only at Tonypandy did the presence of troops threaten an outbreak of violence. More serious were the events of the long, hot summer of 1911. All over the country dockers came out on strike. Men died in Liverpool and Hull when police clashed with demonstrators. One employer voiced the fear of thousands when he said 'It is a revolution; the men have new leaders . . . and we don't know how to deal with them.' Syndicalism seemed to pay off; the *dockers' tanner* went up to eightpence an hour as the employers surrendered. But the new militancy did not last. A monster transport strike during 1912 failed miserably—the TUC and the Parliamentary Labour Party washed their hands of the whole affair. Said Keir Hardie, Labour leader in 1912:

> The effect of the transport workers' strike of this year has been disastrous, and has shown more than anything else could have done the futility of trying to fight the capitalists by what are known as Syndicalist methods.†

Union members lost interest in Syndicalism and turned to the formation of 'big' unions. In 1913, the Transport Workers' Federation, the National Union of Railwaymen and the Miners' Federation formed the 'Triple Alliance' and pledged themselves to joint action if and when this became necessary.

The voice of labour

After the failure of Syndicalism, both the Parliamentary Labour Party and the trade unions turned to more peaceful methods of persuasion and propaganda. Alfred Harmsworth (later Lord Northcliffe) had led the way in the creation of popular newspapers with the *Daily Mail* (1896). Now labour took a leaf from his book. The unions backed the *Daily Herald* (first published 25 January 1911) and two years later the Labour Party created a counterblast to union propaganda with its *Daily Citizen*.

†Quoted *The History of the TUC 1868–1968*, p. 58.

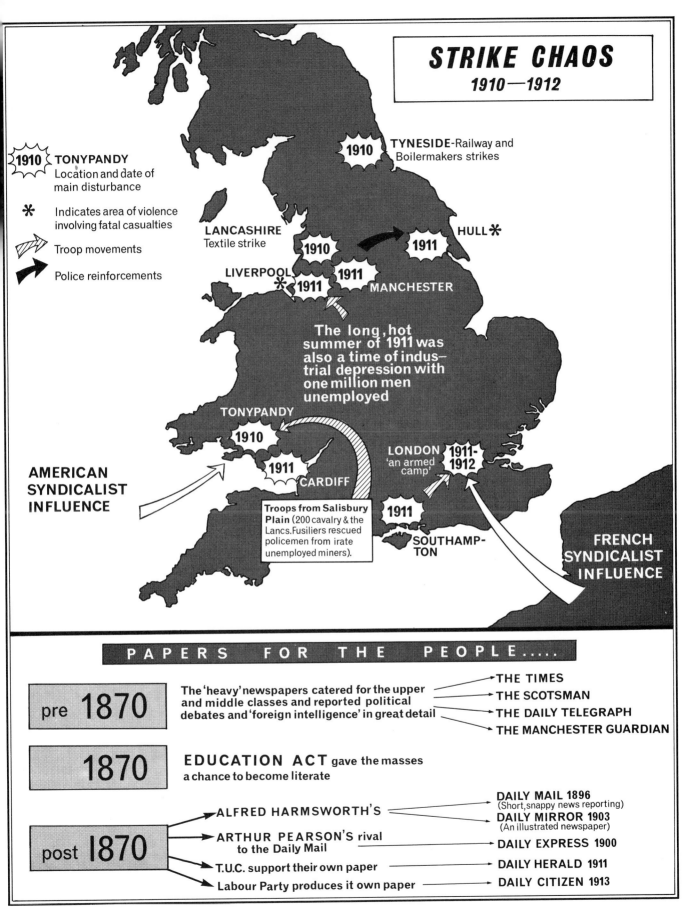

STRIKE CHAOS
1910—1912

1910 TONYPANDY
Location and date of main disturbance

* Indicates area of violence involving fatal casualties

Troop movements

Police reinforcements

1910 TYNESIDE-Railway and Boilermakers strikes

LANCASHIRE Textile strike

HULL *

1910 **1911**

LIVERPOOL
* 1911 **1911** **MANCHESTER**

The long, hot summer of 1911 was also a time of industrial depression with one million men unemployed

AMERICAN SYNDICALIST INFLUENCE

TONYPANDY
1910
1911 **CARDIFF**

LONDON 'an armed camp' **1911-1912**

Troops from Salisbury Plain (200 cavalry & the Lancs.Fusiliers rescued policemen from irate unemployed miners).

1911
SOUTHAMP-TON

FRENCH SYNDICALIST INFLUENCE

P A P E R S   F O R   T H E   P E O P L E.....

pre 1870

The 'heavy' newspapers catered for the upper and middle classes and reported political debates and 'foreign intelligence' in great detail
→ **THE TIMES**
→ **THE SCOTSMAN**
→ **THE DAILY TELEGRAPH**
→ **THE MANCHESTER GUARDIAN**

1870

EDUCATION ACT gave the masses a chance to become literate

post 1870

→ **ALFRED HARMSWORTH'S**
→ **DAILY MAIL 1896** (Short, snappy news reporting)
→ **DAILY MIRROR 1903** (An illustrated newspaper)

→ **ARTHUR PEARSON'S** rival to the Daily Mail
→ **DAILY EXPRESS 1900**

→ T.U.C. support their own paper
→ **DAILY HERALD 1911**

→ Labour Party produces it own paper
→ **DAILY CITIZEN 1913**

40: Law and order—the suffragettes, 1903–1914

Votes for women!

On 10 October 1903 a Mrs Emmiline Pankhurst, active member of the Independent Labour Party, invited friends interested in promoting the cause of women's rights to a meeting in her Manchester home. They decided to band together in a Women's Social and Political Union (WSPU) and to work for women's suffrage. Their activities soon made newspaper headlines; and the *Daily Mail* labelled the women 'suffragettes'. Most of them were middle-class women, dominated by Mrs. Pankhurst and Christabel, her eldest daughter. However, some of the WSPU's members were working-class women and one of them, Annie Kenny, landed in jail when she and Christabel interrupted a political meeting in Manchester with their slogan 'Votes for women!' After this (1905) they moved to London and there pestered Campbell-Bannerman, the Liberal Prime Minister. He was quite sympathetic, but died in 1908. His successor, Asquith, had no time for suffragettes and because of his unhelpful attitude the Pankhursts decided to adopt measures that would bring their cause before the attention of the British people.

'Mild militancy' 1908–9

The suffragettes threw themselves into political demonstrations with great gusto, heckling their opponents at every opportunity. In July 1908 one demonstration got out of hand when they smashed windows at Number 10 Downing Street. Then came a new development. In 1909 Marion Wallace, an ardent member of the WSPU, daubed the inside of St Stephen's Hall with these words taken from the 1689 Bill of Rights:

> It is the right of the subject to petition the King and all commitments and prosecutions for such petitioning are illegal . . .

She finished up in Holloway Prison and there went on hunger strike. The embarrassed authorities felt bound to release her; but this only inspired other imprisoned suffragettes to imitate her example. Scores went on hunger strike and many had to suffer 'forcible feeding'.

People became indignant when they read of the suffering going on inside prisons such as Winson Green, Birmingham; then their indignation turned to admiration when suffragettes chained themselves to railings or, as in the case of the intrepid Muriel Matters, hired a balloon to bombard London with leaflets. Inevitably, the government had to listen to the women's case; but not a single bill to give them the vote managed to scrape through parliament.

The years of violence 1910–14

Now that other methods had failed, about a thousand 'wild women' turned to violence. They decided to attack private property and hoped that the insurance companies, faced with a deluge of claims, would pressure the government into granting women's suffrage. So they attacked private houses, slashed pictures in art galleries, set fire to sports pavilions and poured acid on golf-course greens. An angry government retaliated with the *Cat and Mouse Act 1913* which allowed them to arrest a suffragette, release her when she was weak from hunger strike and then re-arrest her when she was better. But even this paled in comparison with Emily Davison's sacrifice. On Derby Day 1913 she killed herself by running in front of the King's horse.

The end of violence

During 1912–13 the police managed to arrest most of the suffragette leaders who had now lost a lot of public support after their irresponsible actions. Many women who supported 'Votes for women' condemned the militants and the police found no difficulty in banning most of the suffragettes' meetings. Christabel Pankhurst fled to Paris and waged a lonely war against authority. In fact, the militants persisted in their actions right up to the outbreak of war in 1914. Once war was declared, however, the suffragettes renounced violence, changed the name of their broadsheet from *Suffragette* to *Britannia* and poured their immense energy into fanning British hatred of Germany.

The first leaflet raid on London, by suffragette Miss Muriel Matters in 1909. She describes the balloon flight in 'Leslie Baily's BBC Scrapbook'.

THE SUFFRAGETTES IN ACTION — 1903-1914

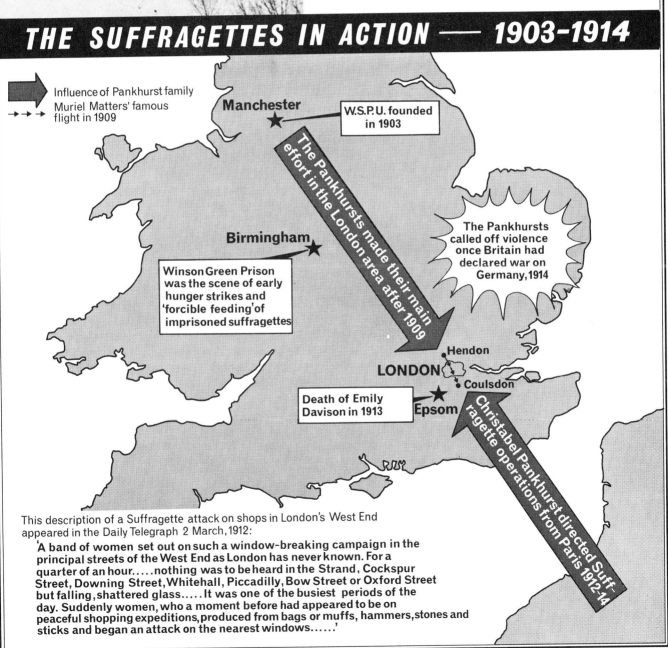

Influence of Pankhurst family

Muriel Matters' famous flight in 1909

Manchester

W.S.P.U. founded in 1903

The Pankhursts made their main effort in the London area after 1909

Birmingham

The Pankhursts called off violence once Britain had declared war on Germany, 1914

Winson Green Prison was the scene of early hunger strikes and 'forcible feeding' of imprisoned suffragettes

Hendon

LONDON

Coulsdon

Death of Emily Davison in 1913

Epsom

Christabel Pankhurst directed Suffragette operations from Paris 1912-14

This description of a Suffragette attack on shops in London's West End appeared in the Daily Telegraph 2 March, 1912:

'A band of women set out on such a window-breaking campaign in the principal streets of the West End as London has never known. For a quarter of an hour.....nothing was to be heard in the Strand, Cockspur Street, Downing Street, Whitehall, Piccadilly, Bow Street or Oxford Street but falling, shattered glass..... It was one of the busiest periods of the day. Suddenly women, who a moment before had appeared to be on peaceful shopping expeditions, produced from bags or muffs, hammers, stones and sticks and began an attack on the nearest windows......'

41: Law and order—the Irish problem, 1912–1914

'Home Rule'

Ever since parliament passed the Act of Union with Ireland in 1800, Irish militants had worked for its repeal. For more than a hundred years, the 'Irish problem' with all its violence and religious bigotry had defied the best brains in British politics. Prime Minister Gladstone publicly announced: 'My mission is to pacify Ireland'. He felt that a policy of 'Home Rule' was the answer. This meant than an Irish parliament based on Dublin would be responsible for all matters apart from foreign affairs and constitutional issues—he was sure that this would give the Irish enough independence to placate them. But he never managed to push either of his Home Rule bills (1886 and 1893) through parliament. The Tories were completely hostile to anything which would diminish Britain's union with Ireland—in fact, they went to the extent of renaming themselves the 'Conservative & Unionist Party'. It wasn't until 1912 that the Liberals (fourteen years after Gladstone's death in 1898) felt it necessary to bring in a third Home Rule bill. The crisis which followed this decision brought the British people to the brink of civil war.

The Irish point of view

Most native Irish were Roman Catholics who favoured a break with Britain. They wanted an independent Ireland free from British rule. They regarded themselves as the citizens of an occupied country, crushed beneath the heel of the Protestant invader who governed them from Westminster, stole their land and denied them basic human rights. Opposing them in the north lived the Ulster Protestants, descendants of the original Scottish and English settlers. They were a minority and feared discrimination if ever a Catholic-dominated parliament came into being at Dublin. So they had a vested interest in maintaining the Act of Union and preserving the authority of parliament at Westminster. On the face of it, there was one obvious solution of the Irish problem. Partition the country into two zones, one Catholic, the other Protestant. Give them both their independence and allow them to go their own ways. But no patriotic Irishman—Catholic or Protestant—would tolerate the division of his country, especially now that the city of Belfast was bigger than Dublin and the centre of the richest industrial area in the country.

Crisis

Led by Sir Edward Carson, the Irish Unionist M.P.s in Westminster were ready to go to any lengths to prevent the passing of a Home Rule bill in 1912. With the connivance of Conservative Party leaders, Carson formed a private army of 80,000 Ulster Volunteers. The southern Irish promptly retaliated with their 'National Volunteers'. Matters worsened during 1913 and by March 1914 Carson was ready to take over the government of Ulster in the event of a civil war. It was at this point that the British government decided to show its teeth. Winston Churchill, First Lord of the Admiralty, ordered a battle squadron to anchor in Belfast Lough. The Royal Navy, plus the regular troops stationed in Ireland, would surely deter Carson's Ulstermen from any warlike action. But to the government's horror, many officers stationed with the cavalry regiments at Curragh Camp said they would resign their commissions before riding north to shoot down protestants. This so-called 'Curragh Mutiny' (March 1914) was the first occasion for more than two centuries on which the British government could not rely on its home-based troops; it gives some idea of the intensity of people's feelings on the subject of union with Ireland.

Civil War?

Disaster seemed round the corner. Both sides were busy smuggling in arms and ammunition; to force a Home Rule bill through parliament at this moment seemed suicidal. Nevertheless, the liberals tried—and the Conservatives howled them down. A very worried King George V summoned the political leaders to a conference at Buckingham Palace. He urged them to seek a peaceful compromise . . . 'the cry of Civil War is on the lips of the most responsible and sober-minded of my people . . .' But it was no good; the conference broke up on 24 July 1914. That day the government tried to decide on its policy when suddenly every man in the Cabinet Room riveted his attention on a message brought in from the Foreign Office. Austria had threatened Serbia with war. Suddenly Ireland and all its troubles seemed unimportant. As Churchill was to write later: 'The parishes of Fermanagh and Tyrone faded back into the mists and squalls of Ireland, and a strange light began immediately, but by perceptible gradations, to fall and grow upon the map of Europe. . . .' War was just a few days away.

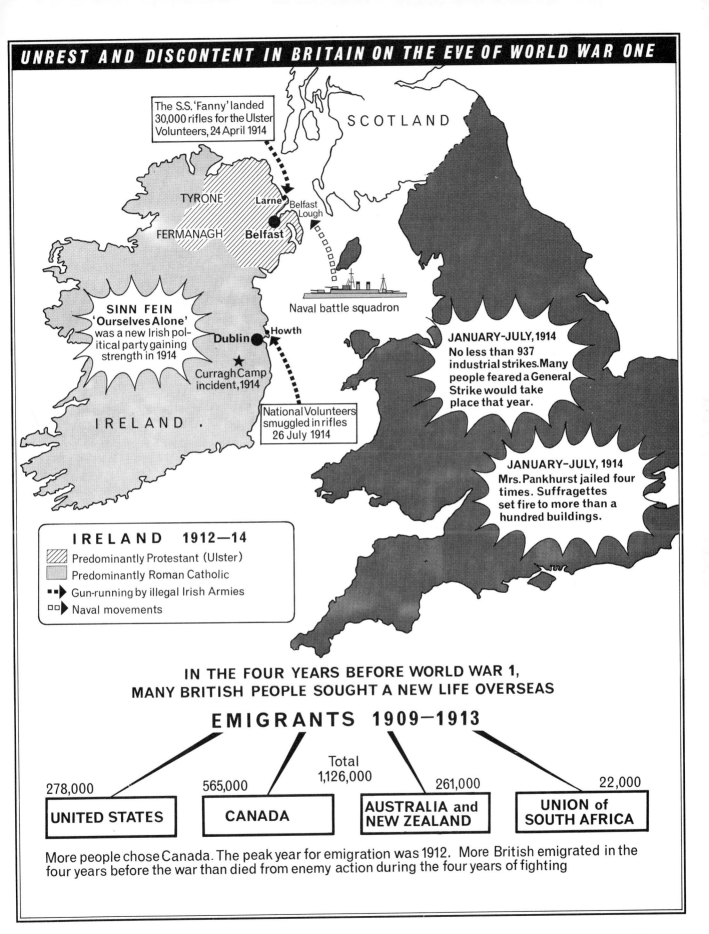

UNREST AND DISCONTENT IN BRITAIN ON THE EVE OF WORLD WAR ONE

The S.S. 'Fanny' landed 30,000 rifles for the Ulster Volunteers, 24 April 1914

SCOTLAND

TYRONE

Larne

Belfast Lough

FERMANAGH

Belfast

Naval battle squadron

SINN FEIN
'Ourselves Alone'
was a new Irish pol-
itical party gaining
strength in 1914

Howth

Dublin

Curragh Camp
incident, 1914

IRELAND .

National Volunteers
smuggled in rifles
26 July 1914

JANUARY–JULY, 1914
No less than 937
industrial strikes. Many
people feared a General
Strike would take
place that year.

JANUARY–JULY, 1914
Mrs. Pankhurst jailed four
times. Suffragettes
set fire to more than a
hundred buildings.

IRELAND 1912—14

- Predominantly Protestant (Ulster)
- Predominantly Roman Catholic
- Gun-running by illegal Irish Armies
- Naval movements

IN THE FOUR YEARS BEFORE WORLD WAR 1,
MANY BRITISH PEOPLE SOUGHT A NEW LIFE OVERSEAS

EMIGRANTS 1909—1913

Total
1,126,000

278,000	565,000	261,000	22,000
UNITED STATES	**CANADA**	**AUSTRALIA and NEW ZEALAND**	**UNION of SOUTH AFRICA**

More people chose Canada. The peak year for emigration was 1912. More British emigrated in the four years before the war than died from enemy action during the four years of fighting

42: Europe at war, 1914

The fear of war

Alongside the social unrest in Britain there also existed the nagging fear that, before long, a terrifying war might break out in Europe. Already the great nations had formed power blocs. Germany, Austria and Italy were in the Triple Alliance; Russia, France and to a lesser extent Britain were in the Triple Entente. Traditionally, the British opposed committing themselves to foreign entanglements. However, in 1904 and 1907, they had settled their differences first with France and then with Russia and, generally speaking, had thrown in their lot with these two countries. Of course, they realized that should any conflict break out between the notorious rivals, Austria and Russia, the 'two armed camps' would drag Europe into a frightful war.

The arms race

After 1906 the Liberals felt that in order to preserve peace it was necessary to prepare for war. With general public approval they poured money into 'Dreadnought' building programmes, for most people believed that victory in any future war would go to those who won a twentieth century version of the Battle of Trafalgar. At the same time, the Liberals created a small British Expeditionary Force (BEF) and trained a volunteer Territorial Army to defend the homeland. All the great powers made similar preparations and yet managed to survive recurring crises. Even when local wars brewed up in the Balkans during 1912–13 the generals and the politicians kept their heads. Nobody mobilized, nobody resorted to force to solve an international issue—until 1914.

The Sarajevo crisis 1914

On 28 June 1914 a Serbian student assassinated Franz Ferdinand, heir to the Austrian throne, during a state visit to Sarajevo. British newspapers, busy reporting the Irish problem, barely mentioned the event until the Austrians, having made impossible demands of the Serbian government, declared war on 28 July. Serbia appealed to Czar Nicholas II for help and he ordered the immediate mobilization of the Russian armies. It was this move which brought in the Germans, together with their complex military scheme called the Schlieffen Plan. They believed that, in the event of a war in the east, it was first necessary to defeat Russia's ally, France. They would accomplish this by means of a surprise sweep through Belgium and then turn round to face the Russian

'steamroller' as it approached East Prussia. Therefore Kaiser Wilhelm II declared war on Russia (1 August) and then France (3 August) and sent his troops into Belgium. On 4 August Prime Minister Asquith announced to a tense House of Commons that, as Britain had a moral obligation to defend Belgium under the terms of the 1839 Treaty of London, he had given the Germans an ultimatum: withdraw from Belgium by 23.00 hours or suffer war. There was no reply; consequently Britain declared war on Germany.

The early battles and the first wartime Christmas

A week after war began the BEF crossed to France. After a brief skirmish with a Uhlan (heavy cavalry) patrol, the British began their march towards the main combat area on 21 August. Their task was the defence of Mons which, quite unknown to them, lay directly in the path of the main German armies. For nine hours, 35,000 khaki clad soldiers armed with their magazine loading Lee-Enfield rifles held the Germans at bay and then retreated—having suffered 1600 casualties. This famous retreat from Mons delayed the Germans long enough for the main French armies to prepare for the autumn battles. After Mons came the battles at the Rivers Marne and Aisne and then the bloodbath of the First Battle of Ypres, or 'Wipers' as it was called by the British soldiers. By December, the armies were dug in and trenches ran from Switzerland to the Channel coast. But it was not just the soldiers who were involved in this war. On the morning of 16 December two German battle-cruisers steamed out of the mist to shell towns on the east coast; and on Christmas Eve a Taube monoplane flew over Dover to drop the first bomb on Britain. In the trenches that night German soldiers put lights on Christmas trees and sang 'Stille Nacht, Heilige Nacht'. Amazed British troops responded with 'We are Fred Karno's* army . . .' and as dawn broke the front line soldiers crawled from their trenches to fraternize in an unofficial truce in *No-man's-land*. Said one German soldier: 'Christmas united the soldiers . . . the men heard the voice of 2000 years back, but the rulers did not. And so the war went on for four years. And millions of young men had to die . . . to die.'†

*Fred Karno was an early silent screen comedian, predating even Charlie Chaplin.
†He was an NCO named Josef Sewald of the 17th Bavarian Reserve Regiment. The quote comes from Leslie Baily's *BBC Scrapbooks*, Vol. 1, p. 214.

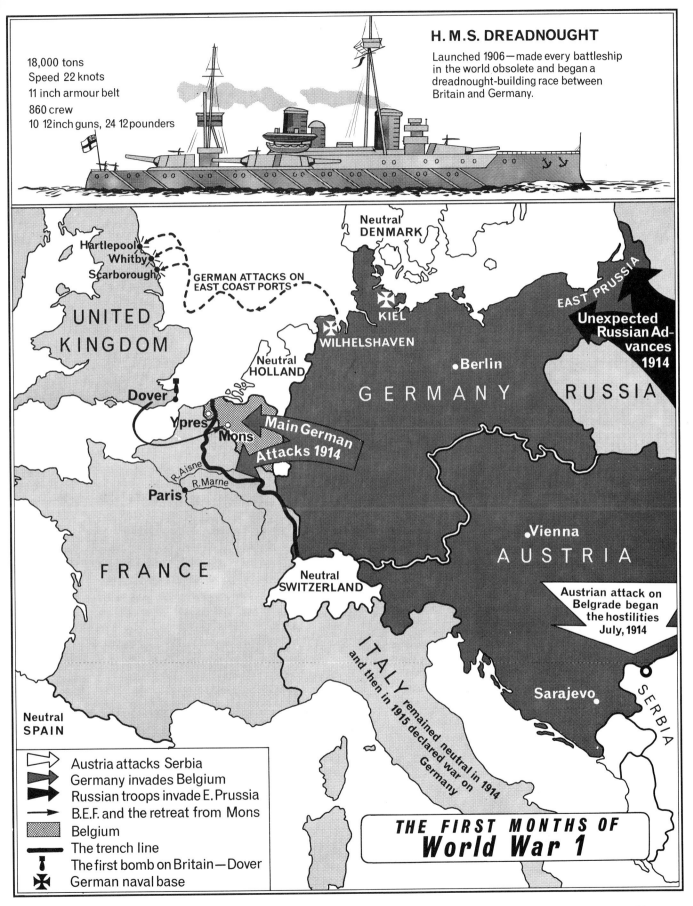

H.M.S. DREADNOUGHT

18,000 tons
Speed 22 knots
11 inch armour belt
860 crew
10 12 inch guns, 24 12 pounders

Launched 1906—made every battleship
in the world obsolete and began a
dreadnought-building race between
Britain and Germany.

Hartlepool
Whitby
Scarborough

GERMAN ATTACKS ON
EAST COAST PORTS

UNITED KINGDOM

Neutral DENMARK

KIEL

WILHELSHAVEN

Berlin

GERMANY

EAST PRUSSIA

Unexpected Russian Advances 1914

RUSSIA

Neutral HOLLAND

Dover

Ypres
Mons

Main German Attacks 1914

R. Aisne
R. Marne

Paris

FRANCE

Neutral SWITZERLAND

Vienna

AUSTRIA

Austrian attack on Belgrade began the hostilities July, 1914

ITALY
remained neutral in 1914
and then in 1915 declared war on Germany

Sarajevo

SERBIA

Neutral SPAIN

⬜➡ Austria attacks Serbia
▨➡ Germany invades Belgium
⬛➡ Russian troops invade E. Prussia
→ B.E.F. and the retreat from Mons
▨ Belgium
▬ The trench line
⌁ The first bomb on Britain—Dover
✠ German naval base

THE FIRST MONTHS OF
World War 1

43: The war in the trenches, 1914–1918

Strategy and tactics

Although men fought the First World War on land, sea and in the air in many parts of the globe, the decisive battles took place on the Western Front. Here the majority of British servicemen spent a part—or the rest—of their lives in a grim, slogging war where artillery barrages could last for days and battles went on for months. On both sides, the generals wanted to break through the enemy's elaborate trench system so carefully guarded by barbed wire and machine guns. Techniques of attack and defence remained largely unchanged for four years. Before an attack the guns fired thousands of shells on the enemy's position, thus giving him ample warning of what was coming. As the barrage lifted, the infantry went 'over the top', crawling out of their trenches to begin the hazardous trudge across *No-man's-land* into the enemy wire. Certain refinements appeared as the war progressed. At the Second Battle of Ypres 1915 the Germans used poison gas; on the Somme in 1916 the British introduced the tank. By 1918 aircraft were participating in land battles, strafing anything that moved in the enemy trenches. Occasionally, engineers burrowed below *No-man's-land* to plant huge loads of explosive; when the plunger went down up went whole trench systems together with their unfortunate occupants.

The soldier's life

After basic training in England and perhaps a spot of battle school in France, the average British soldier moved up into the line with his battalion. He received a shilling a day—paid in francs—and had the satisfaction of knowing that the government allowed his wife 12/6 a week with extra for each dependent child. If he were lucky, he moved into a quiet part of the line where he deepened his trench to the regulation seven feet, scrounged extra duckboards, strengthened the barbed wire and filled lots of sandbags. There was a reasonable chance of survival if he could escape patrol duty and set-piece battles. In attack, however, he ran a very good chance of getting killed. He had to plod forward (without benefit of steel-helmet until late in 1915) irrespective of what the enemy threw at him. With a heavy pack on his back, entrenching tool at his side, weighed down with an ammunition bandolier and perhaps a few Mills bombs, he clutched a Lee-Enfield rifle with a long sword bayonet jutting beyond the muzzle. He was an unwieldy figure and an easy target. In defence, he cowered deep in the earth while the shelling was on; when it stopped he lifted his head to find the enemy just a few yards away. 'Shell-shock' (as mental collapse was often called) and 'trench-feet' (foot-rot resulting from hours of paddling in liquid mud) claimed many victims. It all seemed rather futile—few men had any idea of the current battle situation. Rather more didn't know what the war was about. But all were subject to the iron military discipline which made them carry out their orders—or be shot.

The battles

Most British soldiers experienced the set-piece battles such as those fought at Ypres (1914, 1915, 1917,* 1918), the Somme (1916), the Marne (1914, 1918), Loos (1916), Messines, Vimy Ridge, Cambrai (all 1917), and St Quentin (1918). The turning point came as late as August 1918 at the great Battle of Amiens. Here the entire British Fourth Army of 100,000 troops attacked the German trenches. Every allied soldier was warned of secrecy and received a simple printed instruction: 'Keep your mouth shut!' All supply movements took place at night. As 534 tanks nosed forward RAF planes roared low to drown the noise of the engines. One hour before daylight, 8 August 1918, the assault went in along a 40 mile front. Spearheaded by the superb Canadian and Australian Army Corps, the troops pierced the German trenches and made August 8 a 'black day' for the German Army. For three more months, as the killing reached new heights, the Germans fell back until on 11 November 1918 they surrendered. About 3 million British and Empire troops had suffered death or injury—and they were a small fraction of humanity's total losses in all parts of the globe.

*Known as 'Passchendaele'.

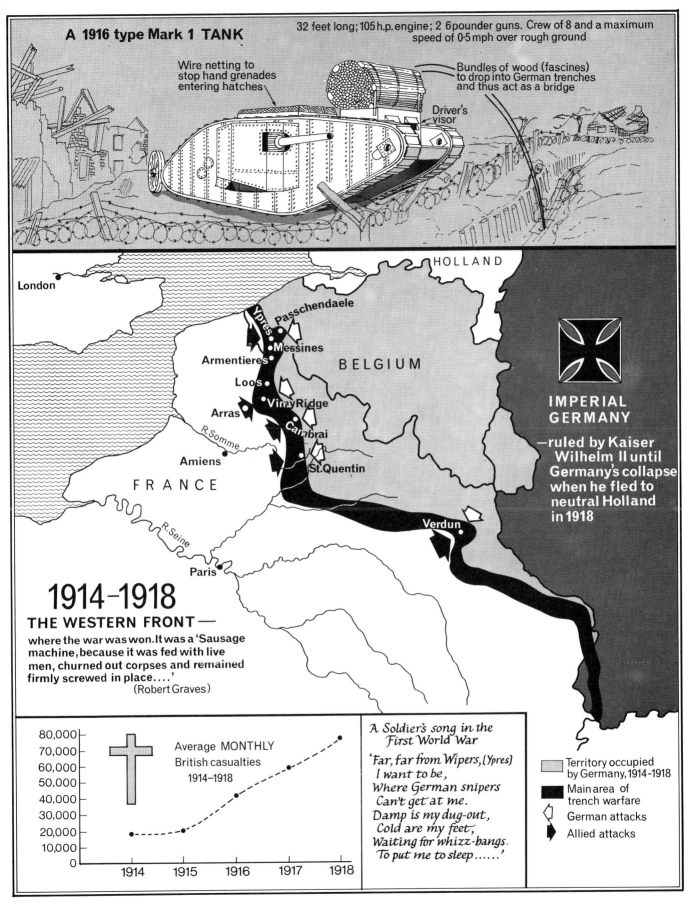

A 1916 type Mark 1 TANK

32 feet long; 105 h.p. engine; 2 6 pounder guns. Crew of 8 and a maximum speed of 0·5 mph over rough ground

Wire netting to stop hand grenades entering hatches

Bundles of wood (fascines) to drop into German trenches and thus act as a bridge

Driver's visor

London

HOLLAND

BELGIUM

Ypres
Passchendaele
Messines
Armentieres
Loos
VimyRidge
Arras
Cambrai
St.Quentin

R.Somme

Amiens

FRANCE

R.Seine

Verdun

Paris

IMPERIAL GERMANY

—ruled by Kaiser Wilhelm II until Germany's collapse when he fled to neutral Holland in 1918

1914–1918
THE WESTERN FRONT —

where the war was won. It was a 'Sausage machine, because it was fed with live men, churned out corpses and remained firmly screwed in place....'
(Robert Graves)

Average MONTHLY British casualties 1914–1918

	1914	1915	1916	1917	1918
80,000					
70,000					
60,000					
50,000					
40,000					
30,000					
20,000					
10,000					
0					

A Soldier's song in the First World War

'Far, far from Wipers, (Ypres)
I want to be,
Where German snipers
Can't get at me.
Damp is my dug-out,
Cold are my feet,
Waiting for whizz-bangs.
To put me to sleep......'

☐ Territory occupied by Germany, 1914–1918

■ Main area of trench warfare

⬦ German attacks

◆ Allied attacks

44: The Home Front, 1915–1918

Shortage of manpower

There was a popular song at the beginning of the First World War which went:

Oh! We don't want to lose you,
But we think you ought to go;
For your King and your Country,
Both need you so . . .

But when the men flocked to join the army in their thousands, they abandoned in the process many jobs which were vital to the war effort. Coalmining and the electrical industry both lost 20% of their manpower; the high explosive and chemical industries were even worse off. This left the government with two unexpected crises on its hands: a shortage of munitions workers *and* a shortage of munitions. Matters came to a head when, in May 1915, an attack on the Western Front was a total failure. *The Times* reported: 'We had not sufficient high explosives to lower the enemy's parapets to the ground . . . the want of an unlimited supply of high explosives was a fatal bar to our success.' Asquith decided on a government reshuffle. He made Lloyd George *Minister of Munitions* and included a Labour spokesman, Arthur Henderson, in his new cabinet. Lloyd George drafted women into the factories, prohibited strikes and put the munitions industry on its feet.

The role of women

But this still left a shortage of manpower especially after the 1916 *Conscription Act* drew more men into the army. Women had to fill the vacancies—there was 500,000 in the factories by mid-1916—and in this way they established their right to earn *respect* as well as a decent living wage. Apart from their contribution to the armament industry, thousands joined the services (WRAFS, WAACS, WRNS) and the nursing organizations; one nurse, Edith Cavell, became a wartime heroine after the Germans shot her for helping allied prisoners to escape. Other women became bus and tram conductresses, delivered milk and worked on the railways.

The role of children

Children played a part in the war effort. Well over half a million left school early to work on the farms and in the factories. Many could earn up to £2 a week—far more than a soldier's pay in the front line! This situation had some harmful effects. One government report in 1917 deplored the increase in juvenile crime and blamed gambling, drinking, a decline in parental control and a lack of discipline. It also noted that children suffered

from long hours of shift work and that they tended to move from one job to another in search of easier money. Undoubtedly, the war brought unprecedented amounts of money into many homes where, in 1914, there had been considerable poverty.

The Easter Rising 1916

To many Irish republicans, the war provided a golden opportunity to throw off British domination forever and they asked the Germans to provide military aid in the form of troops as well as weapons. Easter Sunday 1916 was chosen for the revolt—but at the last minute the Germans called it off by sending an agent, Sir Roger Casement, to Ireland in a U-boat. One group of rebels ignored his warning and on Easter Monday occupied the Dublin GPO and there declared the creation of the *Irish Republic*. British troops moved in and, after four days of hard fighting, forced the rebels to surrender.

Raids, rationing and the 'flu

After December 1916, when Lloyd George became Prime Minister and brought his immense capacity for getting things done into action, the British civilian population faced up to the many miseries which accompanied the First World War. Between January 1915 and June 1918 they withstood Zeppelin and Gotha bomber attacks on 106 occasions. London suffered the worst raid on 13 June 1917 (the 594 casualties were rather less than those sustained by the East Coast towns shelled in December 1914). Dover, because of its proximity to enemy air bases, suffered the most raids. By the end of 1917, there was a sophisticated anti-aircraft defence against the raiders and many were brought down. In addition to these attacks, civilians had to endure food shortages after the indiscriminate U-boat campaigns of 1915 and 1917. Housewives had to queue for food; Lloyd George set up a Food Ministry to encourage voluntary rationing. When this failed, the government imposed food rationing during February-March 1918. Coinciding with this came a virulent influenza epidemic. It began simultaneously in Scotland and France; wave after wave killed 151,000 people before the epidemic ended in 1919. Strangely enough, the most likely person to fall victim to the disease was the young, healthy adult. This is difficult to explain because, although there were food shortages and a 100% rise in prices during the war, the standard of living did not decline. In fact, a 1918 government report stated that in many parts of Britain the families of unskilled workers were rather better fed by the end of the war than they had been in 1914.

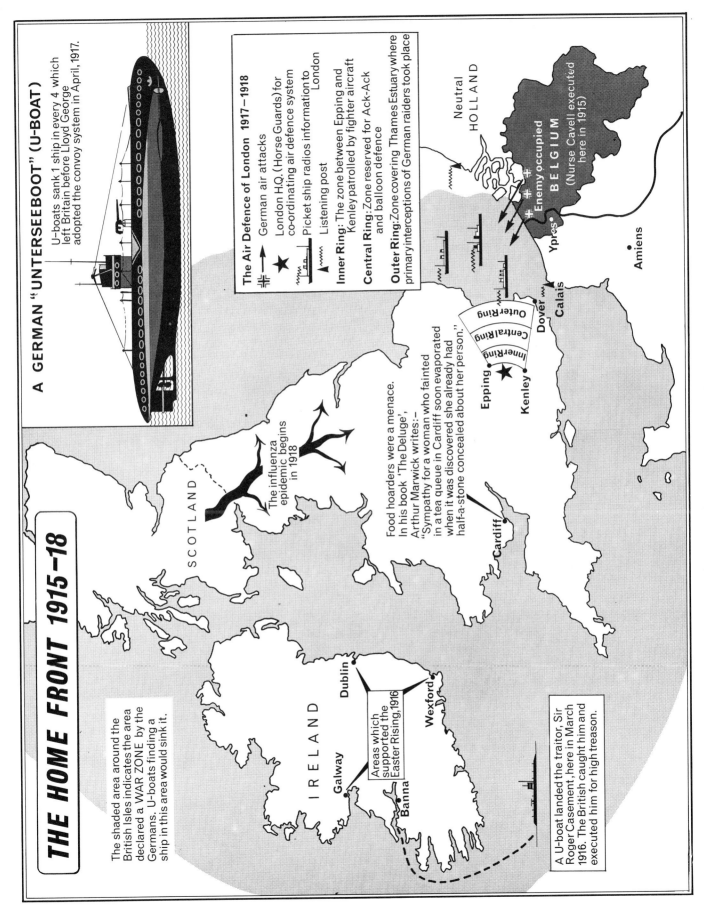

THE HOME FRONT 1915–18

The shaded area around the British Isles indicates the area declared a WAR ZONE by the Germans. U-boats finding a ship in this area would sink it.

A GERMAN "UNTERSEEBOOT" (U-BOAT)

U-boats sank 1 ship in every 4 which left Britain before Lloyd George adopted the convoy system in April, 1917.

The Air Defence of London 1917–1918

German air attacks

London H.Q. (Horse Guards) for co-ordinating air defence system to London

Picket ship radios information

Listening post

Inner Ring: The zone between Epping and Kenley patrolled by fighter aircraft

Central Ring: Zone reserved for Ack-Ack and balloon defence

Outer Ring: Zone covering Thames Estuary where primary interceptions of German raiders took place

Neutral HOLLAND

Enemy occupied BELGIUM (Nurse Cavell executed here in 1915)

Ypres

Amiens

Calais

Dover

OuterRing
CentralRing
InnerRing

Epping

Kenley

SCOTLAND

The influenza epidemic begins in 1918

Food hoarders were a menace. In his book 'The Deluge', Arthur Marwick writes:–
"Sympathy for a woman who fainted in a tea queue in Cardiff soon evaporated when it was discovered she already had half-a-stone concealed about her person."

Cardiff

I R E L A N D

Dublin

Wexford

Galway

Banna

Areas which supported the Easter Rising, 1916

A U-boat landed the traitor, Sir Roger Casement, here in March 1916. The British caught him and executed him for high treason.

45: Government control during the First World War

The role of government

In order to win a war against the industrial and military might of Imperial Germany, the British people had to transform their peacetime economy into one which would enable them not only to outfight but also to out-produce their opponents. World War I was destined to be a war of attrition. To gear the national economy to this end was the task of government and people working together in the closest harmony.

Agriculture

The desperate need for food and fodder illustrates this point. Before 1914 farmers had drastically reduced their cereal acreage in the face of foreign competition. They cut their overheads by employing fewer farmhands and by the time war broke out the trend in British agriculture was to produce more and more dairy products and to rear sheep and cattle for meat. But once the U-boats started torpedoing the food ships as they steamed through the 'war zone', the government had to devise a plan that would reverse this trend. They had to persuade the farmers to produce high-calorie foods—cereals and potatoes—plus plenty of hay for the horses and mules used in France. A government Food Production Department started the planning in 1916; in 1917 the *Corn Production Act* guaranteed the farmers minimum prices for their crops. It worked like magic. The farmers ploughed up land which had been derelict for years as well as their rich pastures. By 1918 there was a general rise of 50% in British food production. Farmers prospered—but not for long. Their affluence depended on how long the government was willing to subsidize British agriculture.

Industry

One of the most important changes in industry was the use of new kinds of automatic machine tools in the new armament factories. Unskilled workers had to produce thousands of rifles and machine guns, millions of bullets and shells accurately and at great speed. The government met this challenge by importing the necessary machinery from America. Almost overnight, a new generation of expert turners, millers and capstan lathe operators appeared. New factories mushroomed—their location was kept on the secret list so well that many of the original sites are forgotten today—and mass production techniques became familiar to thousands of British workers. In this way, another stage in the industrialization of Britain took place—'the gun, aeroplane and tank factories of 1918, in their equipment and layout and in their methods of organization, bore little resemblance to most British factories of 1913 . . .'*

Wages

Now there was a demand for *unskilled*, rather than *skilled* labour, many people who had been on the poverty line in 1914 enjoyed a real increase in their living standards. Near-starvation had been only too common among *fully employed workers* in 1914; but it became a rarity during the war. Admittedly, inflation took away most of the purchasing power of wage increases and, if it hadn't been for the overtime, many workers would have been hard pressed. Nevertheless, most workers were abreast of inflation by 1918. Of course, they didn't save much. A soldier's wife had little to spare. Statistical evidence indicates that 68% of the total increase in wealth during 1914–18 went to those who already possessed 'fortunes of more than £5000'!

Trade unions

Throughout the war, the government was the main employer of labour. It also took control of the coalmines and railways. It supplied the raw materials, provided the orders and paid top prices for the goods. It also insisted that trade unionists worked side by side with unskilled workers (many of whom joined trade unions during the war). The unions did not like this and reluctantly accepted the *1915 Shell and Fuses Agreement* which permitted the dilution of skilled labour with unskilled workers together with the introduction of automatic machinery. In return, the government promised, at the end of hostilities, to dismiss the dilutees (usually women workers) so that men returning from the war would not be out of a job. Not all the unions were co-operative: the Glasgow engineers resisted Lloyd George's munition schemes with strikes and demonstrations before he forced them to collaborate.

*The Economic Effects of the World Wars on Britain, Alan Milward (Macmillan 1970) p. 34.

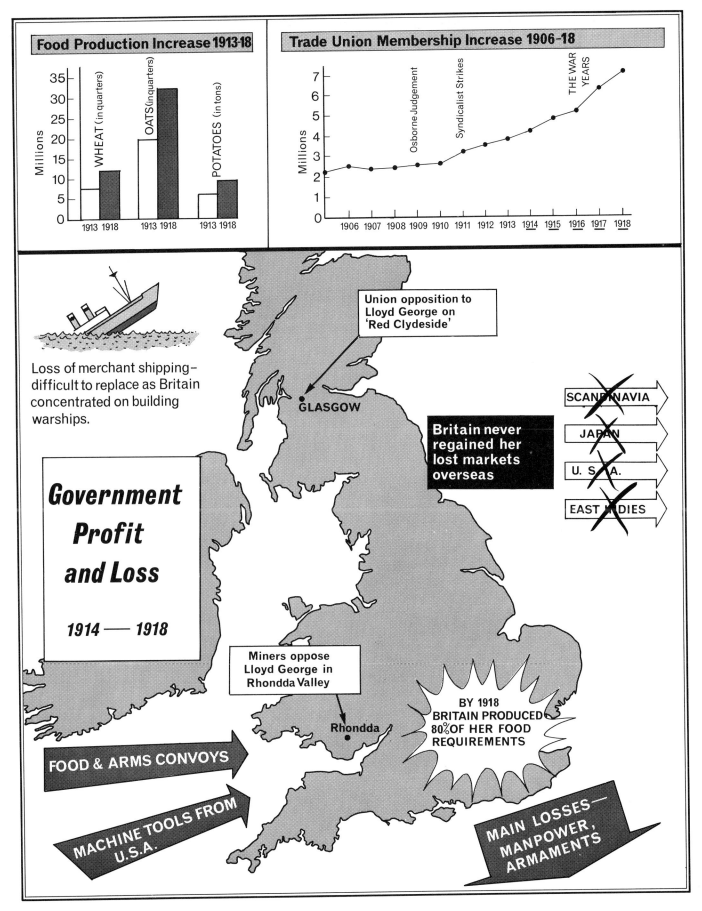

Food Production Increase 1913-18

Millions

- WHEAT (in quarters)
- OATS (in quarters)
- POTATOES (in tons)

1913 1918 · 1913 1918 · 1913 1918

Trade Union Membership Increase 1906-18

Millions

Osborne Judgement
Syndicalist Strikes
THE WAR YEARS

1906 1907 1908 1909 1910 1911 1912 1913 1914 1915 1916 1917 1918

Loss of merchant shipping–
difficult to replace as Britain
concentrated on building
warships.

Union opposition to
Lloyd George on
'Red Clydeside'

GLASGOW

Britain never
regained her
lost markets
overseas

SCANDINAVIA
JAPAN
U. S. A.
EAST INDIES

Government Profit and Loss

1914 — 1918

Miners oppose
Lloyd George in
Rhondda Valley

Rhondda

BY 1918
BRITAIN PRODUCED
80% OF HER FOOD
REQUIREMENTS

FOOD & ARMS CONVOYS

MACHINE TOOLS FROM
U.S.A.

MAIN LOSSES—
MANPOWER,
ARMAMENTS

46: The industrial capacity of the British at the end of World War I

Peace and promises 1918

> Hostilities will cease at 11 hours today. Troops will stand fast on the line at that hour . . . .

For thousands of men on the Western Front this order meant that they would survive the carnage of the First World War. For the civilians at home it meant a moment of joy. In London, Winston Churchill watched as 'from all sides men and women came scurrying into the street. Streams of people poured out from all the buildings. Northumberland Avenue was now crowded with people in hundreds, nay thousands, rushing hither and thither in a frantic manner, shouting and screaming with joy . . . suddenly and everywhere the burdens were cast down'. The time of peace was also a time of promises, promises that came easily to the lips of the Prime Minister, Lloyd George. Already a living legend as the man who had won the war, he was determined to win the peace. 'What is our task?' he cried, 'to make Britain a fit country for heroes to live in!'

General Election 1918

In December he sought re-election and for the first time candidates in the constituencies canvassed the votes of women. By the *Representation of the People Act (February 1918)*, all adult males and women over thirty were enfranchised. Conscientious objectors, many of whom had suffered jail rather than engage in battle against their fellow men, were debarred from voting for the next five years. For the first time in history, the British people formed a democratic electorate, one of the unexpected by-products of the war. Unfortunately, most of the troops were still in France and only about 25% cast their votes—some of these were under 21 but had had special permission to vote because they had seen front-line combat. Nevertheless, the results reflected the people's feelings. Lloyd George and his supporters won 533 out of the 634 Parliamentary seats. It was the biggest majority ever gained.

Britain's potential 1918

Britain emerged from the war still led by her most popular politician. Now he was off to Paris to dictate peace terms to the defeated Germans. He promised to hang the Kaiser (who lived safely in Holland long enough to see Hitler capture Paris in 1940) and make Germany pay for the cost of a war in which the British had spent more than £10,000 million. He felt he had every right to be confident of Britain's future. Over the last four years he had supervised Britain's industrial progress, progress which had been not only remarkable but also the main reason for her survival and victory. The ability of the British to mass-produce war material had been the main test the nation had had to face. By 1918 it seemed that the British could produce whatever was needed. Churchill, then Minister of Munitions, saw this clearly: 'There was very little in the productive sphere that they could not at this time actually do. A requisition, for instance, of half a million houses would not have seemed more difficult to comply with than those we were already in process of executing for a hundred thousand aeroplanes, twenty thousand guns, or the entire medium artillery of the American Army, or two million tons of projectiles.' Three main factors had made all this possible during the war:

1. There had been full employment. The factories and farms as well as the battlefields had created an insatiable demand for men.
2. Because it needed to control heavy industry, coal and transport for the war economy, the government had taken the means of production out of the hands of the private owners.
3. The government had spent money like water. It increased taxation, sold up its overseas investments and borrowed very large loans. Government could afford—for a fairly short period—to spend its capital on war materials and, at the same time, pay workers high wages to manufacture them.

So, by spending a great deal of money, government had given a new lease of life to the traditional British industries: coal, transport, iron and steel—all of which had been in the doldrums before the war. Now the great issue facing the British people was this: could they pass, without too much hardship, from a wartime back to a peacetime economy? Would the markets of the world, many of which had been lost to British goods in the war, be able to absorb all the products of British industry?

Opposite, an armaments factory during World War I

THE INDUSTRIAL CAPACITY OF THE BRITISH PEOPLE IN 1918

Lloyd George's War Cabinet

Poured £7 million per day into the war

Created new industries to prosecute the war

MUNITIONS
LABOUR
FOOD
BLOCKADE
SHIPPING
AIR
PENSIONS
NATIONAL SERVICE

Controlled the means of production

Armament factories which produced, for example - - - - - - -

COAL MINES

RAILWAYS

Equipment for 4 million fighting men

4 million ·303 rifles

250,000 machine guns such as this Vickers

52,000 aeroplanes such as this S.E.5 of No. 92 Squadron

Part 5 – Into the Twentieth Century and the First World War

Spread

38. *The Liberals and the Welfare State***	R. D. H. Seaman	Hill & Fell
39. *The History of the T.U.C. 1868–1968***	published by the General Council of the TUC	
40. *Suffragettes and Votes for Women***	L. Snellgrove	Longmans
41. *Post-Victorian Britain*	L. C. B. Seaman	Methuen
42. *Twentieth Century Germany***	B. A. Catchpole	OUP
*BBC Scrapbook Volume 1***	Leslie Baily	
43. *With a Machine-Gun to Cambrai*	George Coppard	HMSO
44. *Sagittarius Rising*	C. Lewis	Davies
*BBC Scrapbook Volume 1***	Leslie Baily	
45. *The Economic Effects of the Two World Wars on Britain*	A. S. Milward	Macmillan (Advanced discussion)
46. *Post-Victorian Britain*	L. C. B. Seaman	Methuen

**Especially suitable for project and topic work

PART 6

'The Lost Peace'
1919–1939

Although the British people had been on the winning side in World War I, they rapidly discovered that the price of victory was not much different from the price of defeat. However, unlike most European peoples, their democratic institutions survived the post-war depression. Extremist political parties such as the Communists and Fascists found little support for their policies among the British working classes. One reason for this was that the standard of living actually improved during the post-war years. Virtually no *fully-employed* man lived on the poverty-line—as his father may have done in 1914. And though there were armies of unemployed (over 2 million between 1931 and 1935 and never less than a million throughout the Thirties) National Assistance payments and Unemployment Benefit kept the wolf from the door. The worst effects of depression were localized. Areas dependent upon traditional 'nineteenth century' industries such as coal, textiles and iron and steel seemed doomed. But in the south, where consumer industries mushroomed during the inter-war years, there was prosperity in the 'twentieth century' sense. This is why many historians contend that, during this period, '*two* Britains' existed side by side.

Life, therefore, was tolerable for the majority of the population. And for the rest conditions improved, ironically enough, under the threat of war. Heavy industry, though it shared in a general revival of European trade after 1935, benefited from the rearmament programmes first authorized by Prime Minister Ramsay MacDonald. By 1937, the threat of war preyed on many people's minds. They were afraid of massive air attacks—so devastating that gas and high explosive bombs might kill millions of people overnight. They wanted to avoid war, wanted to keep out of international crises such as the Abyssinian conflict and the Spanish Civil War. As far as Nazi Germany was concerned, the people supported Neville Chamberlain's policy of 'appeasement' towards Adolf Hitler. Only when everyone clearly understood that Hitler's promises of 'no more territorial demands in Europe' were totally valueless did a resigned and bitterly disappointed people support their Prime Minister's declaration of war on Germany in 1939.

The Peace achieved by the 'war to end wars' had lasted 21 years—time enough for another generation of young men to grow up and put on uniforms.

47: Industrial crisis during the Twenties

General dissatisfaction

For a decade after the First World War there was an almost total absence of harmony between British workers and their employers. Even the short-lived 'boom years' 1918–20 were plagued with strikes far more serious than those which swept the country just before 1914. Dockers, railwaymen, soldiers home on leave, even policemen showed their deep dissatisfaction with the post-war condition of Britain. Poor wages, a housing shortage, rising unemployment—was this the land fit for heroes? War veterans out of a job did not think so. On Armistice Day 1922 more than 20,000 filed past the Cenotaph. Their banners carried a bitter message: 'From the living victims to our dead comrades who died in vain'. However, the trade recession was an international problem, not a domestic one—and of course the Liberal and Conservative governments failed to find a solution. In desperation the people turned to Labour in 1924. Ramsay MacDonald became the first Labour Prime Minister—but he had no more idea than the rest of the politicians and his government did not survive the year.

The plight of the miners

Miners formed the biggest single group of industrial workers and their protests were the loudest and most concerted. They wanted the government to nationalize the coal industry—and in fact the 1919 Sankey Commission recommended this course of action. Unfortunately the Lloyd George government was not prepared to introduce state control of industry during peacetime. It knocked an hour off the miners' eight-hour day; it continued to subsidize their wages; but it rejected the idea of nationalization. Thus it ignored the fundamental issues: the mines were ill-equipped and obsolete, the owners were penny-pinching men unwilling to pour capital into the industry—only the government had the resources to make the mines a profitable, economic proposition.

The General Strike 1926

In fact, the miners did not do too badly during the years 1921–4 when Europe's coal production declined. But after this date the mines ran at a loss and the owners could see no answer other than cutting the miners' pay. Naturally, the miners set up a howl of protest and in 1925 the government asked the Samuel Commission to investigate the industry. It reported in 1926 and suggested that, in return for better working conditions, the miners must accept either wage cuts or revert to the eight-hour day. 'Not a penny off the pay, not a minute on the day!' came the miners' answer. On 1 May 1926 the owners called a lockout and the whole industry came to a standstill. In waded the TUC with a rather wild threat of calling a General Strike unless the miners received satisfaction. Clearly, Prime Minister Baldwin's Conservative government did not intend to impose any settlement and possibly chose this moment to have a showdown with the miners and the whole trade union movement once and for all. So on Monday 4 May 1926 a very surprised nation awoke to discover that most industrial and transport workers had come out on General Strike.

A state of emergency

Baldwin was ready for the fray. He declared a state of emergency, called out the troops and implemented his detailed arrangements for getting food to the people—he ignored the strikers' statement that they would not interfere with these anyway. Winston Churchill, who had now switched to the Conservatives and was Chancellor of the Exchequer, quite openly called the strikers enemies of the state. Ernest Bevin, a prominent union leader, retorted: 'War has been declared by the government!' Fortunately, there was no war—and very few bursts of violence. Friendly football matches between strikers and policemen received far more publicity. Other strikers watched with bleak amusement the antics of volunteers who drove buses and—with less success—the railway engines. For nine days the TUC maintained the General Strike. Then it surrendered, leaving the miners in the lurch. Months later, starvation drove them back to the pits where they accepted longer hours and smaller wage packets. It was a time of gross social injustice and men spoke of revolution. But revolutions only happen when the government fails to govern. And if nothing else, Stanley Baldwin never lost control of the situation. Later, millions praised him as the man who kept his head and who saw the country through one of its most dangerous moments.

The Trades Disputes Act 1927

Baldwin survived the General Strike; he did not relish another one. So, despite the fact that 1927–8 saw rising European prosperity and a fall in unemployment, he prepared legislation. By the 1927 Trades Disputes Act a general strike, or any other strike called out 'in sympathy' with other workers, was now illegal.

British Coal Exports to Europe 1921—1924

German Coal Exports decline

Polish Coal Exports decline

DENMARK

HOLLAND

BELGIUM

GERMANY

Ruhr Coalfields

POLAND

Poland and Russia at War 1920–21. Coalmining almost ceased in Poland

FRANCE

CZECHOSLOVAKIA

Franco-Belgian armies invaded the Ruhr in 1923 when Germany failed to meet her reparation payments. German mines closed; Britain secured the markets Germany lost 1923–24.

Britain's Coal Exports hinge on events in Europe

SWITZERLAND   AUSTRIA

DEPRESSION IN HEAVY INDUSTRY: Population movements

Glasgow

Edinburgh

Newcastle

Cumberland

Lancashire

NOTTINGHAM

Potteries

BIRMINGHAM
COVENTRY

S.Wales

SLOUGH

London

South Wales lost 5% of its population 1920–1930

London & South East gained 14% in population 1920–1930

Explanation:
1. Britain's basic heavy industries —mining, textiles, iron and steel, shipbuilding — declined in the Twenties.

2. New consumer industries, powered by electricity and oil, grew up near a large affluent population in S.E. England. Unemployed people migrated here – and also to the Midlands.

Example: Slough became a light-industry centre based on the **Slough Trading Estate**. Many South Wales mining families migrated there in the Twenties.

■ Area of heavy unemployment
✪ Important centres of light industry
→ Population movement
■ Areas of relative prosperity

48: The Thirties—depression and recovery

The lack of funds

Lack of government finance dogged all the schemes for social improvement after the First World War. Fisher's Education Act, for example, raised the school leaving age to 14 during 1918 but was never able to implement a scheme to provide day continuation classes for children up to 16. The new Ministry of Health, founded in 1919, could not improve the nation's health services. The family of an insured man either had to pay to go on the local doctor's 'panel' or forgo medical treatment altogether. Only one Minister of Health, Neville Chamberlain, made any significant change in the social services; he abolished the Poor Law and replaced it with Public Assistance Committees at the beginning of 1929. This was the year in which the perennial shortage of money turned into an international calamity and set in motion events which brought millions of British families into a state of poverty.

Economic blizzard 1929–31

In October 1929 share values on America's Wall Street Stock Exchange fell disastrously. While millions of Americans lost their savings, the U.S. government called in its overseas loans. In turn many European bankers withdrew their deposits in Britain and, to meet this sudden drain on cash reserves, the British government devalued the £ sterling during September 1929. Then, in 1932, Britain abandoned her free trade policy and hoped, by creating import duties on foreign manufactures and foodstuffs, to protect agriculture and industry at home. It did not work. Most of the western countries did precisely the same thing so that in the end Britain was no better off. Gradually, international trade stagnated and 30 million people in the western industrial world found themselves out of a job.

Depression in Britain

Nearly 3 million people were unemployed in Britain at the peak of the economic crisis (1932–3). Textile towns, together with all the centres of heavy industry, experienced more short-time and misery than they had ever done in the Twenties. And where the townspeople relied on a single source of employment there was disaster. In Dowlais and Mossend all the industrial plant closed; all of Jarrow's shipyards shut down. Ramsay MacDonald and Stanley Baldwin joined political forces and formed a National Government in 1931—but apart from introducing more wage cuts and inventing the hated Means Test (a device by which an unemployed man might lose his benefit if it were discovered that other members of his family were bringing money into the house) the politicians could do little to improve the miserable prospect of prolonged poverty.

The paradoxes

Mercifully, the worst features of the depression were over by 1935—due mainly to a general increase in European trade prosperity and to the rearmament programme—although money was still short. However, prices of food and consumer goods remained relatively low—a characteristic of a period of 'deflation'. A man lucky enough to be in full employment during 1933 earned around £3 a week; but with this he could buy goods worth £3.10.0 at 1923 prices. In other words, the purchasing power of the £ increased during the depression. And as many workers kept their jobs, many families could afford a few luxuries as well as the essentials of life. In Southern England, where the electrical and car manufacturing industries flourished, there was a building boom. A £5 deposit secured a semi-detached or terraced house. It would have a bathroom and toilet and all mains services. For a few shillings extra the optimistic purchaser could persuade the local council to put in a garage entrance. Inside the house, the three piece suite, the 'wireless' (connected by lots of wires to a big aerial in the garden or on the roof) and the 'hoover' would not be uncommon by 1939. The father of the house probably smoked (most working class children managed to assemble complete collections of cigarette cards in the Thirties), looked forward to a few days at the seaside and, every Saturday night, prayed for a big dividend on the football pools. But in the North, it was a different story. Degrading poverty forced Jarrow's workers to organize their famous Crusade in 1936; hunger marchers swarmed into the capital. Children left school with no hope of a job; skilled riveters and welders remained unemployed for years. Touring Britain's 'distressed areas', J. B. Priestley remarked that the unemployed reminded him of prisoners of war—'the same grey faces, the same shambling walk . . . I hated the whole ugly mean dole system which destroyed self respect and manhood. . . .'*

Conclusions

Britain failed, not entirely because of her own shortcomings, to find markets which could absorb her industrial capacity. Therefore it was the traditional industries which declined; the new chemical, electrical and light engineering industries managed to meet the challenge though everybody suffered to some extent in those years called the Thirties—the 'Devil's decade'.

*Quoted P. Leslie Baily's, *Scrapbook 1918–39*.

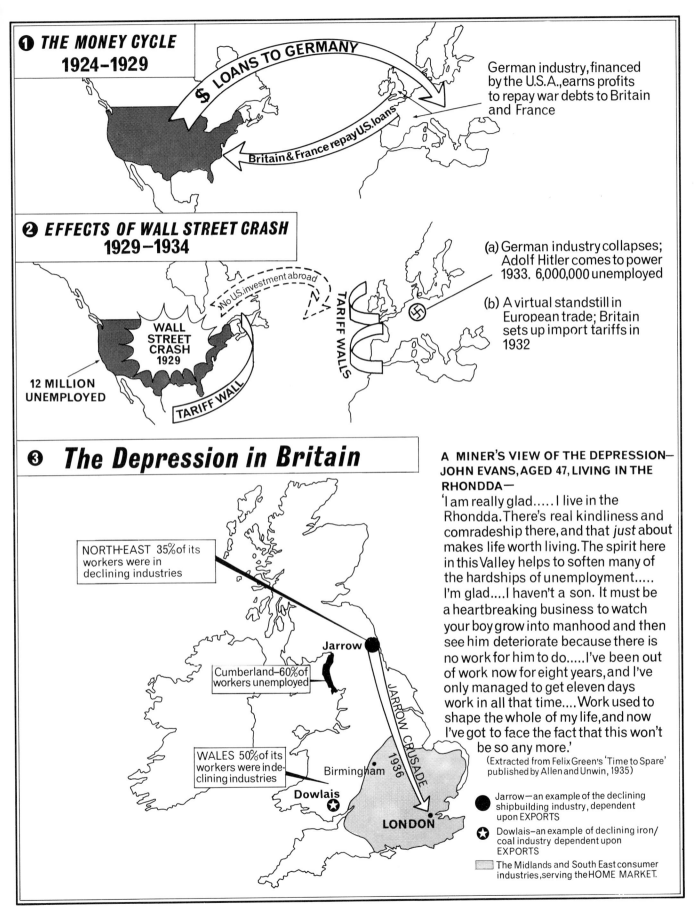

❶ THE MONEY CYCLE 1924–1929

$ LOANS TO GERMANY

German industry, financed by the U.S.A., earns profits to repay war debts to Britain and France

Britain & France repay U.S. loans

❷ EFFECTS OF WALL STREET CRASH 1929–1934

No U.S. investment abroad

WALL STREET CRASH 1929

12 MILLION UNEMPLOYED

TARIFF WALL

TARIFF WALLS

(a) German industry collapses; Adolf Hitler comes to power 1933. 6,000,000 unemployed

(b) A virtual standstill in European trade; Britain sets up import tariffs in 1932

❸ The Depression in Britain

NORTH-EAST 35% of its workers were in declining industries

Cumberland–60% of workers unemployed

Jarrow

JARROW CRUSADE 1936

WALES 50% of its workers were in declining industries

Birmingham

Dowlais ✪

LONDON

A MINER'S VIEW OF THE DEPRESSION— JOHN EVANS, AGED 47, LIVING IN THE RHONDDA—

'I am really glad..... I live in the Rhondda. There's real kindliness and comradeship there, and that *just* about makes life worth living. The spirit here in this Valley helps to soften many of the hardships of unemployment..... I'm glad....I haven't a son. It must be a heartbreaking business to watch your boy grow into manhood and then see him deteriorate because there is no work for him to do.....I've been out of work now for eight years, and I've only managed to get eleven days work in all that time....Work used to shape the whole of my life, and now I've got to face the fact that this won't be so any more.'

(Extracted from Felix Green's 'Time to Spare' published by Allen and Unwin, 1935)

● Jarrow—an example of the declining shipbuilding industry, dependent upon EXPORTS

✪ Dowlais—an example of declining iron/coal industry dependent upon EXPORTS

▨ The Midlands and South East consumer industries, serving the HOME MARKET.

49: Science and society

Motor cars

Motor cars became a familiar sight in Britain after 1919. Thanks to the skill of engineers such as Harry Austin, the internal combustion engine became a highly efficient power unit. Precision techniques developed during the war meant that pistons, valves and bearings could be mass-produced; in fact, as early as 1923 W. R. Morris was using automation techniques to manufacture cylinder blocks. By that date, specialized firms were producing reliable suspension units, carburettors, lighting and ignition systems—clearly the motor car was here to stay. Unfortunately, most people could not afford to buy one. Instead they went on outings to the coast or to what was, for most people, the un-explored countryside. Although Ford's had a £100 saloon on the market by 1935, most purchasers were members of the upper and middle classes. Nevertheless there were more than 2 million cars on the road by 1939 and they constituted a major road hazard. People were careless—road casualties in the 1930s were as serious as those today. Many local authorities built round-abouts, installed traffic lights and 'Belisha beacon' pedestrian crossings in an effort to bring order into the mounting traffic chaos.

Airships and aeroplanes

The evolution of military aircraft during the war led directly to the growth of civil aviation. Britain, in common with most air-minded countries, had an unsuccessful flirtation with airships. The idea of linking the British Empire by means of airship routes was a very attractive one and in 1919 the R-34 airship managed a transatlantic crossing. It took $4\frac{1}{2}$ *days!* Unfortunately, disaster dogged airship development. In 1921 the R-38 broke up 3,500 feet above Hull while undergoing trials. In 1930 the R-101 crashed in France. After these tragedies, the British concentrated on fixed wing, piston-engined aircraft. Already, De Havilland DH4As had flown a regular service between London and Paris. Imperial Airways, founded in 1924, were flying passengers as far as Switzerland. Their famous *Heracles* biplanes never had a fatal accident as they made their majestic flights over Europe. When Short Bros built a huge flying boat for the Britain-Australia route in 1936 it was clear that the dream of world wide air routes had turned into reality.

Cinema

Of course, very few people could enjoy these techno-logical triumphs—though everyone took a keen interest in the exploits of fliers such as Amy Johnson and Alan Cobham. But everybody could enjoy the cinema. Silent films were shown even before 1914 but it was the advent of the *talkies* in 1928 which made the cinema immensely popular. Despite the depression, ornate Odeons and Granadas rose up in or close to working class residential districts. For tenpence or less, a plush seat in a warm, cosy cinema brought you all the thrills of *The Thirty Nine Steps* (1935) or the pleasure of *Snow White and the Seven Dwarfs* (1938). There were choc-ices in the inter-val, when the cinema organist rose from the depths of the pit to lead community singing on his massive, electronic instrument. The 'pictures' provided entertainment every day except Sundays. On Saturday mornings, children flocked to their Odeon clubs to watch Flash Gordon's space adventures and Walt Disney's cartoons. It was the finest escapist entertainment the people had ever had.

Radio and television

Radio made an equal impact upon society. Very few people understood the principles on which radio waves worked—but 75% of the population could receive trans-missions by 1939. London's Radio 2LO opened on 14 November 1922; next day Manchester and Birmingham studios began their broadcasts. By the end of the year the British Broadcasting Company* (BBC) came into existence with a monopoly of broadcasting. It exerted immense social influence bringing as it did the news, plays, music and religion into the homes of the people. It gave politicians direct contact with the electorate; it provided a new teaching aid for schools. Side by side with radio came the rise of the record industry. The 78 rpm records brought classical and light music, jazz and swing within reach of millions. And in 1936 the very first television service opened at Alexandra Palace, thanks to the pioneer work of John Logie Baird and, equally important, the much lesser known figure of Isaac Schoenberg.† Again, very few people could afford a 9 inch television set. But at least a beginning had been made in the development of a new form of mass media destined to be the most dramatic form of home entertainment in the first half of the twentieth century.

*Became the British Broadcasting Corporation in 1927.

†Baird usually gets all the credit for the development of modern television. In fact, though he made the major break-through in 1924 by transmitting moving pictures, it was Isaac Schoenberg (Director of Electric and Musical Industries) who, after 1931, developed the Emitron electric camera which permitted him to transmit a picture of 405-line definition, much superior to Baird's.

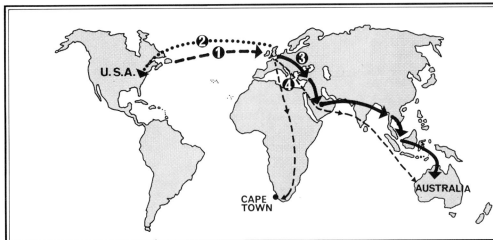

1. Alcock and Brown fly the Atlantic 1919
2. R-34 flies from Scotland to the U.S.A. 1919
3. Amy Johnson's famous flight to Australia (1930) in her little D.H.Gipsy Moth
4. Sir Alan Cobham's flights to Cape Town and back (1925/26) and Australia and back (1926). His 'Flying Circus' (1926-1936) did a great deal to popularise flying in Britain

Milestones in British Aviation ——— 1919—1939

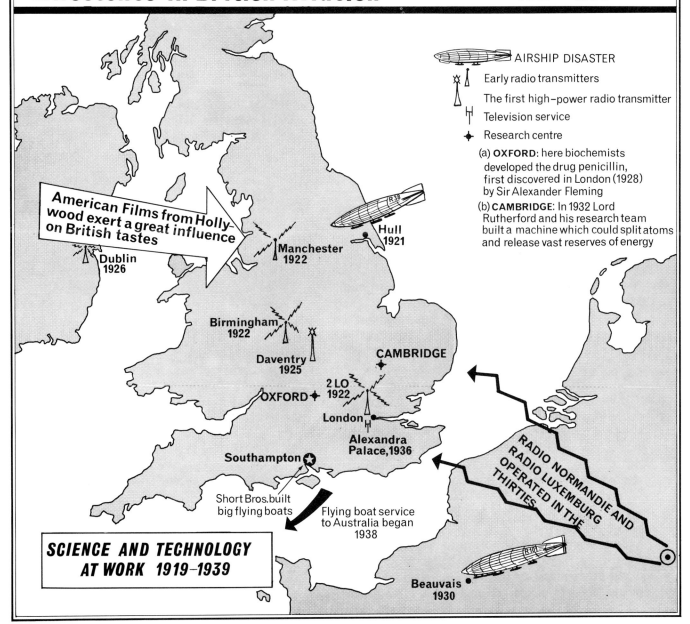

AIRSHIP DISASTER

Early radio transmitters

The first high-power radio transmitter

Television service

Research centre

(a) **OXFORD**: here biochemists developed the drug penicillin, first discovered in London (1928) by Sir Alexander Fleming

(b) **CAMBRIDGE**: In 1932 Lord Rutherford and his research team built a machine which could split atoms and release vast reserves of energy

American Films from Hollywood exert a great influence on British tastes

Dublin 1926

Manchester 1922

Hull 1921

Birmingham 1922

Daventry 1925

CAMBRIDGE

2 LO 1922

OXFORD

London

Alexandra Palace, 1936

Southampton

Short Bros. built big flying boats

Flying boat service to Australia began 1938

RADIO NORMANDIE AND RADIO LUXEMBURG OPERATED IN THE THIRTIES

Beauvais 1930

SCIENCE AND TECHNOLOGY AT WORK 1919-1939

The creation of the Commonwealth of Nations

When Britain declared war on Germany in 1914 she naturally assumed that all members of the Empire would follow suit—as indeed they did. All the Dominions—Australia, New Zealand, South Africa, Canada—together with India made a vital contribution on battlefields all over the world. Moreover, in 1917 their leaders congregated in London to form an Imperial War Cabinet and thus share in the responsibilities of decision-making. Yet in the very same year they also decided that once peace returned Britain ought to 'recognize the right of the Dominions and India to an adequate voice in foreign policy'. They were asserting their right to act as responsible nations in world affairs. They sent their own representatives to the Peace Conference in Paris; they joined the League of Nations; and when Germany agreed to the terms of the Treaty of Versailles 1919, Australia, New Zealand and South Africa took on the task of governing some of the surrendered German colonies. Clearly, the relationship between Britain and her Dominions was changing. In 1926 Lord Balfour, Chairman of the Imperial Constitutional Conference, described the Dominions in these famous words:

> They are autonomous Communities within the British Empire, equal in status, in no way subordinate one to another in any aspect of their domestic or external affairs, though united by a common allegiance to the Crown, and freely associated as members of the British Commonwealth of Nations.

In 1931 the British parliament passed the Statute of Westminster which formally recognized that Britain and her Dominions enjoyed this equality of status. Now the Dominions were free to pass their own laws and to choose their own way in the world.

Ireland

These important changes were not accomplished in an entirely peaceful atmosphere. The failure of Ireland's Easter Rebellion in 1916 had by no means crushed Irishmen's determination to rid themselves of the British. Sinn Feiners won plenty of support—the people elected 73 of them as M.P.s in 1918 and all of them refused pointblank to take their seats in Westminster. One of them was the first woman ever elected to the House of Commons—the Countess Markiewicz. She and her comrades set up their own *Dail Eireann* (Irish Republic parliament) which the British promptly outlawed. It was a tragic situation. Two rival Irish governments, one in Dublin, the other in Westminster, resorted to guerrilla warfare in order to resolve the issue. Irish republicans fought specially recruited British 'Black and Tan' mercenaries. Atrocities became the order of the day. 'General' Michael Collins led Republican 'flying columns' in attacks on the Black and Tans' barracks. The Tans swept down on Republican villages in their armoured cars, hauled suspects out of bed and shot them on the spot. There seemed no solution to the 'Troubles' other than that of partition and so, in 1920, the Government of Ireland Act divided the country into two separate zones of 'Home Rule'. But this didn't satisfy the Southern Catholics and the fighting continued. When King George V visited Ulster to open the Northern Ireland parliament he urged the Irish 'to pause . . . to forgive and forget'. They paused long enough for the *Irish Free State Act 1922* to give Southern Ireland dominion status. But many remained dissatisfied. De Valera, leader of the Republican groups which demanded a free, united Ireland, condemned Michael Collins for giving in to the British on this point. He supported the illegal IRA (Irish Republican Army) which in 1922 gunned down Collins in County Cork. Another year of bloodshed passed before the Southern Irish found peace as well as freedom from British rule.

India

India also sought a greater measure of self-government, but with far less success. Most Indians expected far more independence than the Government of India Act 1919 gave them. They had made plenty of sacrifices during the war. They suffered six million deaths in the post-war influenza epidemics. Frustration caused a wave of protest in the Punjab and in 1919 culminated in the appalling massacre at Amritsar, where General Dyer's Gurkhas shot down 1,500 Indian civilians. Enraged Indians demanded reprisals against the British but the pacifist Mahatma Gandhi, leader of the Indian Congress Party, urged the people to remain calm. He agreed that Dyer's act was 'grave provocation' but insisted that a policy of *'satyagraha'*—civil disobedience—was a much more effective manner of undermining British power. Gandhi spent many months in jail but on release he remained determined to intensify civil disobedience. One of his most famous protests was his march to Dandi were, in 1930, he defied the salt-tax laws by gathering salt from the seashore. He visited Britain in 1931 where he found immense sympathy among the unemployed Lancashire mill-workers.

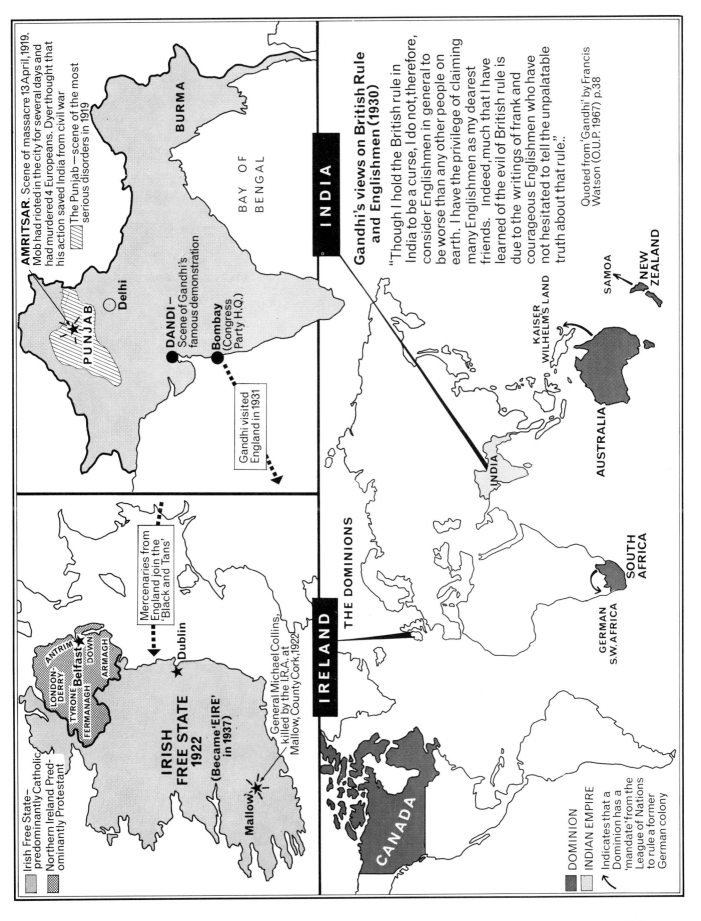

AMRITSAR. Scene of massacre 13 April, 1919. Mob had rioted in the city for several days and had murdered 4 Europeans. Dyer thought that his action saved India from civil war

The Punjab—scene of the most serious disorders in 1919

BURMA

BAY OF BENGAL

Delhi

PUNJAB

DANDI—Scene of Gandhi's famous demonstration

Bombay (Congress Party H.Q.)

Gandhi visited England in 1931

INDIA

Gandhi's views on British Rule and Englishmen (1930)

"Though I hold the British rule in India to be a curse, I do not, therefore, consider Englishmen in general to be worse than any other people on earth. I have the privilege of claiming many Englishmen as my dearest friends. Indeed, much that I have learned of the evil of British rule is due to the writings of frank and courageous Englishmen who have not hesitated to tell the unpalatable truth about that rule..."

Quoted from 'Gandhi' by Francis Watson (O.U.P. 1967) p.38

KAISER WILHELMS LAND

SAMOA

NEW ZEALAND

AUSTRALIA

INDIA

GERMAN S.W. AFRICA

SOUTH AFRICA

THE DOMINIONS

Irish Free State— predominantly Catholic

Northern Ireland Predominantly Protestant

Mercenaries from England join the 'Black and Tans'

ANTRIM

LONDONDERRY

TYRONE

DOWN

FERMANAGH

ARMAGH

Belfast

Dublin

IRISH FREE STATE 1922

(Became 'EIRE' in 1937)

General Michael Collins, killed by the I.R.A. at Mallow, County Cork, 1922

Mallow

IRELAND

CANADA

DOMINION

INDIAN EMPIRE

Indicates that a Dominion has a 'mandate' from the League of Nations to rule a former German colony

51: Politics and people, 1918–1939

The parliamentary parties

Throughout these twenty years, all the major political parties tried to control the nation's economy so that the British people might enjoy a higher standard of living. Unfortunately, British Prime Ministers could exercise very little influence over world economic trends. Lloyd George failed to provide his home fit for heroes; and once the Conservatives withdrew their support from his government in 1922 he and the Liberals crashed from power. In 1924 the Labour government led by Ramsay MacDonald did not even last the year. Baldwin's Conservatives survived a full term of office (1924–9); but although they enfranchised all women over 21 in 1928 this 'flapper vote' did not win the election for them. MacDonald had a second chance to provide the nation with an effective Labour government—but the disastrous Wall Street Crash of 1929 robbed him of any chance of success. Eventually, in 1931, he joined forces with Baldwin to form the National Government—and when his health failed in 1935 it seemed perfectly natural that Baldwin should assume the office of Prime Minister. National government was popular with the people—they voted it in twice in 1931 and 1935. The nation was in effect a 'one party state'; it recognized that it faced a serious financial crisis and was willing to sink its party differences so that a united Parliament might provide a steadying element in times of stress and potential violence. Yet at no time did the British contemplate violent revolution; extremists, though they won plenty of publicity, secured surprisingly little power.

The Communists

The Communist Party of Great Britain, founded in 1920, remained a small but articulate organization in the years between the wars. It attracted plenty of intellectuals—especially writers and poets outraged by MacDonald's alliance with Baldwin. Communists also made converts in South Wales and on Clydeside but failed in their bid for national support. One reason was that their movement was subordinate to the will of the Soviet Union. Their newspaper, the *Daily Worker* (nowadays called the *Morning Star*), was a slave to the *party line* as dictated by Moscow. It was more often satirized than read.

The Fascists

Even noisier than the Communists was the British Union of Fascists. Led by a former member of the Labour Party, Sir Oswald Mosley, the Fascists offered a dynamic leadership to a markedly unenthusiastic British people. Mosley took control of a motley collection of Fascist groups—some of which dated back to the early Twenties—and soon his regiments of blackshirted, jackbooted followers became a familiar sight on the cinema newsreels. He adopted Mussolini's showmanship and Hitler's rhetoric and exploited racial prejudice in order to stir up passion and hatred. His mass meetings, such as the famous 1934 Olympia Rally, were very effective, and his marches attracted plenty of extroverts who loved to parade in their uniforms. In 1936 Mosley organized a mass march into London's East End, home of a large Jewish community. While the police tried to clear a path for the demonstrators, the Communists, in a carefully planned counter-demonstration, whipped up feeling among the local residents. Soon a running battle between the police and the civil population was in full swing, an event unique in London's history between the wars. This was the so-called 'Battle of Cable Street', remarkable in that the two rival factions, Communists, socialists and Jews *versus* the Fascists, never came to blows!

Pacifism, law and order

There was very little support for this kind of political violence and the British people whole-heartedly supported the government's counter-measures. It banned the sale of seditious literature and prohibited the wearing of military-style uniforms by political organizations. Some of the bigger political groups concerned themselves with entirely peaceful objectives. One was Canon Dick Sheppard's Peace Pledge Union, founded in 1935. Members had to sign a pledge renouncing war as a means of settling international disputes and by 1937 more than 130,000 people had taken the 'Peace Pledge'. On all fronts it was a time of lively political activity—and yet most people simply were not interested. Instead, they absorbed themselves in the affairs of the Royal Family. 1936 was the year of the three kings. George V died; Edward VIII abdicated in order to marry Mrs. Simpson; George VI became king in his place. His coronation took place on 12 May 1937. That evening he spoke on the BBC to the peoples of the British Commonwealth of Nations: 'Some of you will travel from one part of the Commonwealth to another and . . . help in the cause of peace. . . .' Prophetic words; millions journeyed to many parts of the Commonwealth between 1939 and 1945, but not in the cause of peace. Britain and her people were a mere two years away from the Second World War.

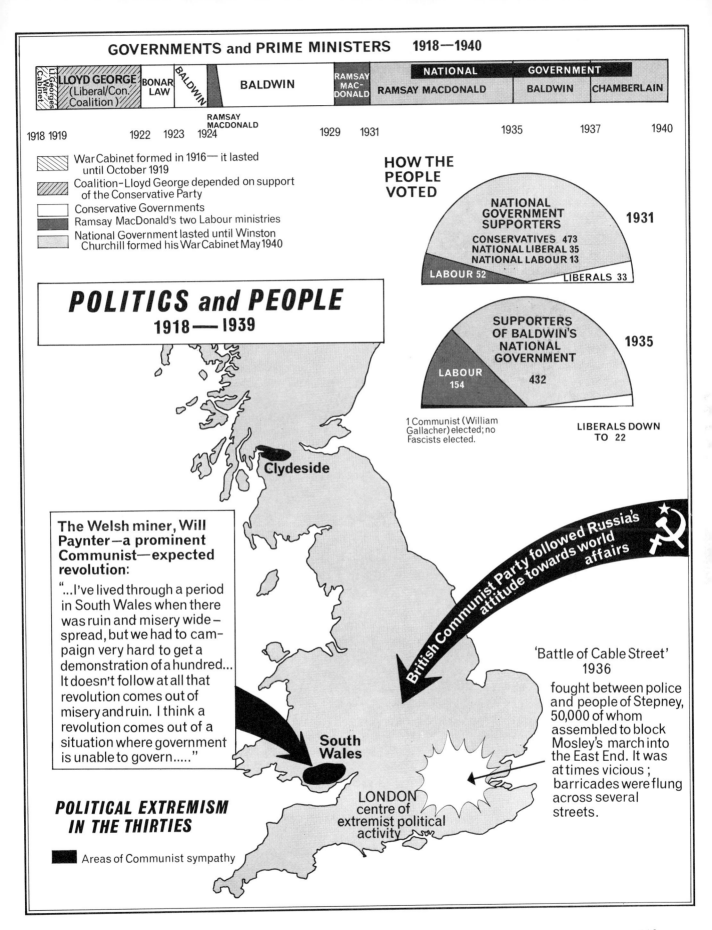

GOVERNMENTS and PRIME MINISTERS 1918—1940

Ll.George's War Cabinet	LLOYD GEORGE (Liberal/Con. Coalition)	BONAR LAW	BALDWIN	BALDWIN	RAMSAY MAC-DONALD	NATIONAL GOVERNMENT		
						RAMSAY MACDONALD	BALDWIN	CHAMBERLAIN

RAMSAY MACDONALD

1918 1919   1922 1923 1924   1929 1931   1935   1937   1940

- War Cabinet formed in 1916 — it lasted until October 1919
- Coalition-Lloyd George depended on support of the Conservative Party
- Conservative Governments
- Ramsay MacDonald's two Labour ministries
- National Government lasted until Winston Churchill formed his War Cabinet May 1940

POLITICS and PEOPLE
1918 — 1939

HOW THE PEOPLE VOTED

NATIONAL GOVERNMENT SUPPORTERS 1931
CONSERVATIVES 473
NATIONAL LIBERAL 35
NATIONAL LABOUR 13
LABOUR 52
LIBERALS 33

SUPPORTERS OF BALDWIN'S NATIONAL GOVERNMENT 1935
LABOUR 154
432

1 Communist (William Gallacher) elected; no Fascists elected.

LIBERALS DOWN TO 22

Clydeside

The Welsh miner, Will Paynter—a prominent Communist—expected revolution:

"...I've lived through a period in South Wales when there was ruin and misery wide-spread, but we had to campaign very hard to get a demonstration of a hundred... It doesn't follow at all that revolution comes out of misery and ruin. I think a revolution comes out of a situation where government is unable to govern....."

British Communist Party followed Russia's attitude towards world affairs

'Battle of Cable Street' 1936

fought between police and people of Stepney, 50,000 of whom assembled to block Mosley's march into the East End. It was at times vicious; barricades were flung across several streets.

South Wales

LONDON centre of extremist political activity

POLITICAL EXTREMISM IN THE THIRTIES

Areas of Communist sympathy

52: Rearmament

The threat from the dictators

It was crystal clear during the Thirties that the League of Nations was no longer any guarantee of international peace. Japan had flouted the League's authority in 1931 when she occupied and absorbed Manchuria. Mussolini successfully defied the League when he invaded defenceless Abyssinia during 1935. Then in 1936 the League did its best to ignore the embarrassing fact that Russia, Germany and Italy were all sending aid to the rival factions fighting the Spanish Civil War. To add to a sense of impending doom, the International Disarmament Conference broke up at Geneva during 1934, the same year in which Adolf Hitler declared himself *Führer* of the German people. He castigated the 1919 Versailles Treaty; poured contempt on the antics of the League of Nations; and spoke ominously of securing *lebensraum* (living-space) in Europe. It was in this uneasy atmosphere that Ramsay MacDonald, for years an ardent pacifist, reluctantly authorized limited rearmament just before he retired in 1935.

'The bomber will always get through'

Stanley Baldwin, Prime Minister again from 1935 to 1937, had no illusions about modern warfare. In 1932 he warned the man in the street that 'there is no power on earth that can prevent him from being bombed. Whatever people may tell him, the bomber will always get through. The only defence is in offence. . . .' He was uttering some of history's oldest advice: if you wish to have peace you must first prepare for war. Very few people wanted to listen to this kind of advice and it was with great reluctance that Parliament authorized spending £186 million on armaments during 1936–7. Indeed Britain was fortunate that many able scientists and engineers, working for private concerns, had progressed so far in research on new offensive and defensive weapons. Some were anxious to prove that fast fighters, armed with up to eight machine-guns, could shoot down enemy raiders before they reached Britain's coastline. The Air Ministry was already impressed by British victories in the International Schneider Trophy air races held during 1927 and 1929 and had invited aircraft manufacturers to build military versions of the high speed seaplanes used to create the new world records. Sydney Camm, chief engineer of the Hawker Aircraft Company, designed the *Hurricane* which first flew at Kingston in 1935. Another brilliant designer, Reginald Mitchell, created the *Spitfire* for the Supermarine Company and the prototype flew at Eastleigh in 1936. Meanwhile, Robert Watson-Watt had despatched an important report to the Air Ministry in 1935. He was the superintendent of the Radio Research Station at Slough and the title of his report was 'Detection and Location of Aircraft by Radio Methods'. His idea was that if enemy aircraft could be located fifty miles beyond the English coast, our fighters could be directed into the best fighting position to await the raiders. This idea was the beginning of radar—one of Britain's most important systems of defence. Soon the tall towers of the radar chain sprouted first at the research stations of Orfordness and Bawdsey and then appeared along much of the east and south coasts. Backing up this complex systems of radar and R.A.F. fighters were the anti-aircraft guns as well as over a thousand look-out posts manned by the Observer Corps.

The Army and Navy

There was no shortage of recruits for the Regular and Territorial Armies—unemployment was the main reason for this. A few new weapons, notably the Bren light machine gun, gave the infantry regiments more hitting power; but in general the infantryman depended on his tried and proven Lee-Enfield rifle. He sometimes travelled in armoured carriers but more often than not in soft-skinned army lorries. Tanks varied in quality—the fast *Cruiser* tanks had a good 2 pounder gun but very thin armour while the big 'I' (Infantry support) tanks had armour plating 70mm thick and were equal in their day to any tank in the world. The most damning criticism of the British army in the Thirties was that very few of its generals had much understanding of the use of all this modern equipment. Lots of cavalry officers looked on the tank as an armoured horse and ignored the advice of brilliant tank-strategists such as Basil Liddell-Hart; he urged that tanks should act as the spearhead of attack in conjunction with air support. He deplored their use in a static role. In contrast, the Royal Navy was well-equipped and well-trained for the sea-battles it *expected* to fight. It had *HMS Hood*, the fastest, most powerful battlecruiser afloat; it had the new heavily armed battleships *HMS Rodney* and *HMS Nelson*. It had submarines, aircraft carriers and scores of escort vessels. The Navy was quite confident of its ability to keep open vital sea-lanes in the event of another major war.

THE NEED TO RE-ARM

The first 'Hurricane'
K 5083 flew in prototype
form on 6 November, 1935

RADAR SCREEN

EIRE

Orfordness
Bawdsey
Slough
Eastleigh   Kingston

HOLLAND

BELGIUM

HITLER'S GERMANY
**Britain's likely
foe**

An early 'I' tank — the 'Matilda' Mark 1
It was slow but very heavily armoured.
This example is armed with
a heavy machine gun

**FRANCE —
Britain's main
ally**

**FASCIST ITALY —
a possible enemy
of Britain**

SPANISH
CIVIL
WAR
1936-1939

A German Messerschmitt Me 109 B (1937)
fighting on General Franco's side in
the Condor Legion, the name given
to the German force in Spain

53: Crisis and war, 1938–1939

Appeasement

In 1938 Hitler's troops marched into Austria and completed the 'Anschluss' or union between that country and Nazi Germany. Though such a move was contrary to the terms of the Treaty of Versailles, nobody was willing to risk a war by imposing the terms of an obsolete and apparently unjust international arrangement. But in September 1938 it was clear that Hitler intended to press his demands for *lebensraum* on Czechoslovakia where several million Germans were living in the Sudetenland. Neville Chamberlain, Prime Minister of Britain since 1937, considered it his duty to maintain and preserve the peace of Europe by appeasing the reasonable demands made by the German Führer. This made him feel obliged to take the initiative in this matter; if he did not, there was the very real risk that France and possibly the Soviet Union might declare war on Germany in order to preserve Czech independence. This was why Chamberlain flew to Germany on three occasions to seek an understanding with Hitler. The first visit was to Berchtesgaden, where Hitler promised not to make any military moves until Chamberlain had arranged a deal with Dr. Beněs, the Czech Premier. A week later, Chamberlain flew to Godesberg and here he offered Hitler a number of proposals acceptable to the Czechs. To his horror, Hitler rejected the lot and said that he would be forced to settle the issue by 1 October 1938. Chamberlain was quite sure that this meant war.

Air raid precautions in Britain

As early as 1935 the Home Office had made plans for specific air raid precautions to be taken in the event of an emergency; in 1937 Parliament passed the *Air Raid Precautions Act* which compelled local authorities to shoulder responsibility for the safety of the civilian population. Now, after Chamberlain's unsuccessful mission to Godesberg, a state of war seemed imminent. Therefore all the ARP arrangements came into effect. Thousands of volunteers offered their services as wardens, ambulancemen, rescue workers and fire-fighters. Unemployed found plenty of jobs filling sandbags and digging slit trenches. On the coast the radar chain went over to a 24 hour watch. High above London, squadrons of *Hurricanes* and *Spitfires* maintained their patrols and a few barrage balloons swaying in the wind gave the people a sense of security. Everybody bought sticky-paper to protect their windows from bomb-blast; hoarded a few tins of corned beef and salmon in case of food shortages and stocked up on torch batteries. Thirty-eight million people received their gasmasks, though the government regretted that it had not had time to design suitable masks for babies. Small structures, reminiscent of bird-tables, appeared in many towns; apparently the paint on them would change colour in the event of a gas attack. Policemen and wardens would pedal their bicycles furiously around the district, blowing their whistles, when this happened. Everyone assumed that war was likely to break out on 1 October 1938—Hitler's deadline. Everyone fervently agreed with the Prime Minister when on 27 September 1938 he spoke to the nation over the radio:

> How horrible, fantastic, incredible it is that we should be digging trenches and trying on gasmasks here because of a quarrel in a faraway country between people of whom we know nothing. . . .

Munich

Next day a miracle occurred. In the midst of a gloomy speech to the House of Commons, Chamberlain received a message from Hitler. He would meet Chamberlain in one last attempt to preserve the peace of Europe. Almost to a man, the members rose to cheer the Prime Minister on his way. Chamberlain flew to Munich and on 30 September he appeased the Führer by handing over to him Czechoslovakia's Sudetenland. On the next day, Chamberlain returned to receive a hero's welcome. After all, surely the sacrifice of Czechoslovakia was a small price to pay for international peace? Chamberlain was certain that it *was* peace. When he managed to force his way through the cheering crowds to Downing Street he came out on the balcony and said:

> I believe it is peace for our time . . .

War

In less than a year Hitler had broken all his promises to Chamberlain. He occupied Bohemia and Moravia in March 1939 and thus completed the destruction of Czechoslovakia. Then he took Memel. After clamouring for Danzig during the summer of 1939, Hitler ordered the unprovoked attack upon Poland, a country whose safety Britain had chosen to guarantee. Chamberlain sent Hitler desperate appeals to call off the blitzkrieg. Eventually, he sent the Führer an ultimatum: give an assurance by 11.00 hours on Sunday 3 September 1939 that German troops will withdraw from Poland. At 11.15 Neville Chamberlain spoke on the BBC to a tense but resigned, British people:

> I have to tell you now that no such undertaking has been received and consequently this country is at war with Germany.

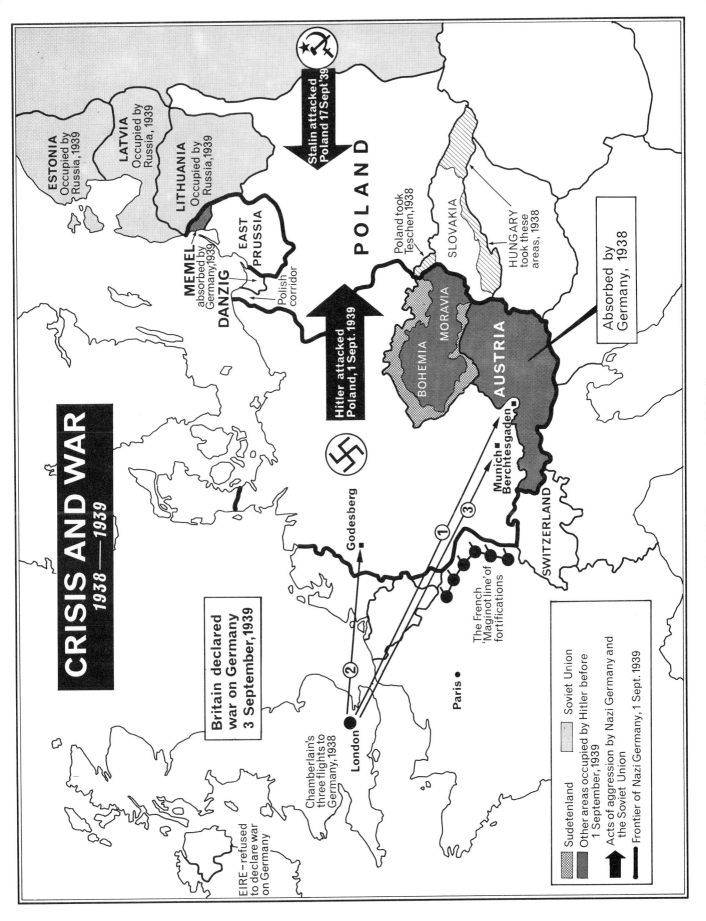

CRISIS AND WAR
1938 — 1939

Britain declared war on Germany 3 September, 1939

EIRE – refused to declare war on Germany

Chamberlain's three flights to Germany, 1938

Paris •

London

Godesberg

The French 'Maginot line' of fortifications

SWITZERLAND

Munich ■
Berchtesgaden ■

Absorbed by Germany, 1938

AUSTRIA

BOHEMIA

MORAVIA

SLOVAKIA

Hitler attacked Poland, 1 Sept. 1939

DANZIG

MEMEL
absorbed by Germany,1939

EAST PRUSSIA

Polish corridor

Stalin attacked Poland 17 Sept '39

POLAND

ESTONIA
Occupied by Russia, 1939

LATVIA
Occupied by Russia, 1939

LITHUANIA
Occupied by Russia, 1939

Poland took Teschen,1938

HUNGARY took these areas, 1938

Sudetenland

Other areas occupied by Hitler before 1 September, 1939

Soviet Union

Acts of aggression by Nazi Germany and the Soviet Union

Frontier of Nazi Germany, 1 Sept. 1939

Part 6 – 'The Lost Peace' 1919–1939

Spread

47. *The General Strike***	R. J. Cootes	Longmans
48. *BBC Scrapbook 1918–1939***	Leslie Baily	
49. *BBC Scrapbook 1918–1939***	Leslie Baily	
50. *Gandhi***	Francis Watson	OUP
51. *The Fascists in Britain***	Colin Cross	Bannie and Rockcliffe
52. *Hurricane Story***	Paul Gallico	Michael Joseph
53. *Map History of the Modern World***	B. A. Catchpole	HEB

**Especially useful for project and topic work

PART 7

The Second World War 1939–1945

During these years the British people had to fight for their very existence. They went to war to stop Hitler's aggression in Europe and not simply, as Prime Minister Chamberlain had told the Germans the day after was began, 'to protect the free and independent State of Poland which this country is in honour bound to defend'.*

There would be 60,000 civilian casualties in Britain as a result of bomber raids and missile attacks. In the unending Battle of the Atlantic and elsewhere 35,000 merchant seamen would die. And on the battlefields of Burma, Libya, Italy, France, Holland, Germany, on every ocean and in the skies 300,000 servicemen would be killed in action. This was to be a war of complex weapons: of 'hedgehogs' versus 'schnorkel' submarines; of bazookas against huge armoured Tiger tanks; of V2s, rocket guns and doodle-bugs—though 'none had a more dominating influence than the heavy bomber'.†

Above all, it was to be a people's war; and the people had a simple war aim. It involved the destruction of Adolf Hitler and all he stood for. There can be no doubt that they achieved this aim. On the very last page of his *English History 1914–1945*, the historian A. J. P. Taylor has written:

No English soldier who rode with the tanks into liberated Belgium or saw the German murder camps at Dachau or Buchenwald could doubt that the war had been a noble crusade. The British were the only people who went through both wars from beginning to end. Yet they remained a peaceful and civilised people, tolerant, patient and generous. Traditional values lost much of their force. Other values took their place. Imperial greatness was on the way out; the welfare state was on the way in. The British Empire declined; the condition of the people improved. Few now sang *Land of Hope and Glory*. Few even sang *England Arise*. England had arisen all the same‡

*The Prime Minister's Broadcast Talk to the German People on 4 September 1939. No. 144 of *Documents Concerning German-Polish Relations and the Outbreak of Hostilities Between Great Britain and Germany On September 3 1939* (HMSO 1939).

†p. 266 *World War 1939–1945*, Peter Young (Arthur Barker Ltd 1966).

‡p. 600 *English History 1914–1945*, A. J. P. Taylor (Oxford 1965).

54: Defeat in the west

The 'phoney war' September 1939–April 1940

Shortly after the Prime Minister announced on the radio that Britain was at war with Germany, air raid sirens wailed in many parts of the country. People who had hurried home from church to hear the broadcast nervously took cover as best they could, for there were very few shelters ready at this time. Then nothing happened; and when the BEF sailed to France, nothing happened. All was quiet on the Western Front. Allies and Germans glared at one another from the fortresses of the Maginot and Siegfried Lines—these were the days of the *Sitzkrieg* or 'sit down war'. No British soldier was killed in action until December when Corporal Priday died in a brief patrol clash. Britain, who had gone to war in the defence of Poland, was unable to give that unfortunate country any military aid whatsoever. Under the combined Nazi-Communist assault, Polish resistance ended in October.

U-boats and surface raiders

For the passengers aboard the s.s. *Athenia* the war brought tragedy within a matter of hours. *Unterseeboot* U-30 fired its torpedoes into her side on 3 September. Six weeks later U-47 audaciously entered the Royal Navy's base at Scapa Flow and sank the battleship *Royal Oak*. But in addition to the danger from submarines, there was also the threat from a big surface raider already at sea when war began. This was the *Graf Spee* and in two months she sank several merchantmen in the Indian and Atlantic Oceans. Eventually, three cruisers—*Ajax*, *Achilles* and *Exeter*—caught her off South America and after a running fight forced her into Montevideo Harbour. On 20 December 1939, three miles off shore, the German crew scuttled the *Graf Spee*. Victory news from this 'Battle of the River Plate' boosted British morale and made the first wartime Christmas more tolerable.

The Home Front

As far as the British people were concerned the war began with one of the most extraordinary population movements in their history. Literally millions sought places of safety in remote parts of the country; thousands of children became evacuees and during September swarmed into the country areas where hardpressed billeting officers persuaded householders to accept mothers and babies as well as primary schoolchildren and teenagers. Evacuation of the children was not a great success and many returned home before Christmas. No doubt many would have stayed in the country had there been the expected German air raids. As it was the Luftwaffe carried out a few desultory attacks on the Orkneys and the Firth of Forth but, on Hitler's explicit orders, refrained from bombing British towns. Meanwhile, the RAF bombarded the Germans with leaflets. This was the highly unprofitable 'confetti war' designed to persuade the German people that their Führer was misguided. But despite the absence of air attack, the British were very conscious that they were at war. They dutifully carried their gasmasks to work and school, passed heavily sandbagged buildings on the way and gazed out of windows plastered with protective tape. At night, the compulsory blackout made life extremely hazardous. Car drivers had to fit visors over their headlights and consequently could barely see where they were going. More than a thousand people died on Britain's roads during *December* 1939!

Blitzkrieg!

During the winter Hitler had decided to occupy Denmark and Norway and on 9 April 1940 a meticulously planned and brilliantly executed invasion of both countries began. The Danes put up no resistance but the Norwegians, despite the fact they they were betrayed by Vidkun Quisling—one of their own politicians, fought on with the help of British troops who landed in the north. Then, in the midst of this campaign, Hitler launched his blitzkrieg in the west. Spearheaded by paratroopers, dive-bombers and tanks, the German Wehrmacht advanced into Holland and Belgium. Scorning the massive defences of the Maginot Line, the Germans pushed through the Ardennes and rolled swiftly towards the English Channel. By 24 May 1940 the troops cut off in the north had one escape route left—evacuation through Dunkirk. Here for nine days the Royal Navy and the 'little ships' took off 337,000 troops. Throughout the evacuation, the Luftwaffe bombed the soldiers on the beaches and huge air battles took place above the burning port. Then, while the troops licked their wounds in England, the Wehrmacht finished off France. Now the British faced the threat of invasion and during June and July they prepared their limited defences. Under the leadership of Winston Churchill, Prime Minister since 10 May 1940, they got ready to 'fight on the landing grounds . . . in the fields and in the streets . . .' They would never surrender in the fight which history was to call the Battle of Britain.

Battle of the River Plate, 1939

- Voyage of Graf Spee
- * Graf Spee victim

Montevideo
x Battle 13 Dec 1939
R.Plate

SHETLANDS
ORKNEYS
← Scapa Flow
← Firth of Forth
Neutral EIRE
BRITAIN

NORWAY
Neutral SWEDEN
DENMARK

FINLAND
allied with
Germany against
Russia, 1941
30 Nov. 1939
Leningrad

ESTONIA
LATVIA
LITHUANIA

SOVIET UNION

9 Apr. 1940
10 May 1940
Dunkirk
HOLLAND
BELGIUM
Warsaw
1 Sept 1939
P O L A N D
17 Sept. 1939

BLITZKRIEG !

- German attacks
- Italian attacks
- Russian attacks
- British evacuations
- ooo SIEGFRIED LINE
- ••• MAGINOT LINE
- Trapped French armies

Paris fell 14 May

FRANCE
Neutral SWITZER-LAND
ITALY
CZECHOSLOVAKIA
AUSTRIA
HUNGARY
RUMANIA
YUGOSLAVIA

Point reached by
German troops when
France surrendered

Neutral SPAIN
Nice
20 June 1940

'OPERATION DYNAMO' ——— DUNKIRK 1940

**Said a crewman from the Gipsy King
(a pleasure boat from Deal):—**

'We went to Dunkirk on May 28th.
We stayed there about 48 hours.
We were under shellfire and
machine-gun fire. We stayed
there until every British soldier
was off the beach.....'

Quoted from Purnell's 'History of
the Second World War', p 244

A thousand ships
saved 337,000 troops

Final defence
perimeter

Embarkation point

Calais

Dunkirk

German
tank attacks

Boulogne

Area held by
Allied troops
at start of
evacuation

55: The Battle of Britain, 1940

Preparation

Throughout June and July 'the Dunkirk spirit' was very much in evidence among the British people. They accepted the food rationing, the tight security and travel restrictions. Everyone expected the Germans to land along the south coast where the main British and Commonwealth defence forces collected. Having lost so much equipment in France, they assembled a motley collection of weapons—some dating back to the late nineteenth century! Local Defence Volunteers (later called the Home Guard) helped out the Army by guarding railway lines and patrolling lonely roads. The RAF had 45 squadrons of *Hurricanes* and *Spitfires* ready for combat by the beginning of July, while the factories were turning out nearly 500 new fighters a month. Across the Channel, the Germans prepared to wrest air supremacy from the British; once they had done this they could attack. Hitler certainly intended to attack. His order, *Preparations for a landing operation against England* (dated 16 July 1940) stated clearly:

> As England, despite her hopeless military situation, still shows no sign of willingness to come to terms, I have decided to prepare, and if necessary to carry out, a landing operation against her. The aim... is to eliminate the motherland of England as a base from which war against Germany can be continued and, if necessary, to occupy the country completely....

Accordingly, Field-Marshal Göring, head of the Luftwaffe, prepared his three *Luftflotten* or Air Fleets for the Battle of Britain.

Stage 1 10 July–7 August 1940

At first the *Luftwaffe* attacked coastal convoys together with a few carefully chosen inland targets. At night, *Heinkel He 111s* dropped mines in river estuaries while other small formations bombed the cities. These tactics brought the Germans very little benefit. They lost 270 planes and many skilled aircrew. Apart from pilots, the RAF could easily make up its initial losses.

Stage II 8 August–23 August 1940

In an effort to destroy the RAF's fighter strength, the Germans now stepped up their bombing attacks. Their first big raid came on *Adlertag*—Eagle Day—when the Luftwaffe flew 1485 sorties against Britain's airfields. Two days later, on 15 August, the three *Luftflotten* made a concerted attack and enjoyed a fair amount of success. In the afternoon, for example, their bombers put Manston and Martlesham Heath out of action. But they still failed to inflict heavy casualties on the RAF. On 18 August they tried another mass raid but again the Germans lost far more planes than they had expected. On these three days, the Germans lost 191 aircraft.

Stage III 24 August–6 September 1940

Both sides needed a respite in order to patch up their depleted forces and to wait for the overcast weather to disperse. On 25 August, the German bombers began heading for military targets on the Thames; but they bombed the City of London in error. For the next week, the air fighting went on at a desperate level and on 1 September RAF losses exceeded those of the Germans. This was the danger point in the battle. If the Germans maintained their tactics they had a chance of winning the battle of attrition. Inexperienced RAF pilots, fresh from the Flying Schools, had little chance against a swarm of *Me 109s;* while on the ground factories and airfields alike were suffering severely from the incessant enemy bombardment.

Stage IV 7–30 September 1940

Firmly believing that invasion was 'imminent', Fighter Command committed all its fighter strength to the battles in the south. When a huge formation of 'bandits' crossed the English coast on 8 September, many people believed that this was the end. Villages rang their church bells (the invasion signal) and the Home Guard moved to action stations. But it was a false alarm. A week later, the Germans tried another huge raid. On 15 September (nowadays called 'Battle of Britain Day') RAF fighters met and broke up the entire German attack and claimed to have shot down 185 of the enemy. In fact German losses were 60 aircraft that day—enough to persuade Hitler that Göring's tactics were far from sound. Hitler decided that the *Luftwaffe* must revert to the original objective of destroying the RAF—and at night to concentrate on the bombing of London. It was an admission of failure. For three months the *Luftwaffe* had battered the British with high explosive and incendiary bombs, shot down or damaged two thousand British fighters and killed or wounded 738 pilots. But by day the RAF had proved itself invincible—even though it was ill-equipped for combat at night. Therefore, Hitler decided to bomb under cover of darkness and so the British people had to steel themselves for the ordeal of the winter blitz 1940–41.

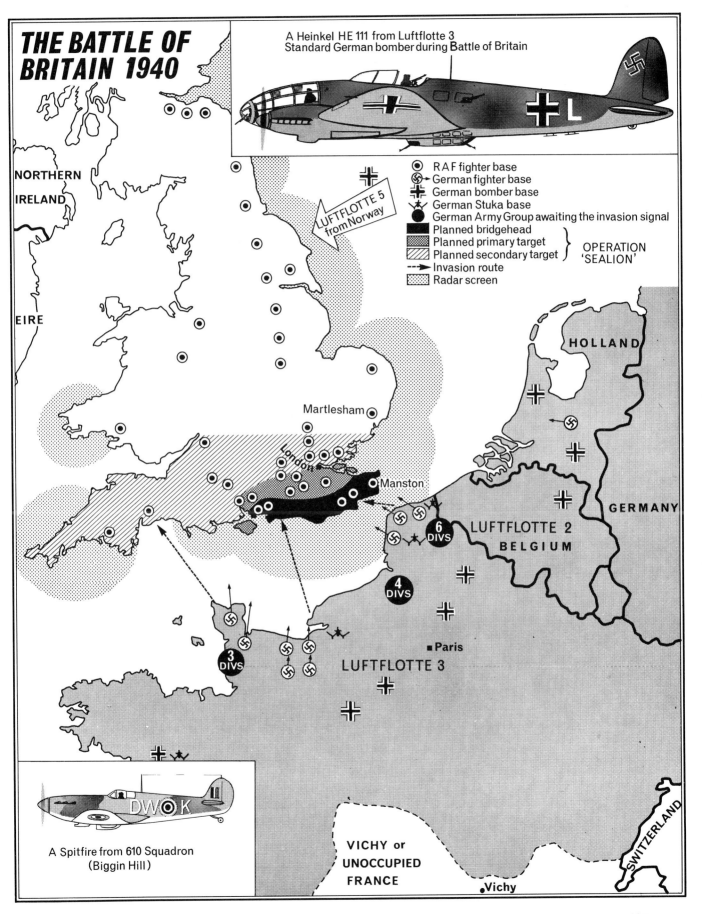

THE BATTLE OF BRITAIN 1940

A Heinkel HE 111 from Luftflotte 3
Standard German bomber during Battle of Britain

◉ R.A.F. fighter base
⊛ German fighter base
✠ German bomber base
✹ German Stuka base
● German Army Group awaiting the invasion signal
■ Planned bridgehead
▨ Planned primary target ⎫
▨ Planned secondary target ⎬ OPERATION 'SEALION'
--→ Invasion route ⎭
▨ Radar screen

NORTHERN
IRELAND

EIRE

LUFTFLOTTE 5
from Norway

Martlesham

London

Manston

HOLLAND

GERMANY

LUFTFLOTTE 2

BELGIUM

6 DIVS

4 DIVS

3 DIVS

■ Paris

LUFTFLOTTE 3

SWITZERLAND

A Spitfire from 610 Squadron
(Biggin Hill)

DW⊙K

VICHY or
UNOCCUPIED
FRANCE

•Vichy

123

56: The bomber's war

Blitz on Britain

From September 1940 onwards, more and more *Dornier*, *Junkers* and *Heinkel* bombers droned over the British coasts under cover of darkness. In their bomb-bays they carried high-explosive bombs, canisters of incendiaries and sometimes the dreaded 'oil-bombs' and parachute mines—the blast from these 'land-mines' could demolish a street of houses. By this time more than two million British families had the protection of an Anderson shelter, a small, corrugated steel structure set into the earth and covered with soil. Because they were secure from anything besides a direct hit, many families used them as bedrooms during the long winter and early spring of 1940–1. Later on, some families used indoor Morrison shelters—steel boxes providing cramped but effective cover. In London, many people had to use the big communal shelters or seek safety down the Tubes. The Tubes were deep but not necessarily safe, owing to the fact that they ran below the sewers and water mains. Direct hits on Marble Arch, Balham and Bank caused some terrible casualties. One of the most remarkable features of the blitz was that it engendered a communal spirit in many people—perhaps for the only time in their lives. People were kind and generous to one another for the simple reason that all were sharing in the same adversity. By the beginning of 1941, 1.5 million people had joined the various voluntary services in addition to a similar number of men already in the Home Guard. Civil Defence services included wardens, rescue teams, stretcher bearers, ambulance workers, police specials and the Auxiliary Fire Service—plus legions of fire-watchers and the indomitable ladies of the Women's Voluntary Service.

The pattern of German attack

Shortly after the blitz began, the *Luftwaffe* perfected a pathfinder force to set fire to the target so that the flames acted as a guide to the main bomber force. On 14 November 1940, Coventry received the first of these systematic raids. For ten hours the *Luftwaffe* showered their target with bombs, destroying the city centre, the cathedral and about a third of the houses. This was 'Coventration'—a form of attack which many cities would soon suffer. At first the Germans tended to concentrate on the main ports, especially those receiving ships coming in from the North Atlantic convoys. Belfast, Bristol, Clydeside and Manchester all had several attacks; the attack on Merseyside lasted eight nights during May 1941 and here civilian morale declined alarmingly. 2000 people died while the docks suffered

very heavy damage. By the spring, most towns experienced air raids as Hitler made one final attempt to inflict injury on the British people before launching his attack on the Soviet Union in June 1941. At the end of it all, one lesson stood out: the blitz hadn't managed to destroy either Britain's morale or her war production. Despite this, Churchill had already decided that Britain must repay Germany with interest. He authorised the creation of a huge bomber force to bring the horrors of war home to the German people.

Bomber Command

Air Marshal Harris became Chief of RAF Bomber Command in February 1942. He immediately began working on his plans to launch a thousand-bomber raid against a single German city. By 30 May he was ready; 1046 RAF bombers took off for Cologne and 910 of these found their way to the target. Here Harris killed 469 civilians for the loss of 39 of his aircrews; he didn't destroy Cologne or its war production. Indeed, it was virtually impossible to destroy any large industrial complex with high-explosive. It was much more likely that air attack would kill large numbers of war-workers. Nevertheless, 'Bomber' Harris persevered and for the rest of the war he subjected the Germans to ever increasing attacks from four-engined bombers such as the *Halifax* and *Lancaster*.

The Americans in Britain

On 7 December 1941 the Japanese made their unprovoked air attack on the American base of Pearl Harbor. Hitler chose to side with the Japanese and very unwisely declared war on the United States. Now the war was truly global. President Roosevelt decided to carry the fighting to Germany by establishing in England the Eighth United States Army Air Force, equipped with four-engined *B.17 Fortresses* and *B.24 Liberators*. So, during 1942–3, East Anglia became the scene of a massive airfield construction programme. Whole farms disappeared under the concrete runways, Nissen huts and control towers seemed to mushroom overnight. Noisy jeeps and command cars hurtled down the country lanes. East Anglians speedily acquainted themselves with the American way of life and made the airmen welcome. Once the Americans had settled in they began their hair-raising daylight missions. At first their huge 'box-formations' suffered badly from enemy fighters; but once the escort-fighters (*P.47 Thunderbolts* and *P.51 Mustangs*) arrived, the American bombers brought death and destruction to Germany until the last days of the war.

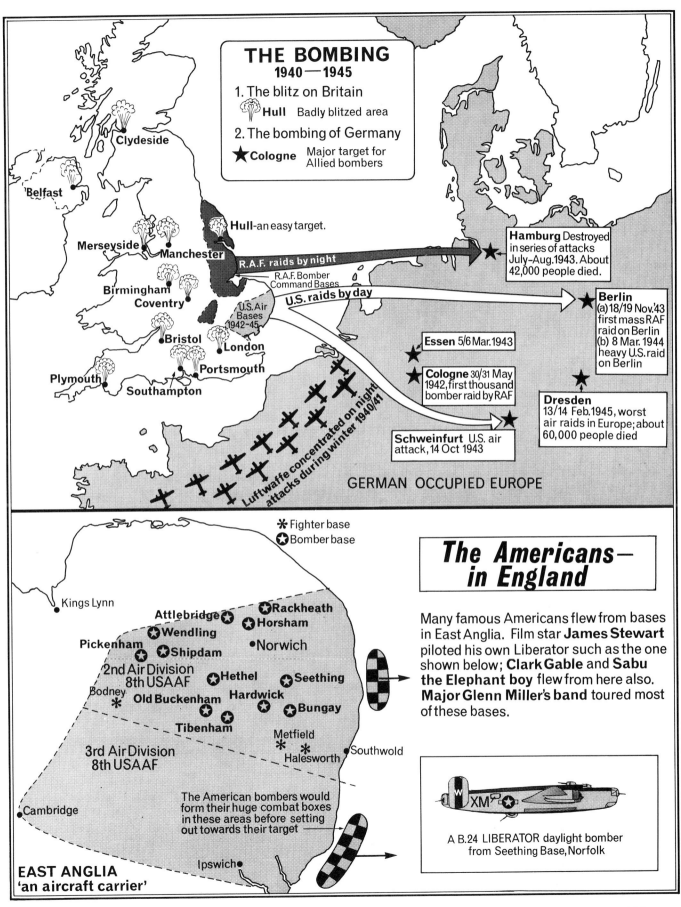

THE BOMBING
1940—1945
1. The blitz on Britain

Hull Badly blitzed area

2. The bombing of Germany

★ **Cologne** Major target for Allied bombers

Clydeside

Belfast

Hull-an easy target.

Merseyside

Manchester

R.A.F. raids by night

R.A.F. Bomber Command Bases

Birmingham
Coventry

U.S. Air Bases 1942-45

U.S. raids by day

Bristol

London

Portsmouth

Plymouth

Southampton

Luftwaffe concentrated on night attacks during winter 1940/41

Hamburg Destroyed in series of attacks July–Aug.1943. About 42,000 people died.

Berlin (a)18/19 Nov.'43 first mass RAF raid on Berlin (b) 8 Mar.1944 heavy U.S. raid on Berlin

Essen 5/6 Mar.1943

Cologne 30/31 May 1942, first thousand bomber raid by RAF

Dresden 13/14 Feb.1945, worst air raids in Europe; about 60,000 people died

Schweinfurt U.S. air attack, 14 Oct 1943

GERMAN OCCUPIED EUROPE

✱ Fighter base
✪ Bomber base

Kings Lynn

Attlebridge **Rackheath**
Wendling **Horsham**
Pickenham **Norwich**
Shipdam

2nd Air Division 8th USAAF
Bodney **Hethel** **Seething**
Old Buckenham **Hardwick**
Bungay
Tibenham

Metfield
3rd Air Division 8th USAAF
Halesworth Southwold

The American bombers would form their huge combat boxes in these areas before setting out towards their target

Cambridge

Ipswich

EAST ANGLIA
'an aircraft carrier'

The Americans— in England

Many famous Americans flew from bases in East Anglia. Film star **James Stewart** piloted his own Liberator such as the one shown below; **Clark Gable** and **Sabu the Elephant boy** flew from here also. **Major Glenn Miller's band** toured most of these bases.

A B.24 LIBERATOR daylight bomber from Seething Base, Norfolk

57: The Battle of the Atlantic

The convoys

The Battle of the Atlantic lasted 59 months and, in the words of Winston Churchill, was 'the dominating factor all through the war. Never for one moment could we forget that everything else depended on its outcome'. Britain desperately needed foreign food and foreign war material. It all had to come by sea; and no matter from which direction the convoys approached Britain they all eventually had to cross the perilous waters of the North Atlantic. Convoys coming from Canada and the USA had the roughest passage of all. *Liberty* ships laden with ammunition, tankers carrying precious aviation spirit would have to run the gauntlet for fifteen days. The ships' crews, knowing full well that they had little chance of rescue when their ship sank, faced dozens of U-boats organized in 'wolf-packs'. These would choose a moment when the convoy was short of air cover or naval escort and then move in to sink half-a-dozen merchantmen in quick succession. Focke-Wulf *Condors*, big four-engined reconnaissance-bombers, would bomb the surviving ships as they neared British waters. And as they steamed into their destinations they still ran the risk of hitting a magnetic mine. Some might be unlucky enough to meet another kind of enemy—the surface raider. And in May 1941 the most powerful battleship afloat entered the North Atlantic to prey on the convoy routes.

Bismarck

Bismarck, together with her companion the heavy cruiser *Prinz Eugen*, had emerged unscathed from the Baltic and had reached the western side of Iceland before being intercepted by the Royal Navy. The battlecruiser *Hood*, pride of the navy, together with the battleship *Prince of Wales* engaged the two German ships. Almost immediately the *Hood* blew up while the *Prince of Wales* broke off the fight. Then the *Ark Royal's* Swordfish torpedo planes attacked and managed to cripple the *Bismarck's* steering gear. This left her an easy target for the guns of two more battleships which had joined in the fray—

the *Rodney* and the *Duke of York*. Eventually, the *Bismarck* fell victim to the torpedoes of HMS *Dorsetshire*. The huge ship sank on 27 May 1941. *Prinz Eugen* escaped.

Defeating the U-boats

Despite this sort of dramatic—if expensive—success, the Allies barely held their own against the German submarines. Convoys leaving St. Johns or Halifax could count on losing six or seven ships before reaching Britain; while at the time of the Allied invasion of North Africa (November 1942) when escort vessels were in short supply losses were even higher. 1943 saw the climax of the Battle of the Atlantic. During March the U-boats made an all-out attack on the North Atlantic convoys in an effort to prevent the assembly of an invasion force in Britain. Two important convoys suffered numerous torpedo attacks and lost 21 merchant ships. This was a disaster and soon a great battle developed between the U-boats and the escort vessels, now equipped with all sorts of elaborate devices to seek out and destroy the enemy. *Asdic* and *radar* located the submarine; 'hedgehog' and 'squid' bombthrowers surrounded the U-boat with explosive charges. Fast frigates and corvettes waited their chance to ram or gun down a surfacing submarine. It was a grim, merciless struggle and the fortunes of one famous convoy, codenamed ONS-5, represent the turning point in the Battle of the Atlantic during May 1943. As the wolf-packs closed for the kill they found themselves pulverized by relentless escort vessels supported by aircraft. One bomber destroyed *U-630*; 'hedgehogs' sank *U-192* and *U-531*; gunfire accounted for the *U-125*; depth charges finished off *U-438* and *U-638*. From this moment onwards the Allied navies gained the upper hand despite the technical refinements that the Germans built into their submarines. Even with *schnorkel* breathing apparatus for their diesel engines, extra anti-aircraft guns and special 'zig-zag' running torpedoes, they couldn't cope with ever-increasing numbers of superbly equipped planes and ships which maintained a constant watch on the shipping lanes.

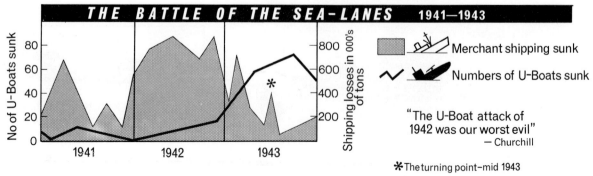

THE BATTLE OF THE SEA-LANES 1941—1943

No of U-Boats sunk

Shipping losses in 000's of tons

Merchant shipping sunk

Numbers of U-Boats sunk

"The U-Boat attack of 1942 was our worst evil"
— Churchill

* The turning point—mid 1943

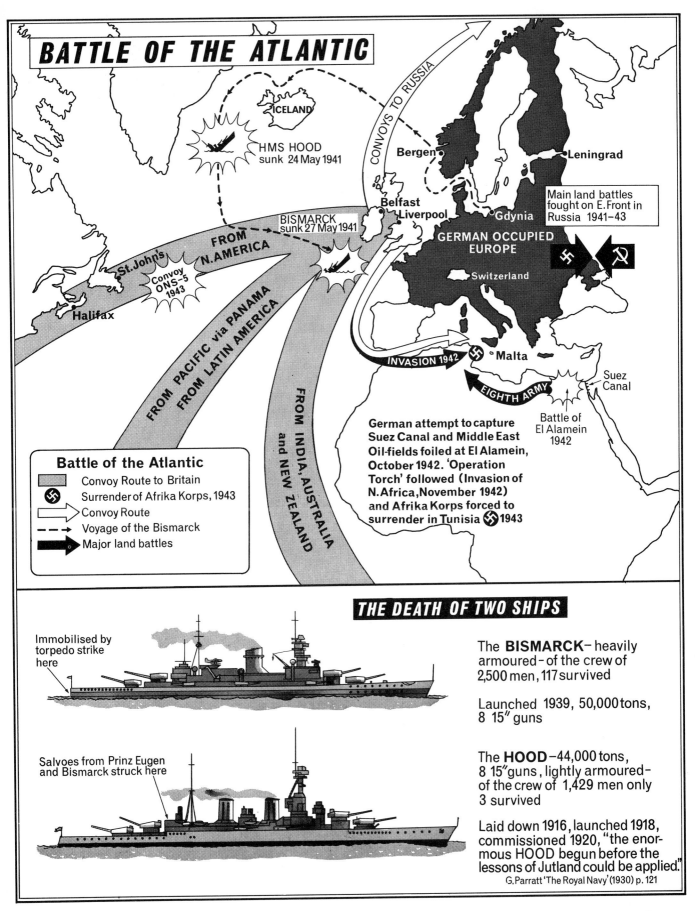

BATTLE OF THE ATLANTIC

CONVOYS TO RUSSIA

ICELAND

HMS HOOD
sunk 24 May 1941

Bergen

Leningrad

Belfast
Liverpool

Gdynia

Main land battles
fought on E.Front in
Russia 1941–43

BISMARCK
sunk 27 May 1941

FROM
N.AMERICA

St.John's

Convoy ONS-5
1943

GERMAN OCCUPIED
EUROPE

Switzerland

Halifax

FROM PACIFIC via PANAMA

FROM LATIN AMERICA

FROM INDIA, AUSTRALIA
and NEW ZEALAND

INVASION 1942

Malta

EIGHTH ARMY

Suez
Canal

Battle of
El Alamein
1942

German attempt to capture
Suez Canal and Middle East
Oil-fields foiled at El Alamein,
October 1942. 'Operation
Torch' followed (Invasion of
N.Africa, November 1942)
and Afrika Korps forced to
surrender in Tunisia 🟢 1943

Battle of the Atlantic

Convoy Route to Britain

🟢 Surrender of Afrika Korps, 1943

➡ Convoy Route

╌╌➤ Voyage of the Bismarck

➡ Major land battles

THE DEATH OF TWO SHIPS

Immobilised by
torpedo strike
here

Salvoes from Prinz Eugen
and Bismarck struck here

The **BISMARCK** – heavily
armoured – of the crew of
2,500 men, 117 survived

Launched 1939, 50,000 tons,
8 15" guns

The **HOOD** – 44,000 tons,
8 15" guns, lightly armoured –
of the crew of 1,429 men only
3 survived

Laid down 1916, launched 1918,
commissioned 1920, "the enormous HOOD begun before the
lessons of Jutland could be applied."
G. Parratt 'The Royal Navy' (1930) p. 121

58: Technology and warfare

Production

By 1943 Churchill's government had fully committed Britain's industrial resources to the task of winning the war against Germany and Japan. These resources had to be supplemented by Lease-Lend material from America—'Put your confidence in us!' cried Churchill in 1942. 'Give us the tools and we will finish the job!' He and his Cabinet, together with the heads of the armed services, decided on general war planning; a Central Statistical Office worked out the manpower and equipment requirements; finally the Ministry of Production organized the supply of goods. In this way Britain became one of the most centralized industrial states ever; she made ruthless use of her resources—far more so than did the 'totalitarian' states of Germany and the Soviet Union. Neither Hitler nor Stalin recruited women for war work as intensively as did the British. For example, without the Women's Land Army wartime agriculture would have failed. Agriculture had been in the doldrums during the Thirties; but after 1940 50% more land came under the plough and 20% more people worked on the farms. Meanwhile, heavy industry, scene of slump and depression during the Thirties, feverishly produced tanks, ships and guns. There was so much overtime going in the North-East that workers there were some of the highest paid in the country. Of course, none of this would have been possible without the consent of the British people. They handed in their aluminium saucepans for scrap, parted with their garden railings and saved newspaper for salvage. In order to save gas and electricity, they solemnly bathed in four inches of tepid water and, obeying the exhortations of that remarkable Food Minister Lord Woolton, dined off potato pie for lunch—and potato scones for tea.

Science and war

Government had also recognized by now the importance of the *boffin*—the World War II scientist. Watson-Watt's radar, for example, had many applications. Night fighters used it to locate bombers; bombers used variations called H2S and *Gee* to locate targets in the dark. Eventually, radar was so important that it became an enemy to outwit. It was found that when aircraft released several tons of 'window' (aluminium foil) this could fool enemy radar operators into thinking that a big concentration of ships was nearby. Throughout the war, British and German scientists worked along remarkably similar lines. Both built tanks that could 'swim' from landing-craft to the beaches; both worked on jet-aircraft, though Frank Whittle's engines tended to be more reliable than those fitted to the remarkable German *Me 262* at the end of the war. In rocketry, however, the Germans had a clear lead and were the first to use supersonic rocket missiles. Both sides managed to produce lots of substitute or *ersätz* materials. They produced tyres from synthetic rubber; parachute lines and glider towing cables from nylon (the first stockings made of this material arrived in Britain with the American troops in 1943); they created electrical insulation from PVC and made widespread use of plastics in ships and aircraft. It is interesting to note that all these new materials were known to scientists before the war—the war provided the impetus for their use. This was equally true of research into atomic fission. British scientists—notably Professor Pierls and Dr. Frisch—did vital work on the atomic bomb during the period 1939–41 but lacked the resources to build the weapon. This was why America took over the project.

D-Day 6 June 1944

The technological superiority of the Allies was never better illustrated than on D-Day 1944 when 'Operation Overland' began the invasion of Europe. Ever since 1941, when Russia had begun to bear the full brunt of the German attack, ill-informed individuals had clamoured for Britain to begin a 'Second Front' in Europe. At that time, the Allies were in no condition to mount an attack on Hitler's European empire. But by 1944 they had achieved air superiority and had collected together an extraordinary range of technical aids. Tugs towed prefabricated 'Mulberry Harbours' to the Normandy beaches—so the invasion troops had an 'instant' port at their disposal. PLUTO (*Pipe Line Under The Ocean*) provided them with petrol supplies; DD tanks swam ashore to give the infantry armoured support; while the British 79th Armoured Division's 'funnies'—bridge-carrying tanks; mine-exploding flails-tanks; 'crocodile' flame-throwers—could deal with almost any obstacle. One which did resist them was the tall, thick hedgerows of the Normandy *bocage*—often concealing a deadly German 88 mm. gun. But an engineer in the U.S. Army invented a Rhinoceros tank equipped with tough steel jaws that could bite a hole in the bocage at fifteen mph and thus clear the way for the troops to break out into the open country beyond the bridgehead.

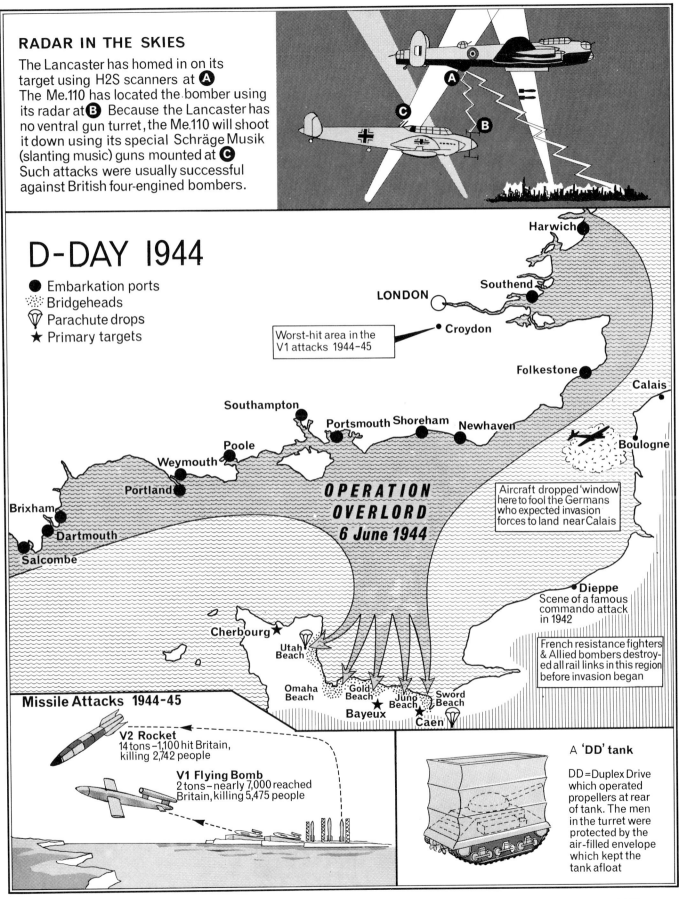

RADAR IN THE SKIES

The Lancaster has homed in on its target using H2S scanners at **A**. The Me.110 has located the bomber using its radar at **B**. Because the Lancaster has no ventral gun turret, the Me.110 will shoot it down using its special Schräge Musik (slanting music) guns mounted at **C**. Such attacks were usually successful against British four-engined bombers.

D-DAY 1944

- ● Embarkation ports
- ░ Bridgeheads
- ⛛ Parachute drops
- ★ Primary targets

Worst-hit area in the V1 attacks 1944–45

Harwich

Southend

LONDON

● Croydon

Folkestone

Calais

Southampton

Portsmouth Shoreham Newhaven

Boulogne

Poole

Weymouth

Aircraft dropped 'window here to fool the Germans who expected invasion forces to land near Calais

Portland

OPERATION OVERLORD 6 June 1944

Brixham

Dartmouth

Salcombe

● **Dieppe** Scene of a famous commando attack in 1942

Cherbourg ★

French resistance fighters & Allied bombers destroyed all rail links in this region before invasion began

Utah Beach

Omaha Beach   Gold Beach   Juno Beach   Sword Beach

Missile Attacks 1944–45

Bayeux   Caen

V2 Rocket 14 tons –1,100 hit Britain, killing 2,742 people

V1 Flying Bomb 2 tons – nearly 7,000 reached Britain, killing 5,475 people

A **'DD' tank**

DD = Duplex Drive which operated propellers at rear of tank. The men in the turret were protected by the air-filled envelope which kept the tank afloat

At no time during the Second World War did the British people lose all faith in the future. No matter what the adversity might be, a sense of humour—epitomised by Tommy Handley's *ITMA* (It's That Man Again) radio show—and a serious belief that Britain must be a better place to live in after the war were present most of the time.

The Beveridge Report 1 December 1942

Sir William Beveridge had the job of conducting a survey into Britain's social insurance schemes and of suggesting some improvements. He was a well-known figure in his day, having appeared with men such as Julian Huxley, Commander Campbell and Professor Joad on the popular BBC Brains Trust programmes. Beveridge published his report shortly after the El Alamein victory which many people hoped marked the turn of the tide in the war against Germany. It was, according to the *Economist*, 'one of the most remarkable state documents ever drafted'. Beveridge preferred to say of it: 'the statement of a reconstruction policy by a nation at war is a statement of the uses to which that nation means to put victory, when victory is achieved.' He wanted to set up a Ministry of Social Security after the war and his report urged the ending of mass unemployment, the provision of a National Health Service for everybody and the payment of family allowances. He proposed to raise the revenue for all this through taxation and flat rate insurance contributions. His report was a best-seller; people certainly wanted the sort of post-war society that Beveridge was describing. However, the government was not so keen. Churchill had previously agreed that, although reconstruction was important, winning the war came first. 'We must be, above all things, careful that nothing diverts or distracts our thoughts and our fullest energies from the task of national self-preservation...' Undoubtedly, Churchill was a great war leader; but people now wondered whether he would be so successful in times of peace.

The 1944 Education Act

This was the government's most important piece of social legislation during the war. By the time it became effective (April 1945), education was in a parlous condition in many parts of the country. Thousands of schoolchildren still suffered from their experiences as 'evacuees'; about 20% of the schools had suffered bomb damage; most had lost their younger members of staff to the armed services. Inevitably, the standard of teaching declined; illiteracy and truancy increased so that many young people left school with serious gaps in their education. R. A. Butler, who introduced the 1944 Act, declared that in future all children would be educated according to their age, aptitudes and abilities. There would be no more fees for secondary education; the school leaving age would go up to 15 in 1947 and to 16 as soon as there were enough teachers and new school buildings. Local Education Authorities must now provide three progressive stages of primary, secondary and further education as well as nursery schools for parents who wanted them. A new Ministry of Education replaced the Board of Education and, in Pamphlet No. 2 (1945), it suggested that secondary education might be divided into a tripartite system of grammar, modern and technical schools—or be offered in 'multilateral' schools. 'In any case free interchange of pupils from one type to another will be made as easy as possible and the decision as to the type of education which was made at the age of about 11 will be reviewed at 13 and even later...' Unfortunately, the system became too rigid for much of this 'interchange'. Most children, after the war, managed to 'fail' the 11 + selection examination; and because of lack of funds and accommodation difficulties they languished in the secondary modern schools which weren't always able to offer them an education that really suited their aptitude and abilities.

Victory in Europe

By the time the Education Act came into force, the war in Europe was drawing to a close. After many setbacks and months of bitter combat, the Western Allies crossed the Rhine and met the Russians who had advanced to the banks of the River Elbe. Already, the Allied leaders had agreed on the post-war division of Europe—in effect the Iron Curtain had already come into existence. So the success of Operation Overlord saved much of Europe from being liberated by the Russians and prevented any hopes that Hitler may have had of holding the Russian threat in the East. On 30 April 1945 the Führer committed suicide. On 4 May General Montgomery received the surrender of German forces in North-Western Europe. Three days later Doenitz, Hitler's successor, formally surrendered at Rheims. On 8 May the British people celebrated *VE Day*—victory in Europe!

Opposite, Farringdon Market, London, after a V2 raid

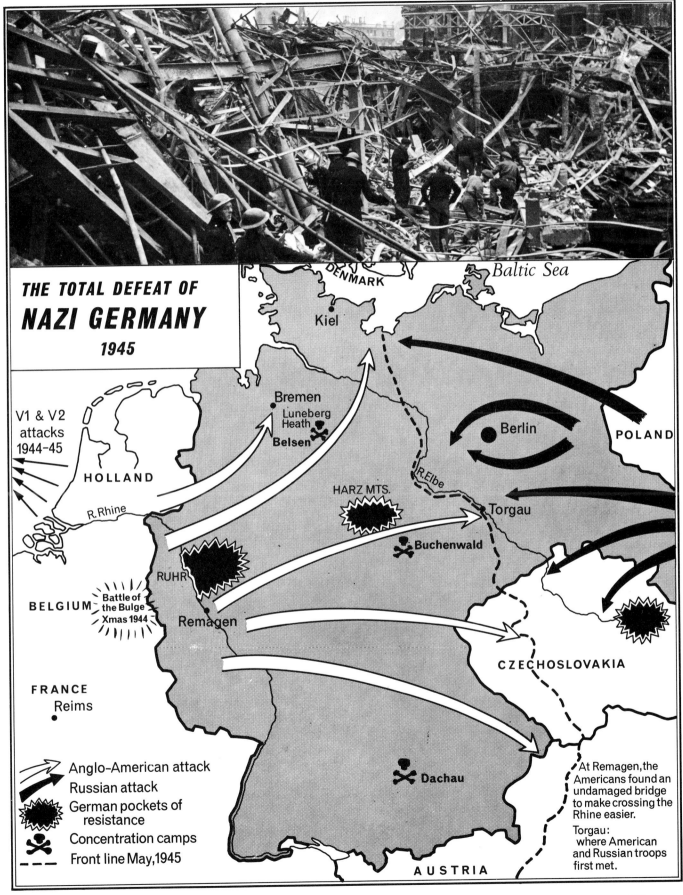

THE TOTAL DEFEAT OF
NAZI GERMANY
1945

Baltic Sea

DENMARK

Kiel

V1 & V2
attacks
1944–45

HOLLAND

R.Rhine

Bremen
Luneberg
Heath
Belsen

Berlin

POLAND

R.Elbe

HARZ MTS.

Torgau

Buchenwald

RUHR

BELGIUM
Battle of
the Bulge
Xmas 1944

Remagen

FRANCE
Reims

CZECHOSLOVAKIA

Anglo-American attack
Russian attack
German pockets of
resistance
Concentration camps
Front line May,1945

Dachau

At Remagen, the
Americans found an
undamaged bridge
to make crossing the
Rhine easier.

Torgau:
where American
and Russian troops
first met.

AUSTRIA

60: The final victory, 1945

The war against Japan

At the end of 1941 Japan struck a series of devastating blows all over the Pacific and the Far East. Pearl Harbor reeled under a surprise attack on 7 December; next day the Japanese invaded Malaya; their bombers sank the two British battleships *Repulse* and *Prince of Wales*. On land, sea and in the air the Japanese reigned supreme, a fact underlined in February 1942 when the biggest British army ever to lay down its arms surrendered at Singapore. By mid-May the situation was desperate; the Japanese had cut the Burma Road to China and threatened to invade British India. Then came the turn of the tide. In the Pacific the Americans began their savage battles against fanatical enemy units defending far-flung coral atolls. In Burma Britain's 'Forgotten Fourteenth Army' repelled the Japanese onslaught in some of the toughest battle conditions in the world. Burma is a land of rivers, mountains, jungles and monsoon rains; more often than not the enemy proved to be malaria or dysentery rather than a Japanese *banzai* charge. Cut off from their main supply bases, the troops became utterly dependent upon regular air-drops. In the words of Lord Mountbatten, Supreme Commander of SEAC (South East Asia Command): '...96% of our supplies to the Fourteenth Army went in by air...315,000 reinforcements were flown in...110,000 casualties were flown out...'—thanks to the skill of the US transport pilots operating in Burma. Under the command of General Slim, the Fourteenth Army held the enemy at bay and then defeated him at the crucial Battle of Kohima (1944). This victory allowed the British and Commonwealth troops to push first to Myitkina and then to Rangoon. By May 1945 they were ready to expel the Japanese from the rest of South East Asia.

The General Election of 1945

Though the war against Japan was still in full swing, millions of British servicemen eagerly looked forward to 'demob-day'. People urgently wanted to get back to normal; the last evacuees trickled back to London and Hull; and there was talk of a general election for the first time in ten long years. Most of the professional politicians anticipated an easy Tory victory. However, the Conservatives' pre-war record in matters such as mass-unemployment, means-test and appeasement had already spelt their doom in the mind of the electorate which, just for a moment in 1945, distrusted the party which stood for capitalism and private enterprise. The people wanted to see a Labour government nationalize the major industries and make Beveridge's Health Scheme a reality. Arranging the election took a long time as 4 million voters were still overseas. Eventually polling day arrived on 5 July 1945 and the long process of collecting votes in—from all over the world—began. Three weeks passed before the results came in—and it was a Labour landslide victory. With 393 seats Labour had an overall majority. On 26 July 1945 Clement Attlee became Prime Minister.

Potsdam Conference

On the very same day the Potsdam Conference called upon the Japanese 'to proclaim now the unconditional surrender of all the Japanese armed forces...The alternative for Japan is prompt and utter destruction...' This conference, held just outside Berlin, had begun as a meeting between Stalin, Harry Truman—the new American President—and Churchill, now replaced by Attlee. Its task was to settle the frontiers of Europe and to bring the war against Japan to a rapid close. One way was to invade Japan, possibly with Russian assistance. Clearly, America would bear the brunt of such an operation and the estimated casualties of up to one million were too high for Truman to consider. Another method was to persuade the Japanese that further resistance was futile—but their failure to respond to the Potsdam Declaration seemed to rule that out. The third way was to give the Japanese people such a shock that they would not have the heart to fight on. And it was here that Truman held a trump card. On the day that the Potsdam Conference opened (16 July) he had heard that an atomic bomb had been successfully tested in Alamagordo, New Mexico.

The atomic bombs

President Truman decided to use the bomb against Japan as a military weapon in order to end the war as quickly as possible. None of the allied leaders disagreed with him. Churchill later said that the question of whether or not to use the bomb was 'never even an issue'. Attlee confirmed this and said that he was not even involved in the decision, as Churchill had already spoken for Britain; 'but if I had been I should have agreed with President Truman...' So on 6 August 1945 the B.29 Superfortress called *Enola Gay* hovered over Hiroshima and released what the Japanese were to call the Pikadon or 'Flash-Boom'. Two days later Russia declared war on Japan. On 9 August another bomb fell on Nagasaki. Japan surrendered.

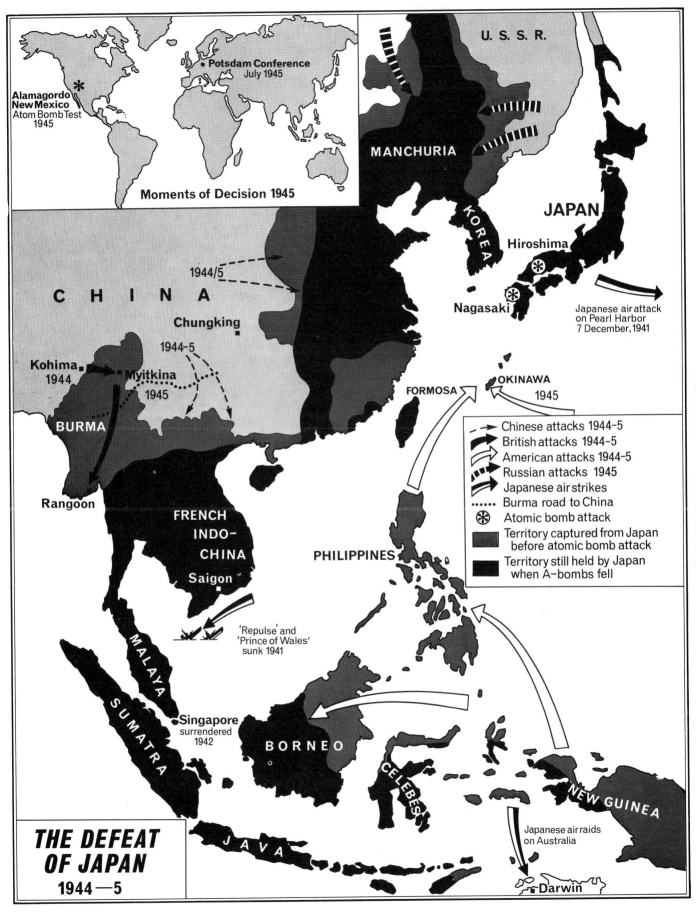

Alamagordo
New Mexico
Atom Bomb Test
1945

Potsdam Conference
July 1945

Moments of Decision 1945

U. S. S. R.

MANCHURIA

KOREA

JAPAN

Hiroshima

Nagasaki

Japanese air attack
on Pearl Harbor
7 December, 1941

1944/5

C H I N A

Chungking

Kohima
1944

Myitkina

1944-5

1945

OKINAWA
1945

FORMOSA

BURMA

Rangoon

FRENCH
INDO-
CHINA

Saigon

PHILIPPINES

'Repulse' and
'Prince of Wales'
sunk 1941

MALAYA

SUMATRA

Singapore
surrendered
1942

BORNEO

CELEBES

NEW GUINEA

J A V A

Japanese air raids
on Australia

Darwin

Chinese attacks 1944–5
British attacks 1944–5
American attacks 1944–5
Russian attacks 1945
Japanese air strikes
Burma road to China
Atomic bomb attack
Territory captured from Japan
before atomic bomb attack
Territory still held by Japan
when A–bombs fell

**THE DEFEAT
OF JAPAN
1944—5**

133

Part 7 – The Second World War 1939–1945

Spread

54. *The People's War***	Angus Calder	Cape
55. *The Narrow Margin***	D. Wood	Arrow Books
56. *Purnell's History of the Second World War***		
57. *Purnell's History of the Second World War***		
58. *The People's War***	Angus Calder	Cape
Luftwaffe War Diaries	Cajus Bekker	Macdonald
59. *The People's War***	Angus Calder	Cape
60. *Purnell's History of the Second World War***		
Hiroshima	John Hersey	Penguin

**Especially useful for project and topic work

PART 8

Winning the Peace 1945–1951

In 1945 the British people went to the polls and elected a Labour government. Prime Minister Attlee formed a ministry to reshape the entire pattern of life in Britain and there can be no doubt that it achieved remarkable success. No country before had experienced such beneficial 'socialization' in so short a time without a revolution. By 1951 Labour had provided everyone with the services of the Welfare State; nationalized several major industries; retained the wartime system of controls and high taxation in an effort to reduce inflation; maintained full employment; and managed to boost British exports. Moreover, the Attlee government made a series of decisions that in the years to come would dictate Britain's role in world affairs. Labour began to put an end to Britain's status as an imperial power; and at the same time deliberately rejected the chance of leading a future European economic union. Ernest Bevin, the colourful and forthright Foreign Secretary, recognized that Britain could no longer afford to 'go it alone', to undertake military commitments without assistance from her allies. He therefore worked to create the North Atlantic Treaty Organization; opposed the extension of communist world power; and committed Britain to the support of American policies. During the 'cold war' he opposed the Russians when they menaced the Western presence in Berlin; and in the Korean 'hot war' he sent out the Commonwealth Division to contain communism in the name of the United Nations Organization.

However, Labour was not always a popular government. People disliked the persistent controls—especially food and petrol rationing. They were also disheartened by the decline of Britain's status in the post-war world. In the 1950 General Election they returned Labour to power—but with a reduced majority. But the next year was disastrous for Attlee and his colleagues. Bevin died during April; Attlee went down with a duodenal ulcer; while the government lost face over the Abadan affair. This arose from a decision by the Persian Prime Minister, Dr. Mussadiq, to nationalize the Anglo-Iranian Oil Company. His attitude compelled the British to abandon their important oil refinery at Abadan and this in turn weakened their prestige throughout the Middle East. Meanwhile, in the Far East, the Korean War had reached deadlock—the government was undoubtedly in the doldrums. It attempted to inject a little life and colour into the drab national scene by staging the Festival of Britain in May 1951. The idea was to commemorate the centenary of the Great Exhibition of 1851—and perhaps emulate some of that exhibition's success. In the words of King George VI, the Festival was to project 'a shaft of confidence' into the rather murky future. No doubt it did this for the Londoners who watched their South Bank enjoy a long overdue face-lift. Lots of visitors to Britain marvelled at the *Dome of Discovery* and the spindly *Skylon* poking hopefully towards the heavens. The Festival closed in September and during October Attlee held another General Election. The result gave the Conservatives a working majority—something which they would retain for the next thirteen years.

61: The health and well-being of the nation 1945–1951

In 1945 the electorate gave the Labour Party a mandate to improve the British way of life. Accordingly, while the government attended to the urgent task of social reform, the people endured continued economic hardship.

Shortages

Life in post-war Britain retained much of its war-time flavour. Food shortages—part of a world-wide problem—came home to the British in the form of bread and potato rationing. There was a serious fuel shortage during the disastrous winter of 1946–47. Widespread blizzards and up to 16 degrees of frost prevented miners and railways alike from getting coal supplies to industry and the housewife. Factories and power stations shut down, gasometers stood empty and street-lighting had to be dimmed. It was the beginning of an 'age of austerity'.

Austerity

Sir Stafford Cripps, Chancellor of the Exchequer 1947–50, urged a policy of public austerity so that he could counteract Britain's serious balance of payments deficit with the United States. American Lend-Lease ceased at the end of the war, but President Truman agreed to lend the Labour government £1,100 million. Now Cripps told the people that they would have to close the 'dollar gap' by boosting the export drive and refraining from asking for increased wages. It was a matter of 'export or die!' This slogan made a brief but highly effective impact on the British. Trade unions agreed to a voluntary wage freeze; production increased and any fear of mass unemployment disappeared. This was helped of course by raising the school leaving age to 15 in 1947 and by calling up all young men at 18 to do up to 2 years National Service in the armed services; these moves kept thousands of people off the labour market. Nevertheless, the people had to submit to a lot of government controls such as clothing, furniture and sweet rationing and, in 1949, to experience the first post-war devaluation of the £ sterling. The effect was to make Britain's exports cheaper abroad, but of course it also put up the cost of living at home.

The creation of the welfare state

Meanwhile, Clement Attlee's government speedily implemented its plans for a social revolution in Britain. A new *National Insurance Scheme* became law in 1946. All adults had to pay weekly insurance contributions to cover themselves against sickness, unemployment and eventually retirement. The state would pay cash benefits in the form of death and maternity grants. Mothers drew their first family allowances in 1946. For those who were destitute a new *National Assistance Board* offered cash relief; in practice these usually went to old people whose pensions never managed to keep up with post-war inflation. Part of the insurance contribution went towards the provision of a genuine *National Health Service*. Everybody who needed medical attention could get it on the National Health no matter what their status or income might be. Clearly the state had accepted its duty to care for the people 'from the cradle to the grave'. However, many doctors resisted the new scheme and Aneurin Bevan, Minister of Health, had several unedifying quarrels with the medical profession before the National Health Service began to function in 1948.

Housing

This was probably the biggest problem facing the Labour government after 1945 and, in general, it failed to find a solution. In the heavily bombed cities, where government assistance was on a niggardly scale, reconstruction was very slow. Britain, a great industrial nation capable of turning out tanks and aeroplanes by the thousand, once more couldn't find the resources to house its own people. Average annual housebuilding figures for 1945–51 fell far below the achievements of the Thirties. This meant that young married couples would put their names down on council housing lists in the knowledge that they would have to wait years for accommodation. Some preferred to buy residential caravans—and thus helped by their demand to create a new industry—while others had to share a house with their 'in-laws'. 'Squatters' took up residence in abandoned Nissen huts which littered the disused airfields. Pre-war terraced and semi-detached houses rocketed in value and began the inflation of property prices which persisted into the Seventies.

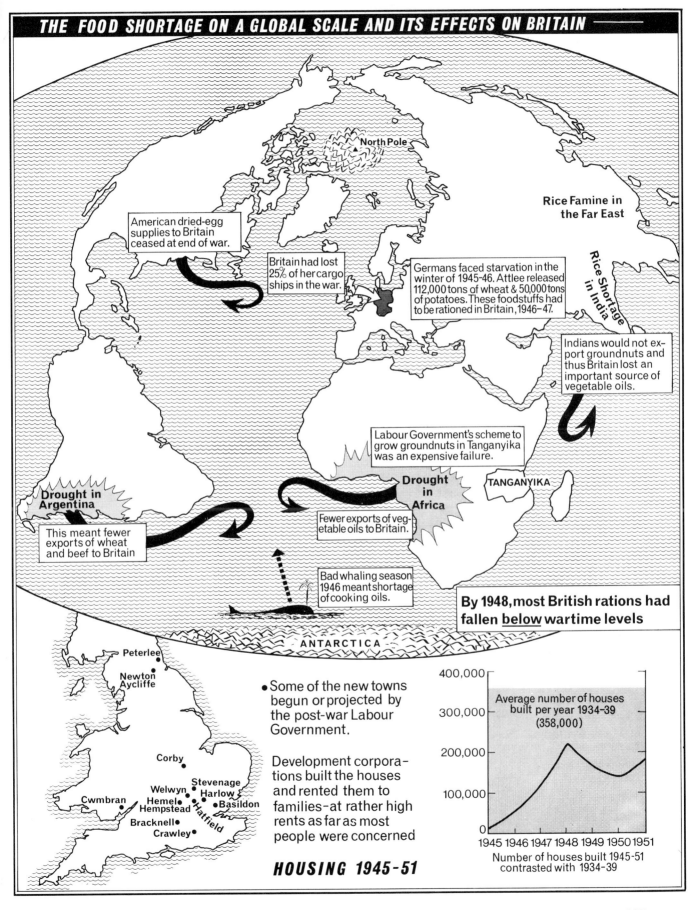

North Pole

Rice Famine in the Far East

American dried-egg supplies to Britain ceased at end of war.

Britain had lost 25% of her cargo ships in the war.

Germans faced starvation in the winter of 1945-46. Attlee released 112,000 tons of wheat & 50,000 tons of potatoes. These foodstuffs had to be rationed in Britain, 1946-47.

Rice Shortage in India

Indians would not export groundnuts and thus Britain lost an important source of vegetable oils.

Labour Government's scheme to grow groundnuts in Tanganyika was an expensive failure.

TANGANYIKA

Drought in Argentina

Drought in Africa

This meant fewer exports of wheat and beef to Britain

Fewer exports of vegetable oils to Britain.

Bad whaling season 1946 meant shortage of cooking oils.

By 1948, most British rations had fallen _below_ wartime levels

ANTARCTICA

Peterlee

Newton Aycliffe

Corby

Welwyn Stevenage
Hemel Harlow
Cwmbran Hempstead Basildon
Bracknell Hatfield
Crawley

• Some of the new towns begun or projected by the post-war Labour Government.

Development corporations built the houses and rented them to families – at rather high rents as far as most people were concerned

HOUSING 1945-51

Average number of houses built per year 1934-39 (358,000)

400,000

300,000

200,000

100,000

0

1945 1946 1947 1948 1949 1950 1951

Number of houses built 1945-51 contrasted with 1934-39

62: Nationalization 1945–1951

'Let Us Face the Future'

This was the title of Labour's election manifesto in 1945. Among other things it called for the immediate public ownership of Britain's means of production—the people as a whole were entitled to share in the profits of British industry. Labour wanted 'a Socialist Commonwealth of Great Britain'—free, democratic, efficient, progressive, its material resources organized in the service of the British people.' Of course, the *nationalization* this implied wasn't something entirely new in British history. The GPO had never known anything else; Baldwin had nationalized the BBC in 1927; BOAC (British Overseas Airways Corporation) had been run as a public company since 1940. Many advanced nations had nationalized certain features of their economies; America, for example, had led the way with her Panama Canal Company and the Tennessee Valley Authority. 1945, however, witnessed the first systematic attack by the state on the 'private sector' of British industry.

The Public Corporations

Between 1945 and 1951 Labour took over the Bank of England, civil aviation, road, rail and canal transport, coal-mining, gas, electricity, iron and steel. A minister in charge of each industry selected a Board; this Board decided on a specific policy; the minister was responsible to parliament for that policy. For example, the British coal industry was hopelessly unprofitable and inefficient. The Reid Committee reported this fact to the government in 1945. If coal-mining were to survive, it needed immediate public investment. Emmanuel Shinwell, Minister of Fuel and Power, was even more emphatic: if the *miners* were to survive the government must nationalize the industry. So on 30 January 1946 parliament created the National Coal Board* responsible for the reorganization of the coal-mining industry throughout the country. In the same year, parliament set up the British Transport Commission** which, according to Alfred Barnes, Minister of Transport, would give the British people the most efficient, comfortable, speedy and cheap transport in the world.

Nationalization and private enterprise

Altogether, the Labour government nationalized about 20% of British industry. Into this relatively small 'public sector' it poured a great deal of money and, had it not been for American generosity, it seems unlikely that Britain could have met the costs of these ambitious projects which coincided with the expensive 'Welfare State' improvements. Between 1948 and 1951 Britain received £2,400,000,000 from America's remarkable Marshall Aid Programme. It helped the government to bolster up the mines and railways, both in desperate need of modernization. The financial aid also helped to maintain full-employment and undoubtedly the prospect of secure jobs persuaded the Trade Unions to keep their wage demands down to a minimum. This helps to explain why, until the end of 1950, British industry's *production costs* remained fairly constant. By that year, the people had attained the target set them by the Labour government—they had boosted the country's exports to 175% of the pre-war figures. To what extent the government could take the credit for this success is open to question. Governments are rarely in a position to control all the factors which influence trade in the modern world. For example, Labour had permitted the car industry to remain in the 'private sector'. By 1950 it was turning out over 900,000 vehicles a year and overseas purchasers snapped up every car they could buy. However, two distinct factors were operating here. First, there was very little foreign competition to worry British car manufacturers. European firms such as Renault and Volkswagen as yet hadn't fully rebuilt their war-ravaged factories. Secondly, the Attlee government deliberately starved the home market of new cars. Very high purchase tax (66.6% on the retail price of the car) and tough hire-purchase restrictions meant that in the late Forties British motorists usually drove a second-hand pre-war 'banger' for which spare parts became increasingly scarce. Generally speaking, the Labour governments of 1945–51 nationalized the basic industries which needed heavy capital investment to come up to date; while at the same time imposing controls on privately owned industries in such a way that their products could be directed into the export markets of the world.

Conclusions

Some members of Attlee's governments had believed that *nationalization* was a magic word, a panacea that would cure the country's industrial ills. In fact nationalization made very little difference to the way industry was run. Very little 'socialization' occurred—there was hardly any 'worker control' of factories and mines. Nevertheless, Labour had reshaped a substantial part of the nation's industrial power and had laid the foundations of Britain's peacetime economy.

*Took up its duties on 1 January 1947
**Took up its duties on 1 January 1948

NATIONALIZATION UNDER THE LABOUR GOVERNMENTS —— 1945-1950 and 1950-1951

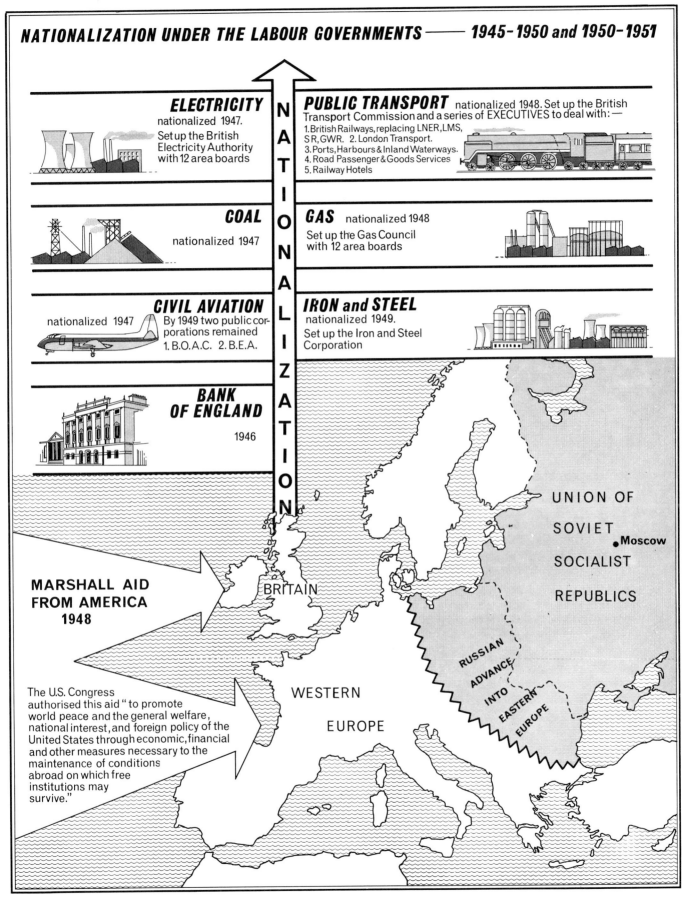

NATIONALIZATION

ELECTRICITY
nationalized 1947.
Set up the British Electricity Authority with 12 area boards

PUBLIC TRANSPORT
nationalized 1948. Set up the British Transport Commission and a series of EXECUTIVES to deal with:—
1. British Railways, replacing LNER, LMS, SR, GWR. 2. London Transport.
3. Ports, Harbours & Inland Waterways.
4. Road Passenger & Goods Services
5. Railway Hotels

COAL
nationalized 1947

GAS
nationalized 1948
Set up the Gas Council with 12 area boards

CIVIL AVIATION
nationalized 1947
By 1949 two public corporations remained
1. B.O.A.C. 2. B.E.A.

IRON and STEEL
nationalized 1949.
Set up the Iron and Steel Corporation

BANK OF ENGLAND
1946

MARSHALL AID FROM AMERICA 1948

The U.S. Congress authorised this aid " to promote world peace and the general welfare, national interest, and foreign policy of the United States through economic, financial and other measures necessary to the maintenance of conditions abroad on which free institutions may survive."

BRITAIN

WESTERN

EUROPE

UNION OF

SOVIET ●Moscow

SOCIALIST

REPUBLICS

RUSSIAN ADVANCE INTO EASTERN EUROPE

139

63: The Cold War

The Iron Curtain

On 4 March 1946, Winston Churchill—no longer a member of the British government—addressed a distinguished American audience in Fulton, Missouri: *'From Stettin on the Baltic to Trieste on the Adriatic an iron curtain has descended across the continent. Behind that line lie all the capitals of the ancient states of central and Eastern Europe.'* In drawing attention to the extent of Soviet advance into Europe, Churchill was inviting the Americans to balance the Russian threat to democracy by establishing a 'United States presence' in Western Europe. When Labour MPs heard of Churchill's statements they asked Attlee for an assurance that these would not influence Ernest Bevin's conduct of British foreign affairs.

The Greek problem

Neither Bevin nor Attlee wished to involve the British people in European power politics. Yet circumstances were already beyond their control. Ever since the liberation of Greece in 1944, skirmishes between Greek communist forces and British troops had become increasingly common. Bevin kept British troops there simply to support those Greek politicians, often corrupt and utterly selfish men, who claimed to be anti-communist. His motives were simple: Greece had to be protected against a communist take-over. If Greece succumbed, Turkey would be the next to go. Then the Russians would sweep into the Mediterranean and threaten British interests in the Middle East. As Britain had defended the oilfields and the Suez Canal against Rommel's Afrika Korps, Ernest Bevin was not going to surrender them now. Unfortunately, he could not afford to maintain a large fighting force in Greece; reluctantly he told President Truman that in March 1947 all British troops would be evacuating the country. Remembering Churchill's Fulton speech a year earlier, Truman came to a decision which was to shape future world history. He decided to appeal to Congress to send dollar aid to Greece and Turkey because *'it must be the policy of the United States to support free peoples who are resisting attempted subjugation by armed minorities or by outside pressures.'* This was the basis of the *Truman Doctrine*—America's determination to contain communism in every part of the globe. It marked the beginning of the Cold War between East and West.

Crisis in Europe 1948

As Marshall Aid poured across the Atlantic, Ernest Bevin put his case before the House of Commons: 'The issue is whether European unity cannot be achieved without the domination of one great power . . . the free nations of Western Europe must now draw closely together. . . . I believe the time is ripe for a consolidation of Western Europe.' But while he was planning the Organization for European Economic Co-operation (OEEC) in order to distribute Marshall Aid, the Cold War escalated into crisis. During 1948 the Russians removed the last vestiges of democratic freedom in Czechoslovakia and pulled her within the Iron Curtain; while in June they closed all road and rail links between Berlin and the West.

The Berlin Airlift 1948–1949

Though the Russians explained the Berlin blockade in terms of 'technical difficulties with communications', they were clearly trying to drive the Western Allies from the city. Once Berlin's housewives entered the Russian sector in search of food and coal, the West would lose face and accept that they must withdraw from the city. However, this was not the Allied reaction. Bevin and Attlee were perfectly willing to help the Americans supply the West Berliners entirely from the air. The RAF provided ground personnel to organize the food, coal, medical supplies and winter clothing urgently needed in West Berlin. American 'Skymasters' and 'Dakotas' took off from British and French airfields and roared along the three air corridors leading to the beleagured city. RAF 'York' transports skimmed low over Berlin houses to land at Tegel Airport; Short 'Sunderland' flying-boats touched down on Berlin's Lake Waan. By April 1949 the West Berliners had a surplus of supplies, for the supply aircraft were coming in at the rate of one a minute. Unquestionably, the airlift inflicted a major Cold War defeat on the Russians and on 12 May 1949 they agreed to end the blockade.

NATO 1949

Even before the blockade ended the Western Allies had taken a step which made the division of Europe even more rigid. On 4 April 1949 Bevin saw his work for European military union crowned with success: Britain, America and ten other countries signed the *North Atlantic Treaty Organization*. But he was less keen to use it as a step towards economic union. He had no wish to surrender any of Britain's sovereign rights. Therefore he was reluctant to join the Council of Europe in 1949; and when the chance came to join the European Coal and Steel Community in 1951, Britain turned it down. Thus the Attlee government rejected the chance of leading Europe from the very beginning; a remarkable decision when, at the same time, it was busily opting out of the responsibilities of Empire.

BRITAIN and EUROPE 1945-49

ICELAND

CANADA

U.S.A.

NORWAY

DENMARK

BRITAIN

Moscow

THE SOVIET UNION

HOLLAND
BELGIUM
LUX.

Stettin
• Berlin ★

GERMANY

★ Warsaw

★ Prague

Vienna
★ Budapest

AUSTRIA

FRANCE

Trieste

YUGOSLAVIA

★ Bucharest

★ Sofia

Fear of Russian expansion into Mediterranean

PORTUGAL

SPAIN

ITALY

GREECE

TURKEY

MIDDLE EAST OIL

M e d i t e r r a n e a n   S e a

1945-47

1945-47

Suez Canal

★ European capital occupied by Red Army
► Communist threat to Greece
▷ British aid and years given
▨ Russian occupied territory
▨ Original NATO countries
— Iron Curtain as it existed in 1946
•••• New line after Yugoslavia was ejected from the Communist Bloc in 1948

THE BERLIN AIRLIFT 1948-49

from Hamburg

ALLIED

RUSSIAN

BERLIN

OCCUPIED

from Hanover

AIR CORRIDORS TO BERLIN

French Sector
✳

British Sector

RUSSIAN SECTOR

American Sector
☆

GERMANY

OCCUPIED

from Frankfurt

GERMANY

〰 Lakes used by flying boats
✳ Tegel
● Gatow } Airfields
☆ Tempelhof

141

64: The end of Empire

India

As early as 1919 the British Labour Party had committed themselves to Indian independence. Now they were in a position to honour their promises and in 1946 Clement Attlee sent a Cabinet mission to India. Their task was to make arrangements for 'Indian Independence Day' scheduled for 1948. To their horror, the British delegates found India to be a land torn by violent religious and racial strife. Moslems and Hindus fought bitter street battles and in the 'Great Killing' of August 1946 more than 4000 people died in Calcutta. Gandhi travelled from town to town, village to village, pleading with his people to end the civil war. He enjoyed phenomenal success—but he couldn't be everywhere at once; it was up to the British to find a rapid solution to the troubles. Attlee appointed Lord Louis Mountbatten as Viceroy of British India. This distinguished war leader and cousin of King George VI persuaded both the Moslem and Hindu leaders that, if they accepted the principle of partition, Independence Day could be brought forward a year. In turn Nehru, the Hindu Congress leader, and Mohammed Ali Jinna, leader of the Moslem League, persuaded their party followers to agree to partition. Though this was not the original wish of the Attlee government, parliament at Westminister passed an act creating *two* dominions—India and Pakistan. At midnight 14 August 1947 British power in the Indian sub-continent ended forever. Unfortunately, independence did not bring peace. The killing went on in the Punjab and in Bengal. In Bihar, for example, where the Hindus were exterminating the Moslem minority, Nehru had to threaten his own people with bombing attacks before they relented. Perhaps the greatest tragedy occurred when Gandhi himself became the victim of his people's passion. As he went to his prayer meeting on the evening of 30 January 1948 a young Hindu refugee assassinated him.

Burma, Ceylon and Eire

Clement Attlee made it plain that he didn't want to force people to stay inside the Commonwealth of Nations. So the Burmese, who doubted the value of dominion status, elected to leave the Commonwealth on 4 January 1948. A month later, and in total contrast, the people of Ceylon accepted dominion status and remained a member of the Commonwealth. Eire, the only Commonwealth member to remain neutral in the war against Hitler, decided to relinquish her ties with the British crown. Symbolically, the Irish chose the thirty-third anniversary of their ill-fated Easter Rising (1916) as their Independence Day. Independence, however, did not solve the problem of the existing partition of Ireland. Plenty of people in Eire, as well as many Catholics living in Ulster, looked forward to the day when the Irish would be united under a *single* government.

Palestine

In 1917 the *Balfour Declaration* had stated that the British government supported the idea of allowing the Jewish people to return to their Biblical home in Palestine. When World War I ended the League of Nations gave Britain a mandate over Palestine together with the task of looking after the welfare of Arab and Jewish people already living there. This situation allowed Britain to admit a number of Jews into Palestine before the outbreak of World War II in 1939. When hostilities ended in 1945, the British had considerable sympathy for the Jews who had managed to survive Hitler's policy of genocide. Statements at the Nuremberg Tribunal, where Nazi war criminals were on trial, revealed that nearly six million Jews had been exterminated in death camps such as Auschwitz and Treblinka. Clearly, the least a horrified world could do was to find the Jews somewhere to live; and no government was more vehement on this point than Clement Attlee's ministry. It stepped up Jewish immigration into Palestine and this, together with the very large number of illegal immigrants, meant that well over the permitted 100,000 Jews were living in Palestine by 1946. Understandably, the Arab residents complained; while the Jews accused the British of keeping *their* numbers down. Once more British soldiers found themselves in the unhappy position of keeping the peace between rival terrorist organizations. They patrolled, guarded key points—and were shot at and ambushed by both sides. In 1946 the Jewish Irgun even blew up British military headquarters in Jerusalem's King David Hotel. British sympathy for the Jews rapidly declined and Bevin referred the Palestine problem to the newly created *United Nations Organization*. The UN advized partition and sent out their mediator, Count Bernadotte. A Jewish terrorist group murdered him. By now the British had had enough. They withdrew from Palestine in 1948, leaving the Jews and Arabs to shoot it out. The Jews immediately proclaimed their state of Israel and successfully resisted every attack launched by the surrounding Arab states. A new and dangerous source of friction had arrived in the Middle East.

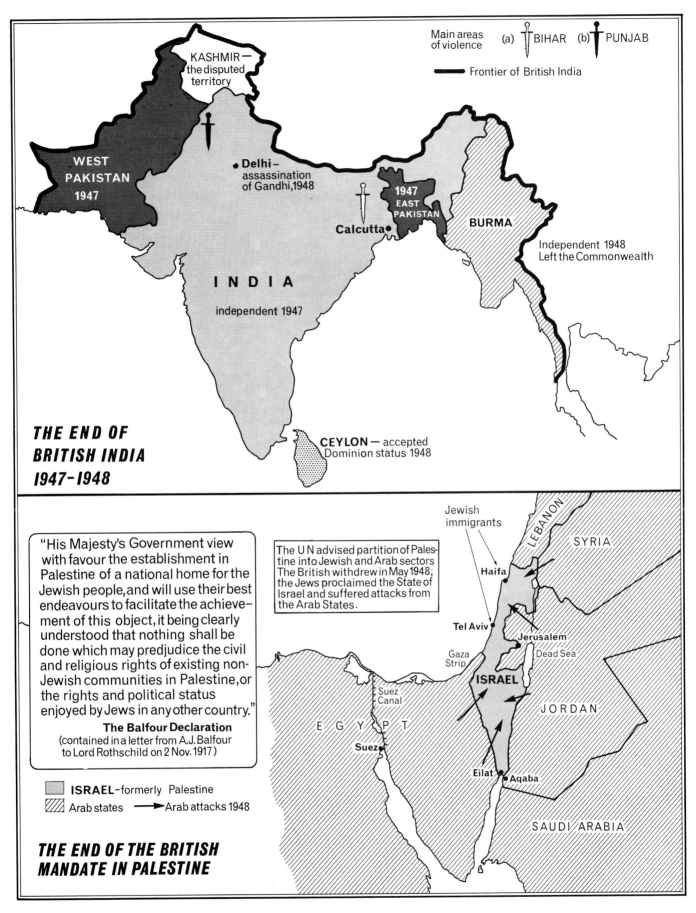

Main areas of violence (a) ⚔ BIHAR (b) ⚔ PUNJAB

━━━ Frontier of British India

KASHMIR — the disputed territory

WEST PAKISTAN 1947

Delhi – assassination of Gandhi, 1948

1947 EAST PAKISTAN

Calcutta

BURMA Independent 1948 Left the Commonweaith

I N D I A independent 1947

CEYLON — accepted Dominion status 1948

THE END OF BRITISH INDIA 1947-1948

"His Majesty's Government view with favour the establishment in Palestine of a national home for the Jewish people, and will use their best endeavours to facilitate the achieve-ment of this object, it being clearly understood that nothing shall be done which may predjudice the civil and religious rights of existing non-Jewish communities in Palestine, or the rights and political status enjoyed by Jews in any other country."

The Balfour Declaration
(contained in a letter from A.J. Balfour to Lord Rothschild on 2 Nov. 1917)

The U N advised partition of Pales-tine into Jewish and Arab sectors The British withdrew in May 1948; the Jews proclaimed the State of Israel and suffered attacks from the Arab States.

Jewish immigrants

LEBANON SYRIA

Haifa

Tel Aviv

Jerusalem

Dead Sea

Gaza Strip

ISRAEL

JORDAN

Suez Canal

E G Y P T

Suez

Eilat **Aqaba**

SAUDI ARABIA

▨ **ISRAEL**-formerly Palestine
▨ Arab states ➝ Arab attacks 1948

THE END OF THE BRITISH MANDATE IN PALESTINE

65:   The war in Korea 1950–1953

The war in Korea represents Britain's biggest military effort since the end of World War II in 1945. Though American forces made the major contribution, the Commonwealth Division played an exceptionally important role in preventing the Chinese conquest of South Korea. Moreover, the war made its impact on British domestic politics; it added to the growing unpopularity of the Labour government and was one of many causes for their defeat in the General Election of 1951.

The outbreak of war

On 25 June 1950 North Korean troops crossed the 38th Parallel into South Korea. Next day the United Nations ordered them to withdraw; and when they refused the UN authorized military sanctions against the communist aggressor. Under the command of America's General MacArthur, troops from many countries in the United Nations arrived in Korea to repel the communist attack.

The progress of the war

MacArthur's troops arrived in the nick of time. North Koreans were poised for their assault on the vital port of Pusan. However, the communists had over-extended themselves and MacArthur managed to inflict a wounding blow on their flank with an amphibious landing at Inchon. Then, with the approval of the UN General Assembly he crossed the 38th Parallel and pushed northwards to within striking distance of the Manchurian border. At this moment two Chinese armies attacked across the Yalu River and drove the UN forces back to South Korea. After many furious battles, the UN counterattacked and forced the Chinese to dig in along a defensive line running across the whole of central Korea. Here on the bare, brown hillsides the Chinese and UN soldiers settled down to wage a bitter, static war that would cost nearly two million lives.

The Commonwealth contribution 1950–1951

British and Commonwealth troops were destined to fight some of the most important actions of the Korean War. Regular troops and National Servicemen, together with tough Australian infantrymen, came out to form the famous 27 Brigade. It led the advance into North Korea during 1950 in the middle of a bitter winter and came within 12 miles of the Manchurian border. 29 Brigade arrived a little later and included in its units the 1st Battalion of the Gloucester Regiment. In April 1951 the Gloucesters made their epic last stand against the Chinese during the Battle of the Imjin River. Sixty thousand Chinese attacked the Commonwealth front; about ten thousand of these became casualties. And of the 622* Gloucesters who bore the brunt of their assault, a mere 46 made good their escape. They had stopped one of the biggest Chinese attacks in the history of the Korean War.

The static war 1951–1953

By the end of July 1951 a static war was in progress in Korea. Both sides were haggling, first at Kaesong and then at Panmunjom, over the exchange of prisoners and the possibility of a cease-fire. In the meantime the killing went on in a fashion closely resembling the trench warfare of 1914–1918. US aircraft dominated the skies over the 38th Parallel, but although they blasted the hillsides with rockets and napalm they rarely managed to hit the Chinese infantry. Enemy trenches were so deep and difficult to spot that they were virtually impregnable. This enabled the Chinese to develop a standard procedure for assaulting the Commonwealth positions. First they poured down a rain of artillery shells and then swarmed up the hillsides. They had little tactical skill but plenty of courage. Rallying to their shrill bugle commands, the communist infantry died by the hundred as they tried to penetrate the Commonwealth bunkers. Such were the tactics adopted by the Chinese for their attack on 'Hill 355' in November 1951. They hurled 6000 shells on the King's Own Scottish Borderers. One 'Kosbie', Pte. Bill Speakman, led the counter-attacks by hurling grenade after grenade at the Chinese. He won the Victoria Cross.

'The Hook' 1953

Just a few weeks before the end of the fighting another terrifying attack fell on the hill called 'The Hook'. It commanded vital lines of communication running south through Korea and the Chinese intended to take it. It had already changed hands on many occasions but when the big attack came 'The Hook' was held by men of the Duke of Wellington's Regiment. The 'Dukes' endured a week of non-stop bombardment before the Chinese charged on the evening of 28 May 1953. After desperate hand-to-hand fighting the Chinese retreated. They never captured 'The Hook'. Two months later the Chinese and UN delegates signed an armistice at Panmunjom. The war in Korea was over.

*Many Gloucesters, including their Commanding Officer Lt. Col. Carne (awarded the V.C. for heroism during the Imjin battle), managed to survive captivity in Chinese prisoner-of-war camps.

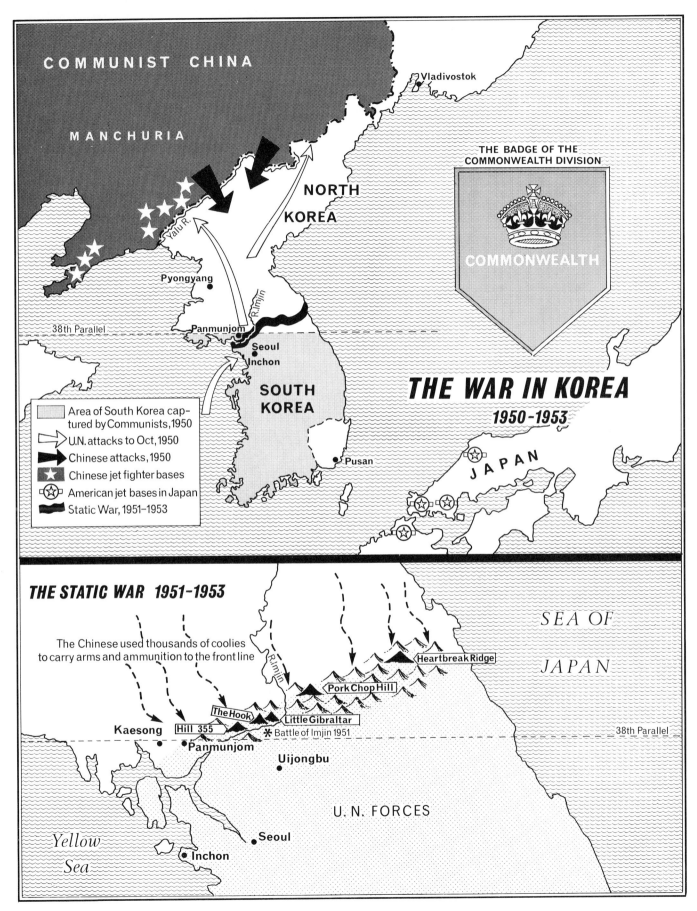

COMMUNIST CHINA

MANCHURIA

Vladivostok

NORTH KOREA

THE BADGE OF THE
COMMONWEALTH DIVISION

COMMONWEALTH

Yalu R.

Pyongyang

R. Imjin

38th Parallel

Panmunjom

Seoul
Inchon

SOUTH KOREA

THE WAR IN KOREA
1950-1953

Pusan

JAPAN

Area of South Korea cap-
tured by Communists, 1950

U.N. attacks to Oct, 1950

Chinese attacks, 1950

Chinese jet fighter bases

American jet bases in Japan

Static War, 1951–1953

THE STATIC WAR 1951-1953

SEA OF JAPAN

The Chinese used thousands of coolies
to carry arms and ammunition to the front line

Heartbreak Ridge

R. Imjin

Pork Chop Hill

The Hook

Little Gibraltar

Kaesong

Hill 355

Battle of Imjin 1951

38th Parallel

Panmunjom

Uijongbu

U. N. FORCES

Yellow Sea

Seoul

Inchon

145

Part 8 – Winning the Peace 1945–1951

Spread

**Especially suitable for project and topic work

PART 9

Britain since 1951

These were the years in which the British people pushed up their living standards to a level unparalleled in their history. After the Korean War ended in 1953, they turned wholeheartedly to the pursuit of pleasure as their earnings increased and more consumer goods appeared in the shops. They took on heavy hire purchase debts, overdrafts and mortgages. Yet despite the arrival of the affluent society, evidence showed that prosperity for the mass of the people was not growing at the rate achieved by other advanced nations. The gap between the rich—1% of the population still owned more than 40% of the total personal wealth!—and the poor seemed to be increasing. Certainly, the immense inequality of incomes together with price inflation were the two main reasons for persistent wage demands by the trade unions, demands which persisted during the unexpected fall in living standards after 1973.

These were also years in which young people played a new and important rôle. Teenagers discovered a new earning and therefore a new purchasing power. And as more of them went to colleges and universities they showed that they had discovered political power. By militant demonstration and by the display of a responsible awareness of the needs of less fortunate members of the community (the latter rarely received much publicity) they persuaded the government that the 18 year old deserved the right to vote.

As modern life became more complex so did government regulations. Wisely, the governments dealt with some of the more dangerous features of the new society. The 70 m.p.h. speed limit, the breathalyser, compulsory seat belts and vehicle testing saved many lives and the government policies—presented on television in terms of 'You know it makes sense'—aroused no opposition. Immigration and the difficult problem of law and order ushered in more legislation; but urgent matters such as conservation and pollution received inadequate attention.

For Britain as a whole, perhaps the greatest change came in her international status. Dean Acheson, speaking in September 1962, touched on some of Britain's problems while at the same time exaggerating them:

'Great Britain has lost an empire and has not yet found a rôle. The attempt to play a separate power rôle—that is a rôle apart from Europe, a rôle based on a special relationship with the United States, a rôle based on being head of a commonwealth, which has no political structure or unity or strength and enjoys a fragile and precarious economic relationship by means of the sterling area and preference in the British market—this rôle is about played out...'

Prime Minister Macmillan's reply was straight and to the point:

'In so far as he appeared to denigrate the resolution and will of Britain and the British people, Mr. Acheson has fallen into an error which has been made by quite a lot of people in the course of the last 400 years.' *

It will be history's task to see which one was right.

* Dean Acheson was the United States' Secretary for Defence. These extracts are quoted by Arthur Marwick on p. 414 of 'Britain in the Century of Total War' published by The Bodley Head 1968.

66 Britain as a world power

Defence in a nuclear age

After fighting a limited war in Korea with conventional weapons, Britain turned wholeheartedly towards a defence system based upon the independent nuclear deterrent. Initially, the plan was to equip V-bombers with a *stand-off bomb* called Blue Steel. Before long, however, the Defence chiefs discarded this in favour of the Blue Streak rocket missile. Then they changed their minds again and decided to buy American Skybolt rockets to which British nuclear warheads could be attached. This was in 1960; two years later the Americans scrapped Skybolt, leaving the British to defend themselves with their obsolete V-bomber force. At the end of 1962 Prime Minister Macmillan met President Kennedy in the Bahamas and there negotiated the Nassau Agreement by which the United States agreed to supply Polaris nuclear missiles for installation in a small fleet of nuclear submarines which Britain would build over the following decade. So much for the British 'independent' deterrent!

Social implications

a) *Cost*:   Britain desperately needed to spend money on hospitals, pensions, housing and roads. Yet the government was calmly squandering millions of pounds in the nuclear arms race. Complex scientific equipment became obsolete almost overnight—and Britain was in no position to meet this sort of expenditure *and* maintain large conventional forces in many parts of the globe. British servicemen were constantly in action—against Greek nationalists in Cyprus, against communist guerrillas in the Malay States, against Mau-Mau in Kenya. All of these campaigns called for highly trained infantry battalions supported by artillery and tactical air strikes.

b) *Conscription*:   Men had to be conscripted for this kind of work and most eighteen-year-olds found themselves called up for National Service. Many derived a great deal of benefit from their life in the armed services; others spent most weekdays blancoing their kit and thought it was a waste of two precious years; quite a lot died in police actions and local wars all over the world. One serious criticism of National Service was the lack of incentive it gave to boys who left school at 15. They knew that conscription was inevitable; many chose to waste the three years before call-up. However, the last National Servicemen returned to 'civvy street' in the early Sixties and by that time the government had run down the armed services from 875,000 men to well under half a million.

c) *Protest*:   One unexpected result of Britain's defence policy was the extent it stirred up peaceful protest. People of all shades of political and religious opinion were deeply concerned by the effects of nuclear tests and the growing threat of nuclear war. Led by distinguished people such as the Reverend Canon Collins, the philosopher Bertrand Russell and the historian A. J. P. Taylor, the Campaign for Nuclear Disarmament (CND)* became an established feature of British life. Every Easter, the CND organized a march to Aldermaston Atomic Weapons Research Establishment to protest against 'the bomb'. After 1962 it extended its activities and set the fashion for public demonstration in the Sixties.

Suez 1956

Only once in this period did Britain try to play a separate power role in world affairs. This was during the ill-fated Suez affair in the autumn of 1956. It arose out of President Nasser's decision to nationalize the Suez Canal. Nasser wanted all British troops out of the Canal Zone—the last ones left in June 1956—and the chance to build the High Dam at Aswan for the benefit of the Egyptian people. He nationalized the Suez Canal simply because Britain and America refused to lend him money to build the dam. Prime Minister Eden regarded Nasser as a latter-day Hitler and the Suez Canal as Britain's vital commerical and naval link in the East. Eden therefore resolved to teach Nasser a lesson. In conjunction with Israeli and French armed forces, British aircraft strafed Egyptian airfields on 31 October. HMS *Newfoundland* sank an Egyptian frigate in the Gulf of Suez. British paratroops dropped outside Port Said on 5 November. Next day there came the cease-fire with the British still 75 miles from Suez and the canal blocked with sunken ships. Faced with the opposition of not only the Egyptians but both the U.S.A. and the Soviet Union, Britain was helpless. It was a major blunder by the Conservative government. Britain gained absolutely nothing; but she lost an enviable reputation as a liberal and law-abiding member of the United Nations Organization.

*C.N.D. founded 1957

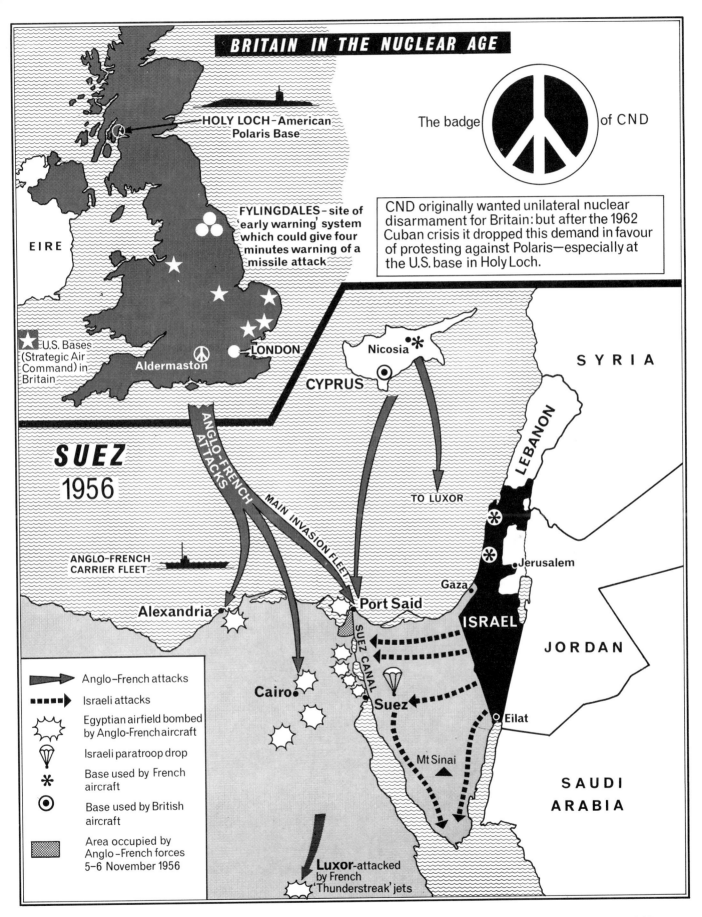

BRITAIN IN THE NUCLEAR AGE

The badge of CND

CND originally wanted unilateral nuclear disarmament for Britain: but after the 1962 Cuban crisis it dropped this demand in favour of protesting against Polaris—especially at the U.S. base in Holy Loch.

EIRE

HOLY LOCH – American Polaris Base

FYLINGDALES – site of 'early warning' system which could give four minutes warning of a missile attack

☆ U.S. Bases (Strategic Air Command) in Britain

Aldermaston

LONDON

CYPRUS

Nicosia

TO LUXOR

SYRIA

LEBANON

SUEZ 1956

ANGLO-FRENCH ATTACKS

MAIN INVASION FLEET

ANGLO-FRENCH CARRIER FLEET

ISRAEL

JORDAN

Jerusalem

Gaza

Port Said

Alexandria

SUEZ CANAL

Cairo

Suez

Eilat

Mt Sinai

SAUDI ARABIA

Anglo-French attacks

Israeli attacks

Egyptian airfield bombed by Anglo-French aircraft

Israeli paratroop drop

✱ Base used by French aircraft

◉ Base used by British aircraft

Area occupied by Anglo-French forces 5–6 November 1956

Luxor-attacked by French 'Thunderstreak' jets

After Suez, the British people saw their Commonwealth evolve into a vague association of independent states all of whom owed allegiance to Queen Elizabeth II. And because many of the emergent states faced massive problems of under-development and over-population they needed generous grants of overseas aid from the British taxpayer.

The wind of change

During World War II African soldiers fought against white men—Germans and Italians. They made new social contacts and discovered fresh political ideas. Ambitious Africans, such as Nnamdi Azikwe and Kwame Nkrumah, had already graduated from American universities and returned to their homelands determined to liberate their peoples from colonial rule. Nkrumah was the first to succeed. In 1952 he became Prime Minister of the Gold Coast; in 1957 his country became independent Ghana. Now the whole of Africa eagerly anticipated the grant of independence from the various imperial powers. Visiting South Africa in 1960, Prime Minister Macmillan neatly summed up the situation in his speech to the white Afrikaner parliament: 'The wind of change is blowing through this continent. . . .'

Political violence

Too often, violence preceded or followed the grant of independence. Tribal jealousies, suppressed for generations, flared again and the whole pattern of political dispute in Africa was entirely different from the verbal cut and thrust associated with Parliament at Westminster. For example, the Mau-Mau movement terrorized white Kenyans and their Kikuyu workers after 1953. While British troops rounded up suspects and restored law and order to the colony, Kenyan independence had to wait until 1963. Nigeria—Azikwe's homeland—managed to achieve her independence in 1960 amidst relative calm. Her tragedy came in 1967 when the Ibo people set up their breakaway state of Biafra. A bitter civil war raged for the next three years until starvation and lack of military supplies forced the Biafrans to surrender in January 1970. However, the African states had no monopoly of political violence. In Malaya communist guerrilla attacks caused a full scale emergency and the fighting delayed independence until 1957. Six years later, the Malays united with North Borneo and Sarawak to form the Federation of Malaysia and immediately came into conflict with President Sukarno of Indonesia. Sukarno sent saboteurs and commandos into Malaysia and British troops, who had fought the Malayan Communist Party from 1948 to 1960, had to spend the years 1963–67 dealing with Sukarno's 'confrontation'*.

South Africa and apartheid

In 1960 news filtered through from South Africa that police had shot down 69 African demonstrators in the native township of Sharpeville. Commonwealth countries had already condemned South Africa for her policy of apartheid—separate social development for black and white peoples—together with all the racial discrimination that this implied. After the Sharpeville Massacre protest reached such a peak that the South Africans abandoned their loyalty to the Queen and in 1961 formed a Republic outside the Commonwealth. But they continued to trade with Britain and South Africa remained a very important export market. The Conservatives permitted several arms deals with Dr. Verwoerd's† Afrikaner government and this provoked criticism from the Labour opposition who contended that strike aircraft such as the Buccaneer could easily be used against the African people in order to enforce apartheid. When Labour came to power in 1964 Prime Minister Harold Wilson stopped the arms deals with South Africa—but almost at once he came up against another highly embarrassing racial issue.

Rhodesia

On 11 November 1965 the Rhodesian Prime Minister Ian Smith issued his Unilateral Declaration of Independence—UDI. As Rhodesia was still a self-governing colony, the UDI was illegal. However, Harold Wilson had vivid memories of the Suez débâcle and had no desire to employ force in order to overthrow the all-white Smith régime. He therefore proposed stringent economic sanctions against Rhodesia hoping, by prohibiting all trade with the colony, to force Smith to surrender. Yet as time went by the policy of sanctions seemed to be having very little effect on the Rhodesian economy. In fact, when the Labour government won the 1974 General Elections the Smith régime still controlled Rhodesia—where 200,000 white people ruled a land populated by nearly 3 million Africans.

*President Sukarno (died 1970) was forced to retire in 1967 and his successor, President Suharto, agreed to end the confrontation with Malaysia the same year.

†Dr. Verwoerd was assassinated in 1966. His successor was Dr. Vorster, who continued to follow the policy of apartheid.

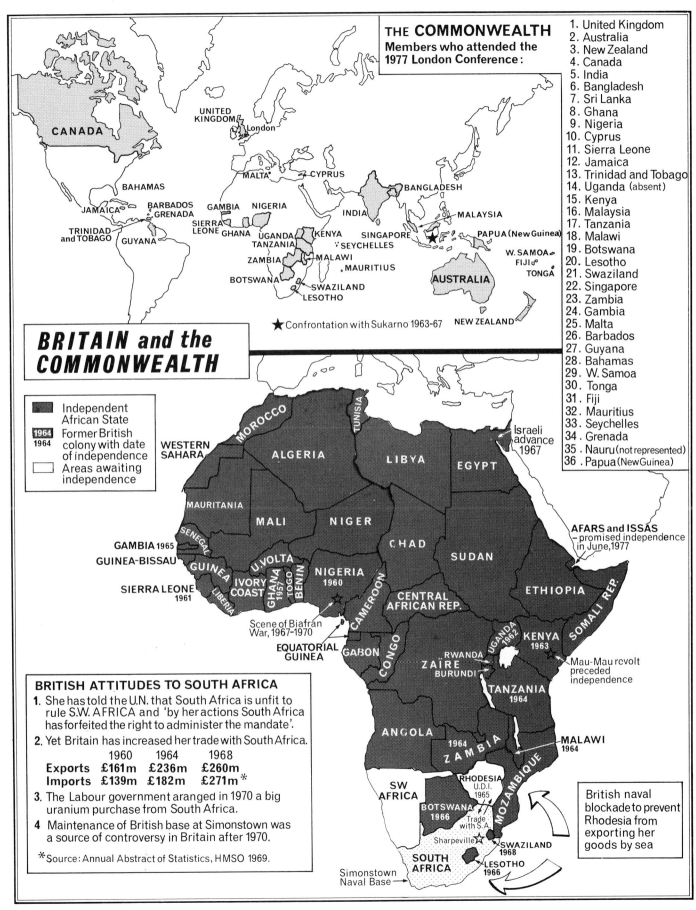

THE **COMMONWEALTH**
Members who attended the 1977 London Conference:

1. United Kingdom
2. Australia
3. New Zealand
4. Canada
5. India
6. Bangladesh
7. Sri Lanka
8. Ghana
9. Nigeria
10. Cyprus
11. Sierra Leone
12. Jamaica
13. Trinidad and Tobago
14. Uganda (absent)
15. Kenya
16. Malaysia
17. Tanzania
18. Malawi
19. Botswana
20. Lesotho
21. Swaziland
22. Singapore
23. Zambia
24. Gambia
25. Malta
26. Barbados
27. Guyana
28. Bahamas
29. W. Samoa
30. Tonga
31. Fiji
32. Mauritius
33. Seychelles
34. Grenada
35. Nauru (not represented)
36. Papua (New Guinea)

★ Confrontation with Sukarno 1963-67

BRITAIN and the COMMONWEALTH

Independent African State

1964 Former British colony with date of independence

Areas awaiting independence

Israeli advance 1967

AFARS and ISSÁS – promised independence in June, 1977

Mau-Mau revolt preceded independence

Scene of Biafran War, 1967-1970

British naval blockade to prevent Rhodesia from exporting her goods by sea

Trade with S.A.

Simonstown Naval Base

BRITISH ATTITUDES TO SOUTH AFRICA

1. She has told the U.N. that South Africa is unfit to rule S.W. AFRICA and 'by her actions South Africa has forfeited the right to administer the mandate'.

2. Yet Britain has increased her trade with South Africa.

	1960	1964	1968
Exports	£161m	£236m	£260m
Imports	£139m	£182m	£271m*

3. The Labour government aranged in 1970 a big uranium purchase from South Africa.

4 Maintenance of British base at Simonstown was a source of controversy in Britain after 1970.

* Source: Annual Abstract of Statistics, HMSO 1969.

68: The British economy

Since 1945 Britain's rate of economic growth has been one of the lowest in Western Europe. To what extent this is due to poor government planning or to circumstances beyond the control of Prime Ministers and their Cabinets has remained a matter of controversy.

Rising prices—the inflationary spiral

Three factors made price rises inevitable after 1945. First, the policy of 'export or die' created shortages in the shops and put up prices. Devaluation in 1949 caused more price increases. Finally, the post-war full employment put trade unions in a strong position to demand higher wages. Desperate for labour, employers readily agreed and passed on their higher production costs to the general public. The post-war inflationary spiral had begun.

Stop-go

No government in a democratic society can control all the factors which determine the people's standard of living. But governments can devise artificial methods of boosting exports in order to preserve a favourable trade balance. If a trade deficit arises because people buy too many home-produced or imported consumer goods, then the Chancellor of the Exchequer 'deflates' the economy by increasing taxes and reducing the amount of money in people's pockets. In 'good times' he can 'reflate' the economy by reducing taxes and giving people more to spend. Unfortunately, such devices create a temptation to manipulate the economy for political purposes. In 1955, for example, the Conservatives reduced taxes in their April budget, won the General Election in May, and then deflated the economy in October by bringing in a host of new taxes. Later on Prime Minister Macmillan told the country that it had 'never had it so good'—it could afford these temporary setbacks. The Labour opposition caustically christened Conservative economic planning as the policy of 'stop-go!'

Recurring crises

After 1956 the problem of the nation's economy developed into the major issue between the political parties. It was a problem complicated by the fact that Britain's pound sterling is a reserve currency. This means that many countries—and individuals—prefer to do their trading in British currency and, moreover, keep large reserves of cash in the Bank of England. But if they suspect that the value of the pound is about to decline they may well exchange their sterling for a more reliable currency such as German marks, American dollars—or even gold. This causes a 'flight from the pound'—an almost annual event in the crisis-ridden years of the Sixties. When the Labour Government came to power in 1964 it was determined to control the inflationary spiral, boost exports, settle the country's overseas debts and build up a healthy economy. At first, Harold Wilson made the mistake of emphasizing that the Conservatives had left him with a £800 million debt—this hardly inspired confidence overseas! Then in 1966 he introduced his prices and incomes *freeze* and tried, by means of the Selective Employment Tax, to divert workers into vital export industries. In 1967 he devalued the pound and tried on television to convince an incredulous British public that it did 'not mean, of course, that the pound here in Britain, in your pocket, or purse, or in your bank has been devalued...' In 1968 he brought in the biggest post-war 'stop' to date by following up a severe April budget with heavy tax increases in November. This was a desperate attempt to save the British economy from sinking further into debt. 'A bitter harvest of socialism' was the Conservative party's judgement; but Wilson weathered the storm with help from the International Monetary Fund. Exports increased—the statisticians discovered that they had been under-estimating Britain's exports for years!—and Wilson was confident of victory in the 1970 General Election. His hopes were dashed; the electorate returned the Conservative party to power.

The Common Market

By the 1957 Treaty of Rome; France, Italy and West Germany joined the three Benelux countries in setting up the European Economic Community—the Common Market. Since then Britain has made three attempts to join. If Britain and her European Free Trade Association (EFTA) partners entered the Common Market they would have unlimited access to a huge, prosperous consumer market and possibly membership of a future 'United States of Europe'. Britain would have the chance of increasing her disappointingly low rate of economic growth just as the Dutch and West Germans have done. Of course, entry to the Common Market would mean higher food prices in Britain; but both the Labour and Conservative parties agreed that these would be quickly offset by rising incomes. Unfortunately, this advantage was not immediately apparent to the electorate after Britain joined the Common Market on 1 January 1973.

BRITAIN JOINS THE COMMON MARKET

1961 Conservatives favoured and Labour opposed entry into the Common Market. Edward Heath opened negotiations.

1963 General De Gaulle vetoed British entry.

1966 Harold Wilson converted to the EEC and announced his 'historic decision' to join in 1967.

1968 General de Gaulle again vetoed British entry. Resigned as President of France in 1969.

1970 Edward Heath, leader of new Conservative government, resumed talks on entry to EEC.

1972 Britain signed TREATY OF ACCESSION in Brussels.

1973 Britain officially a member of the EEC.

1974 Harold Wilson, leader of the new Labour government, promised the British people a *referendum* on whether or not they wished to remain in the EEC and in 1975 they voted to retain their membership.

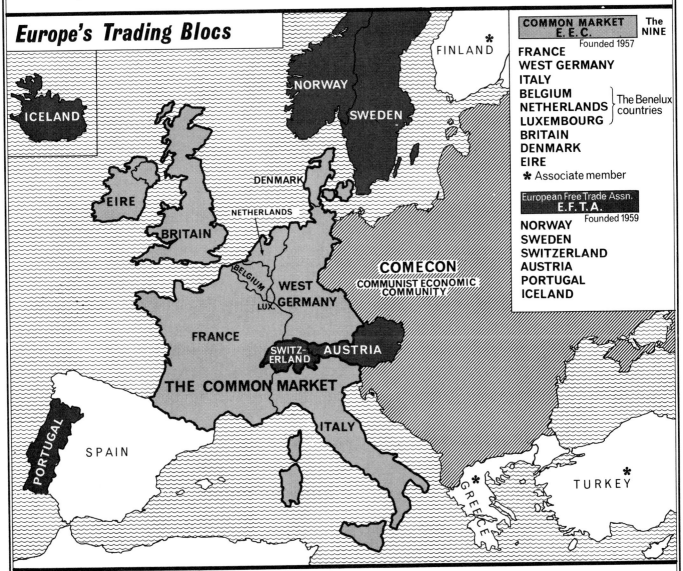

Europe's Trading Blocs

COMMON MARKET E.E.C. The NINE
Founded 1957

FRANCE
WEST GERMANY
ITALY
BELGIUM ⎫
NETHERLANDS ⎬ The Benelux countries
LUXEMBOURG ⎭
BRITAIN
DENMARK
EIRE

* Associate member

European Free Trade Assn. E.F.T.A.
Founded 1959

NORWAY
SWEDEN
SWITZERLAND
AUSTRIA
PORTUGAL
ICELAND

COMECON COMMUNIST ECONOMIC COMMUNITY

THE COMMON MARKET

OTHER OBSTACLES TO BRITAIN'S ENTRY UP TO 1972

1 Britain's agricultural policies: The 1947 Agricultural Act guaranteed British farmers (a) *prices*, (b) *markets*, as well as promising them an Annual Price Review for their products. In this way the British taxpayer has subsidized the farmers who in turn have become highly efficient in terms of mechanization and productivity. This explains why food prices in Britain remained below those of most Western European countries. Common Market members were adamant that Britain should end food subsidies to her farmers.

2 Britain's links with the Commonwealth: She had strong ties with the food-producing countries–especially New Zealand who depended on selling her butter and mutton to British consumers at preferential rates. On the whole, Common Market members were unwilling to see this Commonwealth preference continued.

69: Trade unions, 1951–1974

Since the beginning of the twentieth century the trade unions had unswervingly supported their Labour representatives in Parliament; and when Labour came to power in 1945 it repealed Baldwin's Trades Disputes Act which had declared illegal all sympathetic and general strikes. By the Fifties, however, industrial disputes became increasingly complex and at times threatened the entire economy of the British people. Neither Conservative nor Labour governments secured the full cooperation of the trade unions during the period 1951–74.

Trade unions and the Conservatives 1951–1964

There was little love lost between most trade unionists and the Tory party—traditionally the party of the employers. Nevertheless the TUC insisted that unions must restrict strike activity to matters of wages and working conditions—there must be no ideological war between 'bosses' and 'workers'. Unfortunately, conventional strikes became only too common. National rail and newspaper strikes occurred in 1955; 1956 was the year of Suez and the Hungarian Revolt. Both had important effects on the trade union movement—Suez in particular led to a shortage of oil supplies and a consequent increase in fuel costs. These led the busmen to demand a wage increase of 25/- but the Conservatives, reluctant to encourage a wages 'free-for-all', would offer only a third of this. Consequently, the 1958 London bus strike was a bitter affair which almost developed into a confrontation between the government and the unions. The busmen failed to secure their increase and after this several unions disguised their pay demands by seeking a shorter working week—a device which would give them more overtime. The 1959 printers' strike was a classic example. More serious, perhaps, were the wildcat strikes which swept the country in general and the shipbuilding industry in particular. Demarcation disputes over 'who does what' threatened the national output for quite frivolous reasons. There seemed to be very little contact between the political leaders and the rank and file of the trade union movement. Frank Cousins, the TUC leader, urged the Conservatives to evolve a wages policy and in 1962 a start was made with 'Neddy' —the National Economic Development Council— charged with rethinking the whole basis of the nation's economy.

Trade unions and the Labour governments 1964–1970

In 1964 George Brown, Secretary of State for Economic Affairs, persuaded the employers and the TUC to continue their tradition of *voluntary* wage settlements but to accept, in the event of disputes, arbitration from the new Prices and Incomes Board. Unfortunately, the next three years were years of financial crisis for Britain and the whole basis of an incomes policy collapsed. A seamen's strike in 1966 wrecked the export drive; the same year saw the Labour government impose a pay pause on the unions. Yet 1966 also saw the birth of the Industrial Reorganization Corporation, empowered to aid mergers between important firms in the export business. The IRC provided the cash which allowed Leyland Motors to merge with BMC in 1968, thus creating a motor giant comparable with European organizations such as Renault and Volkswagen. Ironically, it was the motor industry which suffered most from strike action; vehicle production lines are highly vulnerable to wildcat strikes. A whole factory can be brought to a halt in a matter of minutes. Equally devastating were strikes in the car component industry. Prolonged unrest at Pilkington Bros., for example, deprived the motor industry of safety glass during 1970. Export orders as well as home sales declined—and the home market was wide open to foreign competitors who could promise rapid delivery of *their* models.

Confrontation 1969–1974

So serious were the unofficial strikes in upsetting the nation's economy that the Labour government contemplated legislation to control strikes. Barbara Castle, Minister for Employment and Productivity, introduced the White Paper '*In Place of Strife*' at the beginning of 1969. It proposed a 'cooling off' period for unions threatening strike action; offenders might be dealt with by fines or imprisonment. Such radical proposals— in complete contradiction to the tradition of voluntary wage agreements and the right of the worker to withdraw his labour—aroused immense hostility in the unions. Eventually, because of the imminence of the 1970 General Election and the possibility that the TUC might not fund the Labour Party's election campaign, Harold Wilson abandoned his attempt to coerce the unions. Edward Heath was less cautious. During 1970–73 he tried, via an Industrial Relations Act and a *statutory* counter-inflationary policy, to reduce strikes and wage demands to a minimum. Predictably, he antagonized the unions—a factor which contributed to his downfall in 1974. His successor, Harold Wilson, based his policy of national unity and co-operation with the unions upon the much publicized 'Social Contract'.

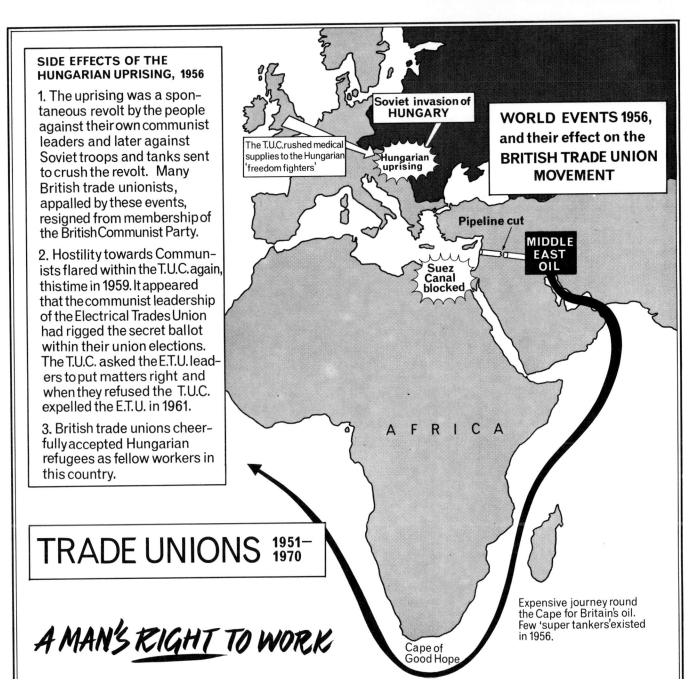

SIDE EFFECTS OF THE HUNGARIAN UPRISING, 1956

1. The uprising was a spontaneous revolt by the people against their own communist leaders and later against Soviet troops and tanks sent to crush the revolt. Many British trade unionists, appalled by these events, resigned from membership of the British Communist Party.

2. Hostility towards Communists flared within the T.U.C. again, this time in 1959. It appeared that the communist leadership of the Electrical Trades Union had rigged the secret ballot within their union elections. The T.U.C. asked the E.T.U. leaders to put matters right and when they refused the T.U.C. expelled the E.T.U. in 1961.

3. British trade unions cheerfully accepted Hungarian refugees as fellow workers in this country.

Soviet invasion of HUNGARY

The T.U.C. rushed medical supplies to the Hungarian 'freedom fighters'

Hungarian uprising

WORLD EVENTS 1956, and their effect on the BRITISH TRADE UNION MOVEMENT

Pipeline cut

MIDDLE EAST OIL

Suez Canal blocked

A F R I C A

Cape of Good Hope

Expensive journey round the Cape for Britain's oil. Few 'super tankers' existed in 1956.

TRADE UNIONS 1951–1970

A MAN'S RIGHT TO WORK

No trade union can give itself by its rules an unfettered discretion to expel a man or to withdraw his membership. The reason lies in a man's right to work. This is now fully recognized by law. It is a right of especial importance when a trade union operates a 'closed shop' or '100% membership' for that means no man can become employed, or remain in employment, with a firm unless he is a member of the union.

If his union card is withdrawn, he has to leave his employment. He is deprived of his livelihood. The courts of this country will not allow so great a power to be exercised arbitrarily or capriciously or with unfair discrimination, neither in the making of rules nor in the enforcement of them.
— Lord Denning, Judge in the Appeal Court, July 1970.

He was referring to a case in which SOGAT (Society of Graphical and Allied Trades) had wrongfully expelled a printer from membership of the union and then forced the employers to dismiss him.

Lack of innovation

A surprising feature of post-war Britain was the relative absence of technical innovation in the country—a sad contrast with the leadership Britain had shown the world in the previous two centuries. There was no lack of scientific discovery and technical brilliance; but too often good designs and valuable ideas perished through lack of financial support or were delayed so long that they became obsolete. Britain's Calder Hall nuclear power station was the first in the field—but soon became obsolete. Several expensive failures occurred in the highly competitive aircraft and missile industries.

TSR-2 and ELDO

TSR-2 was a brilliant aircraft design ordered by the Conservatives as a low level nuclear strike bomber capable of delivering its load at supersonic speeds. Its enormously complex electronic control system meant that each TSR-2 would cost around £6 million. In 1964 the new Labour government decided to scrap the development work—which had cost well over £100 million—and buy American *Phantom* aircraft instead. Having eliminated this expense Britain incurred more in the European Launcher Development Organization—ELDO. This was a plan to put Europe's own communications satellite into orbit and Britain hoped that her *Blue Streak* rocket (which successfully test-fired at Woomera range, Australia in 1966) would form the booster stage of the ELDO project. Unfortunately, development costs again proved exorbitant and, after spending another £100 million, Britain decided to abandon the project during 1970.

Concorde

The supersonic airliner *Concorde* was another expensive project inherited by the 1964 Labour government. Because it was an Anglo-French project guaranteed by an international treaty the Labour government failed to wriggle out of its commitment. Eventually, the French prototype 001 was the first to fly; Britain's 002 made its maiden flight from Filton in April 1969. *Concorde* is designed to carry 130 passengers from Western European capitals to the U.S.A. at supersonic speeds; but the development work was so expensive that some people wondered if the project would ever show a profit.

Natural gas

The exploitation of natural gas had a happier history and represents one of the most dramatic technological changes in post-war Britain. Natural gas was already coming into the country from Algeria when, in 1959, drilling rigs located a big field of gas in the North Sea. British Petroleum made their big strike in 1965, a success marred by the sinking of the rig *Sea Gem* during a vicious December storm. By 1970 large quantities of natural gas were flowing in through the two terminals at Bacton and Easington while the gas boards were busily converting appliances from town to natural gas in one of the biggest investment operations in the history of the British people.

Television and transistors

By 1977 95% of British families owned or rented a television set—more than in any other West European country. Most families could receive ITV transmissions as well as BBC1. The Independent Television Authority dates from 1954 and relies on advertisers for its revenue—it has no share of the TV and radio licence fees. Since 1964 BBC2 has offered an alternative service and was the first—in 1967—to transmit programmes in colour. The widespread use of transistors (an American development) has replaced most valves in electrical equipment. Transistors, together with printed circuits, have reduced the size and power consumption of many electrical goods and have brought radios, record players and tape recorders within the purchasing power of people in general and teenagers in particular.

Mintech

Many new industrial products such as plastics, man-made fibres, non-stick surfaces and light-weight alloys resulted from patient scientific research. They all help to make life more convenient, more enjoyable and symbolise the technological change that has swept over post-war Britain. However, modern technology is expensive* and often needs support from the government's Ministry of Technology—or Mintech. Mintech is prepared to back export industries such as electronics, aviation, hovercraft, computers and the massive British Steel Corporation.† Such help, however, represents one of Britain's great problems of the Seventies: to what extent can Britain's industries become so profitable that they do not need support from the hard-pressed British taxpayer?

*A nationalized industry—formed 1967.
†And sometimes risky e.g. the 1974 Flixborough disaster.

CONCORDE

Public gazes at Britain's Concorde landing at Fairford, Gloucs., after its maiden flight.

Concorde is the most expensive aeronautical project in British history. By 1977 it was in regular service to America and the Middle East.

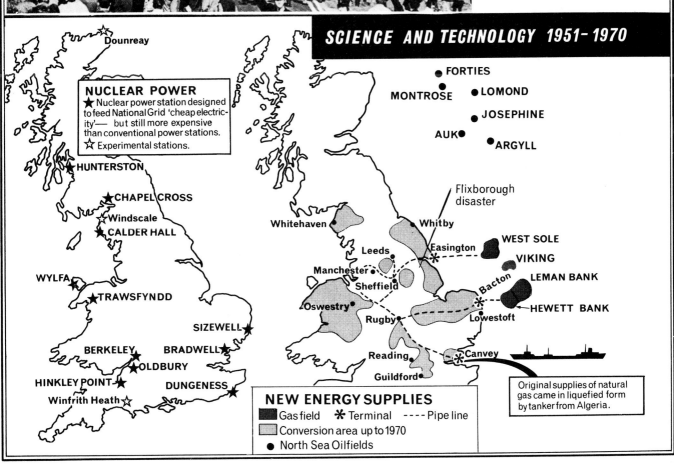

NUCLEAR POWER
★ Nuclear power station designed to feed National Grid 'cheap electricity'— but still more expensive than conventional power stations.
☆ Experimental stations.

Dounreay

HUNTERSTON

CHAPEL CROSS

Windscale
CALDER HALL

WYLFA
TRAWSFYNDD

BERKELEY
OLDBURY
HINKLEY POINT
Winfrith Heath

SIZEWELL

BRADWELL

DUNGENESS

FORTIES
MONTROSE   LOMOND
JOSEPHINE
AUK   ARGYLL

Flixborough disaster

Whitehaven   Whitby
Leeds   Easington   WEST SOLE
Manchester   VIKING
Sheffield   Bacton   LEMAN BANK
Oswestry   Lowestoft   HEWETT BANK
Rugby
Reading   Canvey
Guildford

NEW ENERGY SUPPLIES
■ Gas field   ✳ Terminal   ---- Pipe line
▨ Conversion area up to 1970
● North Sea Oilfields

Original supplies of natural gas came in liquefied form by tanker from Algeria.

157

The affluent society to 1973

Both of Britain's major political parties regard the nation's prosperity as their main priority. Prosperity will enable a better society to use its resources in helping those who, through no fault of their own, cannot help themselves. Undoubtedly, Britain has enjoyed increasing prosperity since the Fifties when commentators began to use the term 'affluent society' to describe the condition in which the British people found themselves. The expression originated with Professor Galbraith* who, in 1958, used it to describe American society where private wealth was growing at the expense of public squalor. However, affluence is not simply a measurement of money. There aren't really many more rich people today than there were in 1938; 'the distribution of capital is still highly concentrated in the hands of a tiny proportion of the population as ever'.† Of course, no-one disputes that the abundance of consumer luxuries has meant a remarkable improvement in the quality of life; but the fact that people can afford to buy them may be due to another important fact—there are 41% more people earning money than there were in 1930. Nowadays, wives and teenagers go out to work; in 1938 they would have found employment hard to come by. Therefore it is the earning power of the British family which has seen the real increase, not necessarily individual wage earners.

Living standards after 1973

By then Britain had one of the biggest inflation problems in Western Europe and, in their search for a solution, the Labour government deliberately cut the living standards of the British people. It did this by increasing most forms of taxation and by charging higher rates for government controlled services such as gas, electricity and postage while, at the same time trying to persuade a disenhanted electorate to refrain from asking for higher wages. It is hard to measure cuts in living standards but they meant that while the cost of living was going up the income people had to spend was going down—by about 1.5% between 1974 and 1976.

Leisure

Nevertheless, workers enjoy much better working conditions and longer, paid holidays. Many can take holidays abroad even though these are often of the cut-price 'package deal' variety. Labour saving devices in the home bring more opportunities for leisure involving the whole family. Children in particular can benefit from the organized school parties which visit holiday centres at home and abroad.

Health

Since 1939 governments have made concerted attacks upon disease and malnutrition—as well as the poverty which is frequently the cause of physical decline. Welfare services and family allowances have benefited the whole population while the practice of admitting the expectant mother to hospital for her first baby has had an amazing impact upon infant mortality rates. The 1938 figures for deaths of infants under the age of 1 year were 55.5 per 1000 live births; thirty years later they had slumped to 18.7 per 1000 live births. In this way, the chances of human survival increased; better medical facilities prolonged life expectancy; and society was left with the problems of decreasing living space and increasing numbers of elderly people. By 1977 there were 9 million old age pensioners in Britain.

Education

By 1970 Labour could make the proud boast that for the first time in her history Britain was spending more on education than on defence. Both Conservative and Labour governments had concentrated upon primary school building so that progressive teachers could deal with the needs and interests of the youngest children. The importance of primary education was becoming more widely accepted and great attention was paid to children's creativity and to the development of reading and number skills. Secondary schools became a subject of political controversy by the 1950s. Many teachers supported the Labour view that selection at 11 + was unsound and that children needed the facilities that large comprehensive schools could offer. After Labour came to power in 1964 it issued the famous Circular 10/65§ in which Anthony Crosland, the Education Minister, asked LEAs to submit plans for 'going comprehensive'. By 1970 about 33% of secondary schoolchildren were in comprehensive schools. All secondary schools during the period sent more students to colleges and universities—where during the period 1965–69 there was a 'population explosion'. Students themselves began to play highly publicized roles in politics and, less conspicuously, made valuable contributions to community service in pockets of poverty which survived the reforms of the Welfare State.

*See Professor Galbraith's 'The Affluent Society' 1958.
†See Pollard & Crossley 'The Wealth of Britain' pp. 265–266.
§ Withdrawn by the Conservatives in 1970. But the 1976 Education Act required LEAs to implement comprehensive schooling.

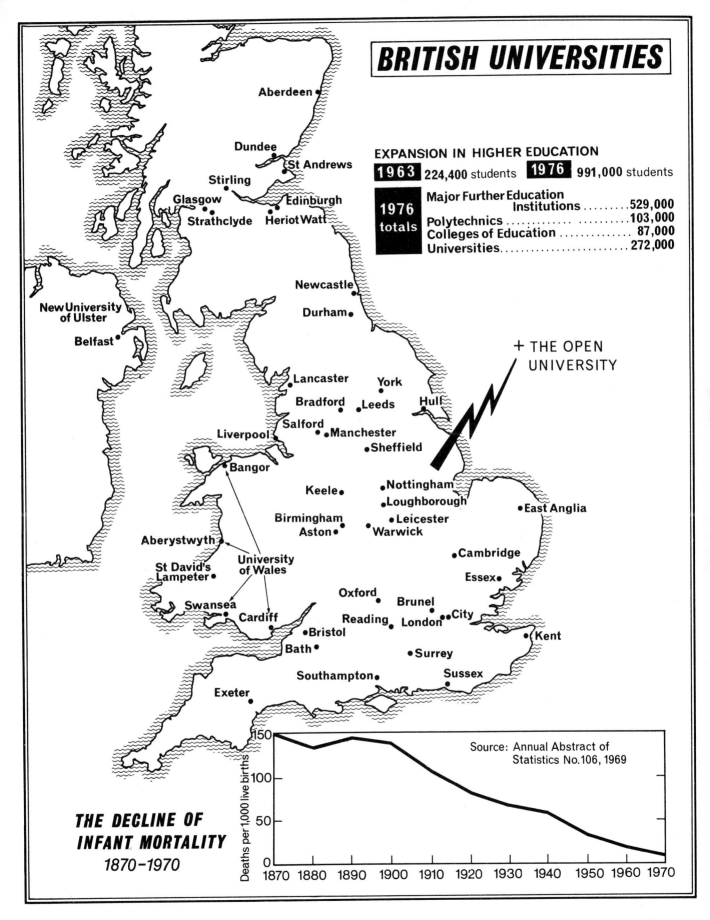

BRITISH UNIVERSITIES

Aberdeen

Dundee

St Andrews

Stirling

Glasgow

Edinburgh

Strathclyde

Heriot Watt

EXPANSION IN HIGHER EDUCATION

1963 224,400 students   **1976** 991,000 students

1976 totals

Major Further Education Institutions	529,000
Polytechnics	103,000
Colleges of Education	87,000
Universities	272,000

Newcastle

Durham

New University of Ulster

Belfast

+ THE OPEN UNIVERSITY

Lancaster

York

Bradford

Leeds

Hull

Salford

Liverpool

Manchester

Sheffield

Bangor

Keele

Nottingham

Loughborough

East Anglia

Birmingham

Leicester

Aston

Warwick

Aberystwyth

Cambridge

University of Wales

St David's Lampeter

Essex

Swansea

Oxford

Cardiff

Brunel

Reading

London

City

Bristol

Kent

Bath

Surrey

Southampton

Sussex

Exeter

THE DECLINE OF INFANT MORTALITY
1870–1970

Source: Annual Abstract of Statistics No.106, 1969

Deaths per 1,000 live births

150

100

50

0

1870 1880 1890 1900 1910 1920 1930 1940 1950 1960 1970

72:   The hazards of modern life: (1) the elements

In many respects the period 1951–70 symbolized man's mastery over his environment. Earth moving plant gouged out motorways across the countryside, new bridges spanned the Severn, Tay and Forth, skyscraper flats* and office blocks reared up in city centres. Occasionally, however, the elements brought death and disaster to communities of the British people.

Lynmouth

At 8.30 p.m. on Friday 15 August 1952 a cloudburst broke over Exmoor. Within an hour more than 5 inches of rain had cascaded on the moor, transforming tiny brooks into raging torrents. Racing down to the coast, the flood-waters channelled themselves into two river beds —the East Lyn and the West Lyn. In turn the rivers funnelled the tidal wave into the picturesque holiday village of Lynmouth. Huge boulders, tree trunks—debris of all descriptions—crashed into the streets. Cottages and shops collapsed, the Beach Hotel disintegrated and 34 people died in the chaos. Lynmouth's flood disaster caught the sympathy of the nation which, within a matter of months, was to suffer an even worse ordeal.

The East Coast floods

At the end of January 1953 an Atlantic depression, codenamed *Liz*, was tracking across the north of the British Isles. It was creating areas of exceptionally low pressure and soon fierce northerly gales began to blow down the centre of the North Sea. On Saturday 31 January gusts up to 120 m.p.h. were hitting the anemometers on the Orkney Islands and storms developed round Britain's coasts. The first tragedy was the sinking of the British Rail ferry *Princess Victoria*. Bound for Larne, the ship had 129 passengers and 49 crew on board. She capsized in the Irish Sea and a mere 44 survivors were picked up; 'the greatest disaster suffered by any British Merchant vessel in peace-time for a quarter of a century.' By now the hurricane force gales were battering Eastern Scotland where damage reached 'catastrophic proportions'. Even more significant, the winds were also banking up a mass of water, drawn from the Atlantic Ocean, into the North Sea. This water was being whipped up into a frenzy by the unceasing wind and at the same time being forced down into the narrow gap between Holland and the East Coast. This unusual concurrence of events led to the 'great tide' of 1953 which killed hundreds of people on both sides of the North Sea. The 'great tide' hit the East Riding first and smashed through the sea defences at Easington.

Moving down to Lincolnshire and Norfolk, the flood-waters poured through the Wash and trapped hundreds of bungalow dwellers. 67 people died outside Hunstanton. By midnight, Southwold and Felixstowe were inundated. Tragedy at Felixstowe occurred when the River Orwell burst its banks and drowned 28 people—many of them trapped in flimsy 'prefabs'. The greatest concentration of floodwater was in Essex and disaster struck the Blackwater Estuary and Canvey Island. As the tide surged past the Nore it overran the Isle of Sheppey and Sheerness Dockyard. HMS *Berkeley Castle*, a frigate, and HMS *Sirdar*, a submarine, were in dry dock. In rushed the floodwater causing both vessels to overturn—fortunately without casualties. Conditions were even worse in the Low Countries. For Holland it was the worst flood disaster for five centuries. Even her sophisticated sea walls were no match for the 'great tide'. About 1,800 people died.

The rescuers

On Monday 2 February Winston Churchill informed Parliament: 'As one might expect after the experiences of two world wars, organizations of all kinds . . . reacted immediately to the call. . . . All the resources of the State will be employed. . . . to meet this emergency'. From all directions volunteers and members of the armed services converged to fill sandbags and rescue the survivors. The Household Cavalry arrived from Windsor, the RASC brought their amphibious DUKWs, the USAF lent their huge trucks with engines that had high water clearance. The RAF formed prodigious feats of sandbag filling and eventually the breaches in the sea defences were repaired.

Aberfan

During 1966 almost an entire generation of schoolchildren died in the little village of Aberfan. It was the worst disaster of its kind ever to take place in Britain. A coal tip, poised above the village, had stood for fifty years; unknown to anyone, a spring inside it was turning the tip into a mountain of sludge. Just below it stood Pantglas Primary School. The critical moment arrived on the morning of 21 October. The sludge engulfed the school, killing most of the 250 children on roll. The event stunned the nation, underlining the hazard of manmade evils which pollute the environment of the British people.

*One of these, Ronan Point (a block of flats in Newham, London), suffered partial collapse in May 1968–four people died.

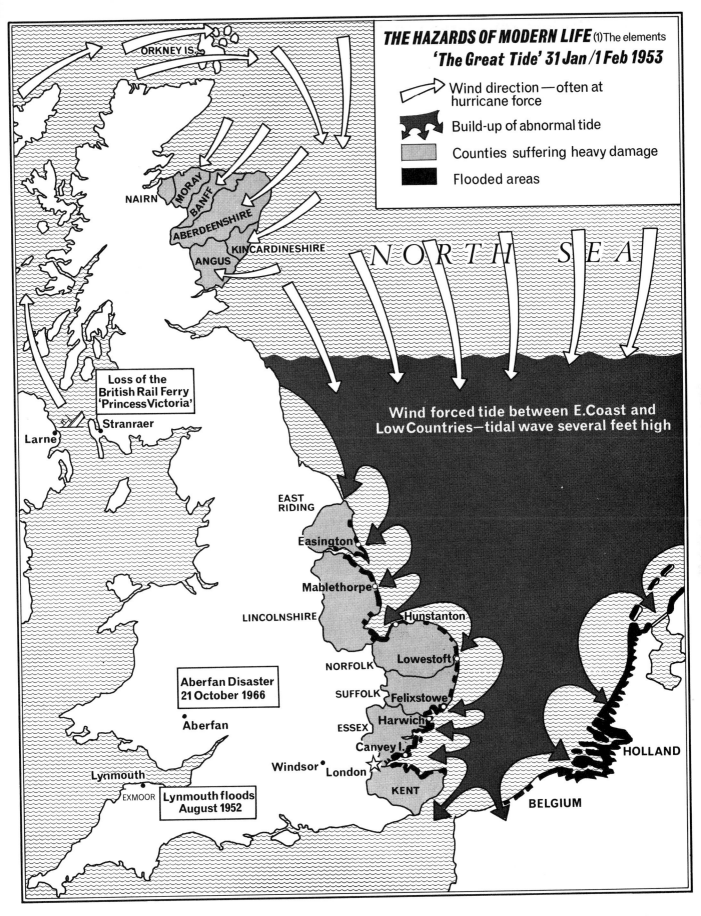

THE HAZARDS OF MODERN LIFE (1) The elements
'The Great Tide' 31 Jan / 1 Feb 1953

Wind direction — often at hurricane force

Build-up of abnormal tide

Counties suffering heavy damage

Flooded areas

ORKNEY IS.

NAIRN

MORAY
BANFF
ABERDEENSHIRE
KINCARDINESHIRE
ANGUS

NORTH SEA

Loss of the
British Rail Ferry
'Princess Victoria'

Stranraer

Larne

Wind forced tide between E. Coast and
Low Countries—tidal wave several feet high

EAST
RIDING

Easington

Mablethorpe

LINCOLNSHIRE

Hunstanton

Lowestoft

NORFOLK

SUFFOLK

Felixstowe

Aberfan Disaster
21 October 1966

Aberfan

Harwich

ESSEX

Canvey I.

Windsor • London

HOLLAND

Lynmouth

EXMOOR

KENT

BELGIUM

Lynmouth floods
August 1952

161

73: The hazards of modern life: (2) pollution

'Fall-out'

Atmospheric testing of atomic bombs after 1945 faced world health with the threat of poisonous 'fall-out'. Scientists engaged in the 1958 International Geophysical Year investigations began to measure the fall-out from atomic air bursts and discovered that the radiation particles—carried by winds high up in the atmosphere—were a menace to all forms of life. By 1962, research revealed that dangerous deposits of strontium-90 in human bone structure were tending to increase. Within a year Prime Minister Macmillan joined with President Kennedy (U.S.A.) and Premier Khrushchev (U.S.S.R.) in signing the 1963 Partial Test Ban Treaty. This prohibited nuclear tests in the atmosphere but allowed them to continue underground. Unfortunately, neither General de Gaulle nor Chairman Mao Tse-tung would sign the treaty and continued to authorize atmospheric tests.

Lung cancer

Scientists made other significant discoveries in 1962. In March the Royal College of Physicians issued a report confirming a belief many people had held for years: smoking was a direct cause of lung cancer. Heavy smokers were four times as likely to die from lung cancer than non-smokers. Despite this information, relatively few smokers abandoned their cigarettes; teenagers continued to take up the habit and hoped to minimize the chance of polluting their lungs by smoking tipped cigarettes.*

Smog

About 4000 people died during London's 'great smog' of 1952. Most of them already suffered from respiratory diseases; the smog simply hastened their deaths. Scientists believed that the killer quality in smog arose from water droplets forming around smoke particles. People inhaled these and damaged their lungs. It seemed that smoke was the villain. Parliament accepted the idea and in 1956 passed the Clean Air Act. This authorized local authorities to create 'smoke free zones'. When smog hit London again in 1962 750 people died, a significant improvement which seemed to be due entirely to the reduction of smoke in the atmosphere.

Other sources of pollution

It has been said that 'inventing the automobile was man's greatest achievement; its functioning his greatest failure.' As yet there is no evidence in Britain that carbon monoxide fumes from car exhausts present a major health hazard. However, the accumulation of hydrocarbons, nitrogen oxides and diesel fumes assailing drivers sitting in traffic jams can reduce their reaction times and may therefore be a contributory cause of road accidents. Sewage effluent is a greater threat. Hundreds of miles of Britain's rivers are seriously polluted; a crash programme to develop better forms of sewage disposal is now regarded as vital. Similarly, industrial waste can destroy the 'balance' of life in the rivers and sea. Such disturbance of the *ecology* of a region is now a world-wide problem and during 1969–70 people increasingly realised the importance of conserving the balance of nature.

Conservation

During 1969 a number of farmers and conservationists met at Silsoe to discuss methods which, whilst permitting agriculture to become even more efficient, would still encourage the preservation of flora and fauna in the British countryside. After all, although this is the second half of the highly industrialised and urbanised twentieth century, more than 80% of Britain still remains essentially rural. And despite the fact that many farmers have destroyed hedgerows and copses, drained ponds and marshes in an effort to improve their productivity everyone agreed that it was not too late to save the amenities of the British countryside. As a result, the government agreed to train Ministry of Agriculture advisers in conservation methods. So at least a start had been made. In the following year Prime Minister Harold Wilson set up a Royal Commission on Pollution,† underlining the seriousness of problems which, a few years before people hadn't thought were important.

*The Labour government 1966–70 banned the advertising of cigarettes on television.
†1970 was also 'European Conservation Year'.

RESIDENTIAL & COMMERCIAL CAUSES OF POLLUTION

SEWAGE — the main source of river pollution

SULPHUR DIOXIDE — as yet not too dangerous. Produced by small factories and office/domestic central heating systems.

HYDROCARBONS — unburned petrol from car exhausts
— while pylons do not enhance the scene

AGRICULTURAL & INDUSTRIAL CAUSES OF POLLUTION

CHEMICAL WASTE — can kill river and sea life
BRICKWORKS — produce fluoride which pollutes grass
ALUMINIUM SMELTER — another major source of fluoride pollution
DIESEL FUMES — a major cause of air pollution
PESTICIDES — can kill wild life and disturb ecology of area
— quarries spoil the countryside

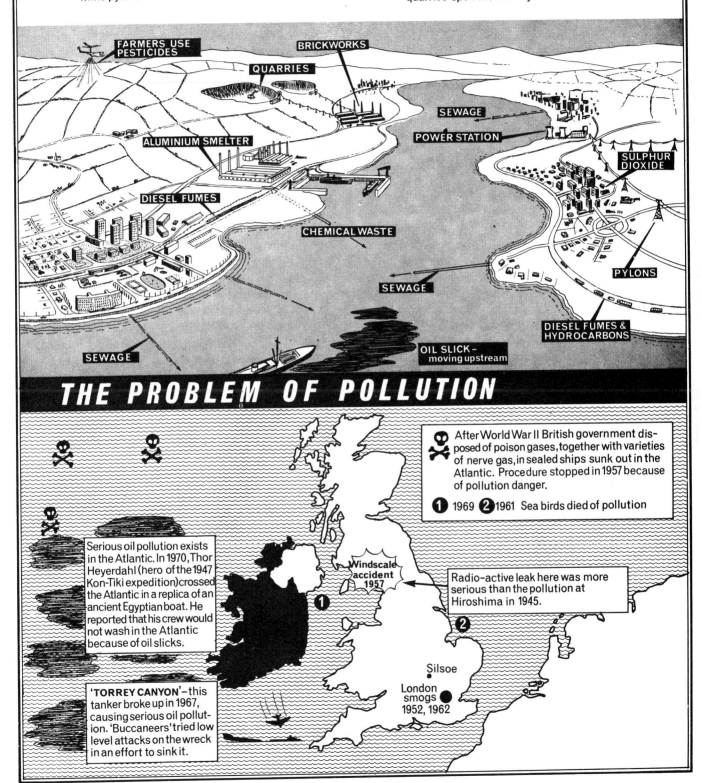

THE PROBLEM OF POLLUTION

After World War II British government disposed of poison gases, together with varieties of nerve gas, in sealed ships sunk out in the Atlantic. Procedure stopped in 1957 because of pollution danger.

❶ 1969 ❷ 1961 Sea birds died of pollution

Serious oil pollution exists in the Atlantic. In 1970, Thor Heyerdahl (hero of the 1947 Kon-Tiki expedition) crossed the Atlantic in a replica of an ancient Egyptian boat. He reported that his crew would not wash in the Atlantic because of oil slicks.

Windscale accident 1957

Radio-active leak here was more serious than the pollution at Hiroshima in 1945.

Silsoe

London smogs 1952, 1962

'TORREY CANYON' — this tanker broke up in 1967, causing serious oil pollution. 'Buccaneers' tried low level attacks on the wreck in an effort to sink it.

Recent British history has thrown up two disturbing situations. One is the problem of violence in Northern Ireland; the other is reaction to the arrival of Commonwealth immigrants.

Violence in Ulster

a) 1968–1970

Ever since George V opened Northern Ireland's first parliament in 1921, voting arrangements in Ulster have discriminated against one third of the population—the Catholics. Cut off from Protestants as children because they attend Catholic schools, Catholics grew up to resent bitterly their inadequate representation on local councils and their substandard accommodation. Moreover, in Londonderry—where Catholics form a majority—they endured constant unemployment and naturally blamed the Ulster Unionist government for this state of affairs. And all over the province, Catholics feared the Ulster B-Specials—the armed police whose job it was to prevent IRA raids across the border with Eire. Serious disorder in the province broke out in August 1968, when the Apprentice Boys of Londonderry provoked Catholic attacks. During 1969 civil war flared in parts of Belfast and Londonderry until conditions warranted the intervention of British troops with their CS-gas and "snatch squads." Soldiers and civilians alike suffered wounds and occasionally death. By 1970, the Ulster Defence Regiment had replaced the notorious B-Specials and 11,000 troops guarded the trouble spots where incidents were becoming progressively serious.

b) 1970–1977

As violence increased, the new Conservative government suspended Ulster's constitution and tried to rule the unhappy province directly from Westminster. But by 1974 300 British soldiers and many more civilians had died in gun-battles, bomb explosions and terrorist raids, some of which had begun to spill over into England.* Labour policies after 1974 brought no respite to Ulster. In 1976, 296 people died; and by 1977 the elusive bombers and gunmen were tying down 14,000 British troops in Northern Ireland.

The immigrants

Traditionally, West Indians have emigrated to the USA. World War II changed the pattern principally due to the desire of Jamaican servicemen† to settle in Britain. In addition, Pakistanis and Indians arrived in the mid-

Fifties, as did Greek and Turkish Cypriots fleeing from their war-torn island. By 1960, about 300,000 had arrived—most of them relatively skilled, hard-working people. The Notting Hill race riots (1958) were the only sign of serious racial tension. Such tension was usually due to the crowding of immigrants into sub-standard houses, a situation which could damage community relations. But it was serious enough to make the Conservatives consider immigration control—and this in turn sparked off an influx of about 200,000 immigrants before the first Commonwealth Immigrants Act became law in 1962. These immigrants flocked to "labour shortage areas" such as London, Yorkshire and the West Midlands. They took jobs which were usually unpleasant, poorly paid with inconvenient shift work. But they were not robbing the British of their jobs—immigrants will naturally take the vacancies which others spurn, just as they have done in the foundries and plastics factories of Common Market countries.

Problems of integration

After 1962 immigration became a major political issue. Many of the new immigrants came from rural areas in Jamaica and Pakistan and found it difficult to adapt to an urban life. Then there came the tragedy of the Kenyan Asians, victims of Kenya's policy of Africanization. These Asians had no future in Kenya and held British passports. Nevertheless, the Labour government felt compelled to keep them out of Britain and passed the 1968 Commonwealth Immigrants Act which prevented any Asian from settling unless he already had family connections in the country. Then the government relented and offered an entry permit to any *expelled* Kenyan Asian. This inconsistent policy aroused Enoch Powell MP to make his controversial speeches about immigration and in turn forced the government to pass the 1968 Race Relations Act (reinforcing the 1965 Act) which outlawed discrimination in housing, employment and public places. In 1976 the Labour government passed a new Race Relations Act. This defined a new offence: incitement to racial hatred in public places by spoken or written words.

*Such as the bombing of the servicemen's coach and the destruction of public houses frequented by servicemen and women in Guildford (1974); and the six-day Balcombe Street Siege in 1975.
†One, P/O Capstick, fought in the Battle of Britain.

Opposite, British troops on a sweep through the Catholic 'Free Belfast', July 1970

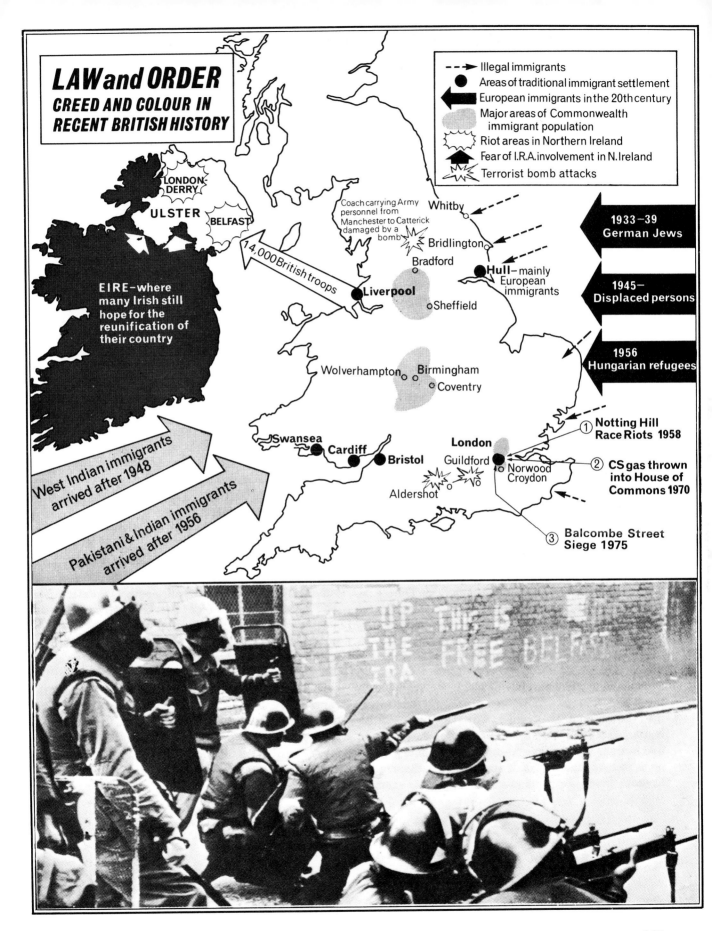

LAW and ORDER
CREED AND COLOUR IN RECENT BRITISH HISTORY

Legend:
- ➔ Illegal immigrants
- ● Areas of traditional immigrant settlement
- ⬅ European immigrants in the 20th century
- Major areas of Commonwealth immigrant population
- Riot areas in Northern Ireland
- Fear of I.R.A. involvement in N. Ireland
- Terrorist bomb attacks

LONDON-DERRY

ULSTER

BELFAST

EIRE—where many Irish still hope for the reunification of their country

Coach carrying Army personnel from Manchester to Catterick damaged by a bomb

14,000 British troops

Whitby

Bridlington

Bradford

Liverpool

Sheffield

Hull—mainly European immigrants

1933–39 German Jews

1945– Displaced persons

1956 Hungarian refugees

Wolverhampton

Birmingham

Coventry

Swansea **Cardiff**

Bristol

Aldershot

London

Guildford

Norwood Croydon

① **Notting Hill Race Riots 1958**

② **CS gas thrown into House of Commons 1970**

③ **Balcombe Street Siege 1975**

West Indian immigrants arrived after 1948

Pakistani & Indian immigrants arrived after 1956

165

75 : People and politics, 1951–1974

Population movements

In many respects, the economic and political structure of Britain seems subject to as much change as it was two hundred years ago. The distribution of population, for example, is by no means settled. Many people living in the industrial north look for greater opportunities by moving to the affluent Midland towns or to the increasingly popular residential areas of South East England. As most who seek advancement tend to be better educated, the areas from which they move are made even poorer by their departure. Prime Minister Wilson tried to combat this undesirable state of affairs by defining certain parts of Britain as "development" or "intermediate" areas. He subsidized these by offering grants and tax concessions to industrialists who would help in the development of these regions. However, co-operative employers frequently found that their own skilled workers didn't want to make the move. The government discovered this harsh fact for itself when it established the new Mint at Llantrisant. London's own Mint was old-fashioned and ill-equipped to strike the new coins needed for D-Day (Decimal Day) 15 February 1971. So it offered the mint workers the chance of moving with their families to the new £7 million plant, with its superb working conditions and housing facilities, just outside Cardiff. Stubbornly, nearly all the London mint workers refused to uproot themselves.

Regionalism

This parochial atmosphere entered politics. During the Sixties the Welsh, Scots and Northern Irish considered that government at Westminster had very little interest in the special problems of their own regions. Consequently, several nationalist movements started on the 'Celtic fringe' of Great Britain. Most famous was Plaid Cymru, the Welsh Nationalist Party. During 1966 the Welsh Nationalist Gwynfor Evans managed to win the Carmarthen by-election; in 1967 the Scottish Nationalists emulated his feat by winning the Hamilton by-election. These events prompted the Labour government to take some action. It appointed a Parliamentary Commissioner—or 'Ombudsman'—in 1967 to examine particular problems brought forward by MPs. It produced arguments to convince the Scots that they simply hadn't the financial ability to run their own affairs. Finally, it pacified the Welsh by holding the spectacular investiture of Prince Charles in Cardiff during 1969. Probably the most persuasive argument against regional self-government in Britain came from the violence that was blighting Northern Ireland. However, in both 1974 elections Scottish and Welsh nationalists made a strong showing and their case was strengthened by the existence of oil and gas in their coastal waters with the promise of economic viability.

The political parties

a) 1951–1970

Despite the spasmodic disenchantment with government at Westminster there were few radical changes in the organization and conduct of British politics. The imprisonment of Miss Bernadette Devlin MP (found guilty on three charges of incitement to riot and one of rioting in the Londonderry disturbances) in Armagh Jail during 1970 and the throwing of CS gas canisters on to the floor of the House of Commons the same year were both symptoms of the troubles in Ulster. Politics remained dominated by the Labour and Conservative parties. Four Tory Prime Ministers ruled Britain during the thirteen years 1951–64. Then the electorate opted for a change and chose a Labour government. Six years later and after unceasing economic crisis, the electorate reverted to the Conservatives—now led by Edward Heath who presented an entirely different image of Conservatism from that offered by previous leaders. This comeback was despite the unhappy Tory record over Suez in 1956, over the Vassall spy case in 1962, and over the 1963 Profumo scandal. No other political party was capable of winning the allegiance of the electorate. Though millions voted for the Liberals, they won fewer and fewer seats in parliament. Students noisily supported ultra-Left wing policies and opposed apartheid and the war in Viet Nam with great vigour and no effect. Their famous Grosvenor Square "demo" in May 1968 came to little; but their threats to demonstrate caused the cancellation of the South African Springbok cricket tour in 1970. But although they had the vote as a result of the 1967 Latey Committee's recommendation to lower the legal age of majority to 18, they made little impact on the outcome of the 1970 General Election.

b) 1970–1974

These were years in which people's disenchantment with politics and politicians became even more intense. An unending economic crisis seemed to dominate national life, especially after the War of Yom Kippur which raged in the Middle East during 1973. Arab-Israeli conflict led directly to huge increases in the price of imported oil. This created an 'energy crisis' which made its impact on everybody's life in the winter of 1973–4, memorable for its power-cuts, three-day working week, sudden shortages of household goods in shops and supermarkets—and the victory of Harold Wilson in the General Elections of 1974.

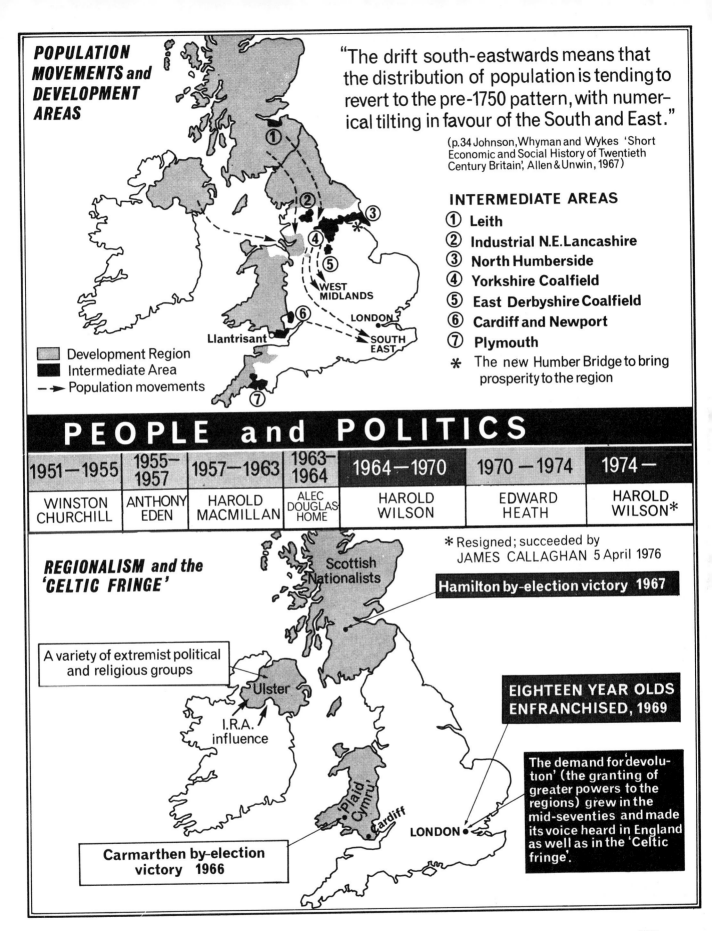

POPULATION MOVEMENTS and DEVELOPMENT AREAS

"The drift south-eastwards means that the distribution of population is tending to revert to the pre-1750 pattern, with numerical tilting in favour of the South and East."

(p.34 Johnson, Whyman and Wykes 'Short Economic and Social History of Twentieth Century Britain', Allen & Unwin, 1967)

INTERMEDIATE AREAS

① Leith
② Industrial N.E. Lancashire
③ North Humberside
④ Yorkshire Coalfield
⑤ East Derbyshire Coalfield
⑥ Cardiff and Newport
⑦ Plymouth
✱ The new Humber Bridge to bring prosperity to the region

WEST MIDLANDS
LONDON
SOUTH EAST
Llantrisant

☐ Development Region
■ Intermediate Area
-→ Population movements

PEOPLE and POLITICS

1951—1955	1955—1957	1957—1963	1963—1964	1964—1970	1970—1974	1974—
WINSTON CHURCHILL	ANTHONY EDEN	HAROLD MACMILLAN	ALEC DOUGLAS HOME	HAROLD WILSON	EDWARD HEATH	HAROLD WILSON✱

REGIONALISM and the 'CELTIC FRINGE'

✱ Resigned; succeeded by JAMES CALLAGHAN 5 April 1976

Scottish Nationalists

Hamilton by-election victory 1967

A variety of extremist political and religious groups

Ulster

I.R.A. influence

EIGHTEEN YEAR OLDS ENFRANCHISED, 1969

'Plaid Cymru'
Cardiff

LONDON

The demand for 'devolution' (the granting of greater powers to the regions) grew in the mid-seventies and made its voice heard in England as well as in the 'Celtic fringe'.

Carmarthen by-election victory 1966

The poverty trap

When the Labour Party returned to office in 1974 it made the usual promises to end inflation, stop strikes and reduce unemployment. But, above all, it promised to make Britain a more equal society, to help the ever-increasing numbers of people living below the poverty line. Usually, poverty is the result of low pay. Yet Harold Wilson's wage restraint policy (the *Social Contract*) held down *all* wages at a time of inflation—so it hardly helped people already caught in the 'poverty trap'. Four million were still taking home wage packets well below the 'minimum wage targets' set by the trade unions: £25 in 1974, £30 in 1975. Then, in April 1976, Harold Wilson announced his resignation. He left behind a Labour Government (he called them 'the most experienced and talented team in this century') which would need all its skill to solve the social and economic problems which faced the British people. 1.5 million were unemployed at the end of 1976; even more were badly housed.

The economic problem

James Callaghan, the new Labour Prime Minister, had to cope with declining industrial production and with a 20% annual rise in inflation. He agreed on a 'wages standstill' with the unions; and by 1978 the inflation rate was below 10%. With union support and the 'Lib-Lab' alliance with David Steel's Liberal Party (March 1977) he seemed set to carry through the long overdue social and economic reforms. In the event, the trade unions failed him. Strikes and high wage settlements overturned his pay guidelines. Inflation shot up again. At the next General Election (3 May 1979) the British people elected a Conservative government led by Mrs. Margaret Thatcher, Britain's first woman Prime Minister.

Britain and the European Economic Community

In the *1975 Referendum* the British had confirmed their membership of the EEC. Nevertheless, they were alive to the problems this caused. Historically, they had always depended upon cheap imported food and cheap energy. Everyone knew that oil prices would never be cheap again; but need food prices be so high? The EEC said yes. Most of its members were food producers and they needed heavy subsidies. If Britain wanted to buy her food elsewhere then she would have to pay import levies to the EEC as well as her very heavy contributions to the Community's budget. But Britain couldn't afford this. EEC membership had not led to industrial prosperity; in fact, Britain had already lost over half of her home market to foreign car manufacturers. So Britain's special needs were hard to reconcile with those of the other eight members. One way of making progress was through the European Parliament. All member countries held elections in June 1979 and Britain sent 68 representatives to Strasbourg in the hope of exercising some influence over the EEC's budgetary and agricultural policies.

Law and order

(i) *The Provisional IRA:* the war in Northern Ireland changed significantly towards the end of the seventies. Indiscriminate bombings (such as the Ideal Home bomb attack in March 1976) went out of favour once the *Prevention of Terrorism Act (1976)* enabled the Home Secretary to expel suspected terrorists from Britain. Instead, the IRA chose individuals as their targets. Consequently, a small group of professional killers continued to engage over 14,000 British troops in Northern Ireland. Each and every murder—and there were 2,000 deaths during the seventies—shocked the British people; but none more so than the killing of Airey Neave (in March 1979) and the assassination of Earl Mountbatten in August the same year.

(ii) *International terrorism:* this also became a war—an extension of, or a substitute for, diplomacy. London was the scene of vendettas between rival foreign groups. First, Colonel Gadaffi, the Libyan Head of State, allowed his murder squads to eliminate political enemies in the British capital. Then, in May 1980, terrorists, hostile to the rule of the Ayatollah Khomeini, occupied the Iranian embassy in London. Special Air Services troops launched a carefully planned assault on the embassy, killed or captured the terrorists within the building and released the surviving hostages.

(iii) *Race relations:* some black Britons (especially those in the 16–24 group) justifiably felt underprivileged. Discriminated against in housing and employment, they fell foul more than most of Section 4 of the *1824 Vagrancy Act* (the 'sus' law *) and many were arrested 'on suspicion'. The National Front had also provoked disorder, sometimes with tragic results as in the case of the Anti-Nazi League demonstration against the National Front in Southall, 1979.

* Parliament repealed the 'sus' law in 1981.

THE EUROPEAN ECONOMIC COMMUNITY AT THE TIME OF THE DISPUTE OVER BRITAIN'S BUDGETARY CONTRIBUTION 1979—80

In May 1980 Mrs Thatcher persuaded the EEC to reduce Britain's budgetary contribution by £717 million. This protracted and much publicized bargaining highlighted differences in the opposition Labour Party regarding Britain's continued membership of the EEC.

Assassination of Earl Mountbatten 1979

Bristol Riot (1980) against poverty and discrimination

Southall Riot 1979

Luxembourg Conference 1980

European Parliament

SURPLUS, HEAVILY SUBSIDIZED FOODS SOLD TO RUSSIA

NORWAY

SWEDEN

Moscow

DENMARK

N.I.

EIRE

NETHERLANDS

BRITAIN

GERMAN DEMOCRATIC REPUBLIC

POLAND

SOVIET UNION

BELGIUM

GERMAN FEDERAL REPUBLIC

CZECHOSLOVAKIA

Strasbourg

SWITZ–ERLAND

AUSTRIA

HUNGARY

ROMANIA

FRANCE

ITALY

YUGOSLAVIA (death of Marshal Tito, 1980)

BULGARIA

ALBANIA

PORTUGAL

SPAIN

GREECE

TURKEY

☆ Greece, Spain and Portugal wanted to join the EEC

Mrs Thatcher's complaint at the Luxembourg Conference 1980 was that the EEC was producing food it did not need at a high cost to the members—especially Britain. And then it was selling off its 'mountains' (surpluses) at a loss! For example, butter cost 80p per lb. to produce, but was sold to Russia at 31p per lb! The Russians retailed it to their own people at £1.15 per lb! 'We have to change this!'

A suggestion from Madron Seligman, European Parliament member: Why not buy more cars, cameras and TV/audio equipment from the EEC—rather than from Japan? We would not have to pay EEC import duties on Japanese goods if we did this.

TWO BRITISH PRIME MINISTERS

Prime Minister James Callaghan, complete with garlands and sitar, during the opening of the Bharatiya Vidya Bhavan Indian Cultural Centre in West Kensington, 19 July, 1978. Both political parties were increasingly keen on winning the votes of minority ethnic groups in Britain.

Margaret Thatcher in the spring of 1980 after one year in office as Britain's first woman Prime Minister, when inflation topped 20%.

169

77: Britain, the Commonwealth and the world, 1978–1980

The 1979 Commonwealth Conference

By the time the Commonwealth leaders assembled at Lusaka in August 1979 a whole array of world problems awaited their attention: the Palestine problem; the continued partition of Cyprus; the racial policies of South Africa; the build-up of US and Soviet power in the so-called 'Zone of Peace', the Indian Ocean; and, more recently, Viet Nam's invasion of Cambodia (Kampuchea) and the retaliatory Chinese invasion of Viet Nam. But towering above all of these was the unresolved problem of Rhodesia and the civil war raging inside this British colony between the armed forces of the illegal Smith government and the black nationalist guerrillas of the Patriotic Front. There was every chance that Soviet or Cuban forces might become involved. The Solomon Islands, Tuvalu (Ellice Islands) and Dominica had all won independence in 1978; the Gilbert Islands became independent Kiribati in 1979. When would Rhodesia become independent Zimbabwe? Commonwealth leaders said that this longstanding problem threatened the entire fabric of the Commonwealth itself but they all agreed with Malcolm Fraser, Australia's Prime Minister: 'I think it is clear that if a non-violent solution to the problem of Zimbabwe is to be found, it will involve flexibility on all sides ... We are all in favour of majority rule.' Prime Minister Margaret Thatcher endorsed his statesmanlike approach and when the Conference communiqué came out it placed the settlement of Rhodesia squarely on the shoulders of Great Britain.

The British response

Mrs. Thatcher reacted swiftly. A top-level conference assembled in Lancaster House, London, under the guidance of the Foreign Secretary, Lord Carrington. Two leaders of the guerrilla *Patriotic Front*, Joshua Nkomo and Robert Mugabe, attended. After weeks of debate it was decided to send Lord Soames as Governor to 'Zimbabwe-Rhodesia' where he would organize a cease-fire, bring the guerrillas out of the bush, hold free elections and establish Zimbabwe's independence under majority rule. There have been lesser tasks.

Independent Zimbabwe

Helped by Commonwealth forces and British policemen, Lord Soames secured the cease-fire in December 1979 and persuaded the Patriotic Front guerrilla units to come out into the open and enter assembly points inside the frontiers of Zimbabwe-Rhodesia. Lord Soames then began arranging free elections which would be contested by Robert Mugabe's *Zimbabwe African People's Union* (ZAPU), Joshua Nkomo's *Zimbabwe African National Union* (ZANU) and Bishop Abel Muzorewa's *United African National Council* (UANC). This bid for black majority rule was entirely successful and on 18 April 1980 Zimbabwe became the forty-third independent member of the Commonwealth. For Britain, it had been a long and somewhat shameful period in her colonial history and the struggle had cost at least 30,000 lives. Britain could take little credit for the independence victory; most credit went to the blacks who had for so long resisted Ian Smith's illegal UDI. Certainly, British determination had speeded up the events of 1979–80 but many people must have endorsed a remark by Lord Carrington, when Mr. Robert Mugabe became Zimbabwe's first Prime Minister, that 'something of a miracle has occurred'.

Reactions to world crises

(i) *The American hostages in Teheran:* in 1979 Iranian students, acting in support of the Ayatollah Khomeini's revolutionary government, seized the US embassy in Teheran and refused to release fifty diplomatic hostages until the Americans returned the Shah of Iran* for trial and acknowledged that the embassy was a cover for Central Intelligence Agency operations. Displaying admirable restraint, President Carter hoped that his western allies would sever diplomatic relations with and impose economic sanctions on Iran. Then, in April 1980, came the abortive American rescue attempt. Mrs. Thatcher sympathized with the motives behind the unsuccessful rescue attempt but said she could not support any military operations.

(ii) *The Soviet invasion of Afghanistan:* in December 1978 the USSR had signed a *Treaty of Friendship* with the Marxist rulers of Afghanistan. A year later, about 80,000 Soviet combat troops fanned out across this mountainous country to winkle out rebellious Muslim tribesmen. Britain expressed alarm at this latest example of Soviet expansion, though her most tangible reaction was to advise athletes not to attend the 1980 Moscow Olympics.

* He died in the summer of 1980.

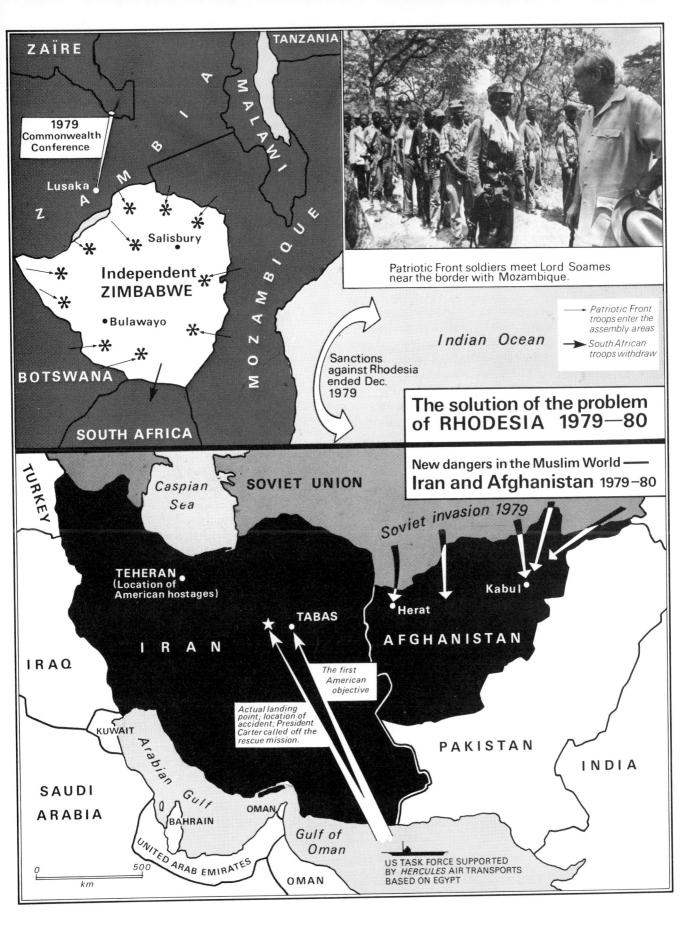

ZAÏRE

TANZANIA

1979
Commonwealth
Conference

MALAWI

Z A M B I A

Lusaka

Salisbury

Independent
ZIMBABWE

MOZAMBIQUE

•Bulawayo

BOTSWANA

SOUTH AFRICA

Patriotic Front soldiers meet Lord Soames
near the border with Mozambique.

Indian Ocean

→ *Patriotic Front
troops enter the
assembly areas*

➡ *South African
troops withdraw*

Sanctions
against Rhodesia
ended Dec.
1979

The solution of the problem
of RHODESIA 1979—80

New dangers in the Muslim World —
Iran and Afghanistan 1979–80

TURKEY

Caspian
Sea

SOVIET UNION

Soviet invasion 1979

TEHERAN •
(Location of
American hostages)

TABAS

Kabul •

Herat •

AFGHANISTAN

IRAQ

I R A N

*The first
American
objective*

*Actual landing
point; location of
accident; President
Carter called off the
rescue mission.*

KUWAIT

PAKISTAN

INDIA

Arabian Gulf

SAUDI
ARABIA

OMAN

BAHRAIN

Gulf of
Oman

UNITED ARAB EMIRATES

0   500

km

OMAN

US TASK FORCE SUPPORTED
BY *HERCULES* AIR TRANSPORTS
BASED ON EGYPT

171

78 : Adversity and triumph : British government policies, 1981–1982

Government economic policies

During 1981–82 Prime Minister Margaret Thatcher was determined to continue with her monetarist policies. These included the 'slimming down' of overstaffed industries, cuts in public spending sectors, such as the Civil Service and local authority support grants. The aim was to make British exports competitive and reduce inflation; the effect was to reduce the annual inflation rate well below 10% at the cost of mounting unemployment.

Political change

Unemployment and short-time working meant radical social adjustment for many British families faced by redundancy, low incomes and the inability of school leavers to find work. This state of affairs provoked all sorts of political reactions at grass-root and national levels. In May 1981 the 'People's March for Jobs' briefly caught the public imagination but lacked the impact of its predecessor, the 1936 Jarrow Crusade.* Splits in the Labour Party appeared when the extreme left-wing Revolutionary Socialist League—Militant Tendency— began to dominate local politics in trade union and constituency branches. Four ex-Labour Cabinet Ministers (Roy Jenkins, Shirley Williams, William Rodgers MP and David Owen MP) formed their breakaway Council for Social Democracy in January 1981. As the *Social Democratic Party*, it attracted a number of Labour MPs and allied itself with David Steel's Liberal Party.

Unrest and frustration

Racial hostility, unemployment and inadequate community policing were some of the factors behind the riots that hit British cities during the summer of 1981. The worst was at Toxteth in Liverpool, and in July 1981 Secretary of State Michael Heseltine, now with special responsibility for Merseyside, began a long overdue examination of the condition of Britain's inner cities. Mrs. Thatcher emphasized (March 1982) that Conservative policies were bearing fruit: increases in productivity, lower inflation, smaller wage increases and falling interest rates meant that 'we were beginning to see the regeneration of our industry'. Ironically, some Scottish workers found themselves at the mercy of superpower politics. The planned closure of Coulport's *Trident* servicing base and the US embargo on the sale of British equipment to the Soviet natural gas pipe-line threatened many jobs.

The Falklands, 1982

For a few months the British people were united in their response to Argentina's invasion of the Falkland Islands and South Georgia (2–3 April). Argentina renamed the islands *Las Malvinas* and, while the UN passed resolutions but did little else, the Prime Minister ordered the despatch of a task force to the South Atlantic. Ocean-going trawlers from Hull, P & O cruise ships, the Cunard liner *Queen Elizabeth 2*, North Sea ferries and container ships all sailed to join the Royal Navy's warships spearheaded by the two aircraft-carriers *Invincible* and *Hermes*.

The liberation

SAS men and Royal Marines reoccupied South Georgia on 25 April. On 1 May a Vulcan bomber from Ascension Island attacked Port Stanley airstrip, while Harriers strafed parked aircraft and fuel dumps there and at Goose Green. Marines and paratroopers then landed at Port San Carlos (20 May), captured Darwin and Goose Green and then footslogged across the marshy countryside in drenching, bitterly cold rain. Both sides paid a heavy price during intense fighting on land, sea and in the air. The Royal Navy lost *Sheffield, Antelope, Ardent* and *Coventry*; Argentina lost the cruiser *General Belgrano* and the submarine *Santa Fe*. Argentine conscripts suffered heavy casualties, as did the Welsh Guards who were caught just as they were disembarking from *Sir Galahad* at Bluff Cove by daring Argentine fighter-bomber pilots.

The surrender

After their successful assault on Argentine defences outside Port Stanley, culminating in a victory for the Scots Guards at the *Battle of Tumbledown Mountain*, the British and the Gurkhas were prepared to attack the Argentine troops occupying the capital. But on 14 June General Menendez surrendered to his opposite number, General Moore. The liberation was complete—an outstanding operation in British military history and a moment of triumph in a period of almost unrelieved adversity.

* See pages 106–7.

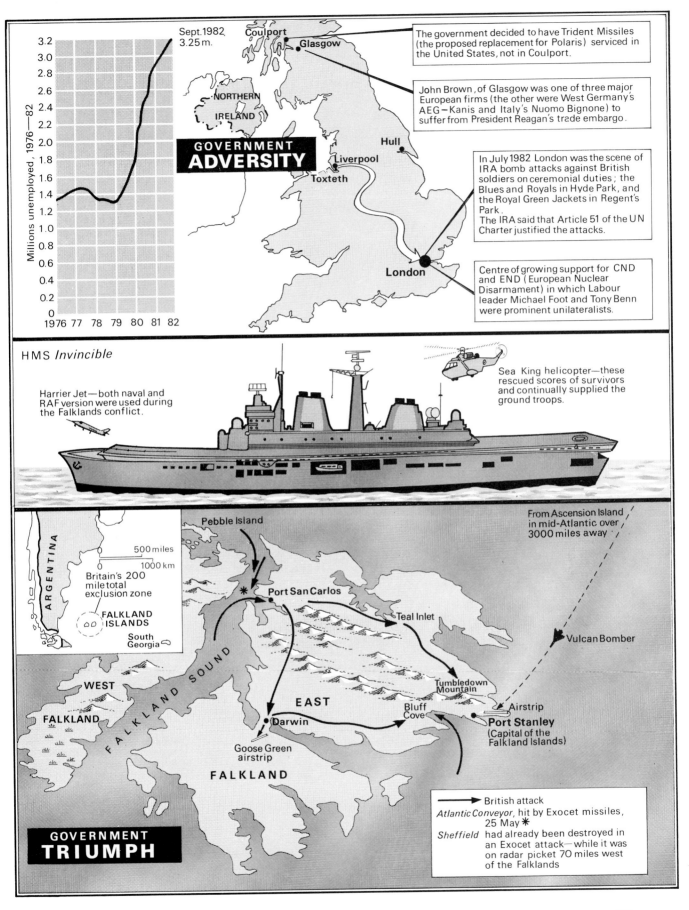

GOVERNMENT ADVERSITY

Millions unemployed, 1976—82

Sept.1982 3.25 m.

The government decided to have Trident Missiles (the proposed replacement for Polaris) serviced in the United States, not in Coulport.

John Brown, of Glasgow was one of three major European firms (the other were West Germany's AEG–Kanis and Italy's Nuomo Bignone) to suffer from President Reagan's trade embargo.

In July 1982 London was the scene of IRA bomb attacks against British soldiers on ceremonial duties; the Blues and Royals in Hyde Park, and the Royal Green Jackets in Regent's Park.
The IRA said that Article 51 of the UN Charter justified the attacks.

Centre of growing support for CND and END (European Nuclear Disarmament) in which Labour leader Michael Foot and Tony Benn were prominent unilateralists.

Coulport
Glasgow
NORTHERN IRELAND
Hull
Liverpool
Toxteth
London

HMS *Invincible*

Harrier Jet—both naval and RAF version were used during the Falklands conflict.

Sea King helicopter—these rescued scores of survivors and continually supplied the ground troops.

From Ascension Island in mid-Atlantic over 3000 miles away

Pebble Island

Port San Carlos

Teal Inlet

Vulcan Bomber

ARGENTINA

500 miles
0   1000 km
Britain's 200 mile total exclusion zone

FALKLAND ISLANDS

South Georgia

WEST FALKLAND

FALKLAND SOUND

EAST

Tumbledown Mountain

Bluff Cove

Airstrip
Port Stanley
(Capital of the Falkland Islands)

Darwin

Goose Green airstrip

FALKLAND

GOVERNMENT TRIUMPH

→ British attack
Atlantic Conveyor, hit by Exocet missiles, 25 May ✳
Sheffield had already been destroyed in an Exocet attack—while it was on radar picket 70 miles west of the Falklands

Part 9 – Britain 1951–1982

Spread

66. *Britain, Europe and the Modern World***	Paul Richardson	Heinemann Educational Books
The Suez Affair	Hugh Thomas	Weidenfeld & Nicholson
67. *Britain, Europe and the Modern World***	Paul Richardson	Heinemann Educational Books (see especially Chapter 16 'The making of modern Africa')
68. *Documents on British Economic and Social History 1945–1967***	Peter Lane	Macmillan
69. *History of the TUC 1868–1968***		published by General Council of TUC
70. *Men, Machines and History*	S. Lilley	Lawrence and Wishart
71. *The Wealth of Britain*	Pollard and Crossley	Batsford
72. *The Great Tide***	H. Grieve	County Council of Essex
Lynmouth Flood Disaster	E. Delderfield	ERD Publications
73. *Keesing's Contemporary Archives*		
74. *Holy War in Belfast*	Andrew Boyd	Anvil
75. *The Labour Government 1964–70***	B. Lapping	Penguin
76. *Labour and Equality* (especially Ch. 1)	N. Bosanquet and P. Townsend (eds.)	Heinemann Educational Books
77. *Keesing's Contemporary Archives*		
78. *The Struggle for the Falkland Islands* (for the historical background up to 1886)	J. Goebel	Yale University Press
Fight for the Falklands! (for the events of 1982)	J. Laffin	Sphere

**Especially useful for project and topic works.

Index

177